Astrology Inside Out

Astrology Inside Out

by Bruce Nevin

Para Research
Rockport Massachusetts

Astrology Inside Out
by Bruce Nevin

International Standard Book Number 0-914918-19-2

Type set in 10 pt Paladium on a Compugraphic Editwriter 7500
Typesetting by Betty Bauman
Graphics by Robert Killam, Marlene Comet

Printed by R.R. Donnelley & Sons Co.
on 55-pound Suretone II

Published by Para Research, Inc.
Whistlestop Mall
Rockport, Massachusetts 01966

Manufactured in the United States of America

First Printing, May 1982, 5,000 copies

Contents

Table of Figures

Introduction

Astrology is tremendously exciting. The delight you will experience in learning astrology is something like the pleasure of learning a foreign language well, and journeying to places where that language is spoken. It is the psychological equivalent of getting contact lenses, when you didn't even realize that you had limited vision.

Even if you never "do" astrology, in the sense of casting and interpreting horoscopes for people, its rich symbolism will open doors of perception and deeply enhance your understanding of yourself and others.

The language of symbols has seemed foreign to many of us for too long. Its native regions have been for us a "darkest Africa" of imagination, intuition, the subconscious and the occult. In this book you will learn the symbol-language of astrology. You will discover that it is in a very deep sense your native tongue. You will experience a homecoming.

How can I convey the excitement of astrology? Should I speak of seeing in the patterns of the solar system the inner trellis on which the psyche shapes itself? Of hearing behind the stately cycles of the planets in their orbits the pulsing cross-rhythms of the dance of life itself? Of the great vision of universal harmony that has inspired astrologers and sages in all times and places?

Words. Mere words, however evocative, will not do. And they are not necessary. The natural attraction that you feel toward astrology is proof that you are ready for it. This book is designed to help you fulfill your desire for wholeness, for that is the real source of the attraction.

It may be that your involvement with astrology doesn't completely "make sense" in terms of your customary ideas about your life. Think about it for a moment. There is more to life than "knowing about" things in theory and asking for proof in terms of words and ideas. There is a kind of *direct knowing*, what was once called *gnosis*, that proves itself in experience.

For instance, "knowing about" riding bicycles in a theoretical sense won't keep you from falling over. You can't apply the theory without direct, intuitive experience of your own inner center of gravity, and your own dynamic interactions with the bicycle. On the other hand, a child needs some instruction, some theory, before taking off on a two-wheeler. What we call "know-how" is a combination of both these kinds of knowledge working together.

This book will help you to know astrology directly as well as theoretically. It will give you practice interpreting your own living experience in astrological terms. With this book, you will learn astrology from the inside out.

As soon as you read about a new topic of symbolism or theory, you will be shown ways of applying it to events and experiences in your life. You will discover how mundane objects and relationships have rich depths of symbolic meaning. You will learn to discover and explore these meanings somewhat as one does with dream symbolism. You will learn literally to converse with the living symbols in your life through visualization and meditation.

The form of meditation suggested is a kind of conversation with your mind. By choosing a specific person, object, event or image, you determine the topic of the conversation. Having brought it to the attention of your mind, you simply sit quietly and wait expectantly. Patiently, but expectantly.

You will keep an astrological journal. This is not the usual kind of journal or diary, so if you are among those who have tried unsuccessfully to establish a habit of diary-keeping in the past, be prepared for something different.

Your astrological journal is simply a loose-leaf notebook with dividers labeled for the different elements of astrology as you learn them. Later, with the exercises that depend on your memory, it will be useful in aiding your recall of the past, and in time it will become a resource that you will treasure.

If meditation or contemplation is completely new to you, or if you want better understanding of the form of meditation suggested here, there is a more complete account in Appendix 2.

Appendix 1 contains a brief summary of the theory of astrology that is embodied in this book, for readers who want it all to make sense in terms of contemporary science. And finally, Appendix 3 gives directions for obtaining horoscopes, both your own and those of others.

You will not need your horoscope to develop your skill and fluency with astrological symbolism in Part I of this book. The astrological dynamics of all sorts of decisions, conflicts and predicaments will spontaneously become apparent to you without its help, as your growing astrological insight transforms stress into creative energy, and problems into opportunities.

In Part II, your own horoscope will begin to speak to you directly, in the language of astrology. You will understand the messages of your horoscope, because the symbols of astrology and the symbols of your own personal experience will be deeply connected at their roots.

You can use this book in many ways. If you are a beginner, I suggest that you read through it once, skimming through the exercises which make up much of the bulk of the book. Then work through the book on a deeper level, learning from the "inside out" as you carry out the exercises.

You may want to use the book to enrich your relationship with another person, or in a group, role-playing the different parts of one another's horoscopes. Use it as a stimulus and organizing framework for your personal journal-keeping. Modify and adapt the exercises to meet your changing needs; use them to teach others. Test the theory of astrology that is offered here in the subjective laboratory of personal experience, and develop your own refinements.

Let this book be a continuing resource for you, as it has been for many of my students in its manuscript form.

Engage in the exercises fully and honestly. Find other students of astrology with whom to talk and share insights. Read astrology books. Many suggestions for reading are scattered through this book, and are gathered for your convenience in the bibliography at the end.

When you come across yet another astrological doctrine (there are quite a few), take it from the realm of theory to the experience of "direct knowing," using the skills of visualization and meditation that you will learn here. Take your time. Allow your mind to unfold toward truth in a natural, organic process, like a flower unfolding in sunlight. Before assuming that what you have heard or read is correct, see how consistent it is with your current grasp of theory and with your own experience. Conversely, before you assume that an astrological opinion is wrong, consider that you might not have understood at a deep enough level.

This is the book I looked for but could not find when I first awoke to my inner attraction to astrology. Writing it has been a deep pleasure and a vehicle for tremendous personal growth. I hope it serves you well.

Part I. Astrology Inside and Outside

In Part I, you will discover that you do not need your horoscope to use astrology in your life. You will gain considerable fluency in the astrological symbol-language, learning to know the houses (Chapter 1), the planets (Chapter 2) and the signs (Chapter 3) as active qualities and energies in your life, rather than just memorizing words and meanings. You will learn to interpret your experiences in terms of the astrological energies that underlie them, without reference to a horoscope.

Then, when you turn to your horoscope in Part II, you will be well-prepared to interpret its messages in terms that are appropriate for your life and your chosen way of living it. When you read the detailed "delineations" of various horoscope factors in other astrology books, you will be prepared to sift the wheat from the chaff. You will be able to read between the lines to find meanings that are for you alone. And when you interpret other people's horoscopes, you will know how to do the same for them as well.

The exercises, particularly those in Part I, ask you to meditate on certain objects, events or ideas. What is meant here is a very easy form of contemplation. In the introduction to the book, I characterized this meditation as a kind of conversation with your mind. By choosing a particular object for your meditation, you set the topic of the conversation, then simply wait quietly and patiently for whatever your mind has to offer in response.

The mind is notoriously vagrant. When it wanders, just remind it gently of your chosen topic and wait attentively. Pay particular attention to sensory images—not just pictures but sounds, smells, tastes, feelings and so forth. You will find that your mind loves attention. It will chatter away as it ferrets around in its packrat hoard, offering you treasures and trash more or less related to your chosen topic. Ignore the trash and ignore the chatter. Don't let your mind change the subject: if something seems like a treasure but is not clearly related to your chosen subject, put it aside for another session. Don't indulge in annoyance, just pay attention with patience and with love, and eventually you will tame your mind.

The regular practice of meditation, even the easy, relaxed form recommended here, has many fringe benefits. When your mind is domesticated, so to speak, you will appreciate what I mean. (When accidents happen in your favor, just remember to thank your subconscious mind.)

At the end of each session, when you have picked out some treasures that have a genuine connection with your chosen topic, review them slowly and carefully in your memory; then jot down a few key words as reminders on a pad of paper that you keep handy for the purpose. Later, you will develop these jotted notes more fully in your astrological journal.

The journal is a loose-leaf notebook, with dividers labelled for the different elements of astrology as you learn them. As you accumulate your brief notes of meditation sessions in your journal, it will become an invaluable tool for you.

In Appendix 2 is a more complete discussion of meditation or contemplation as done in the exercises in this book.

1

The Twelve Houses:
Your Circle of Experience

Everything moves through cycles. Your life is made up of interwoven, overlapping cycles. You can see how many cycles in your life are coordinated with obvious cyclic events in the world around you. For example, you can see how your cycle of waking and sleeping is coordinated with the rising and setting of the Sun. This is also true of more subtle cycles in your life. The exercises in this chapter will help you to recognize and use them.

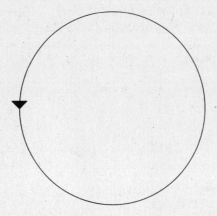

Figure 1. A Cycle

The image of a complete cycle in astrology is a circle. The counterclockwise direction of movement through the cycle is seen as an arrow curving back on itself (figure 1). The tip of the arrow touches the point on the left-hand side of the circle where one cycle ends and another begins.

Every cycle has phases. The waxing and waning phases are the strongest of these. They divide the cycle into two equal parts (figure 2).

Somewhat weaker quarter-phases result from dividing each of these half-phases in two. The peak of growth and development in the waxing phase is a

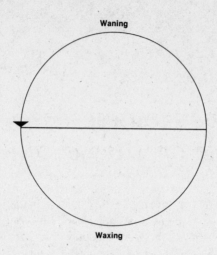

Figure 2. Waxing and waning phases

watershed point dividing it into two parts. Appropriate images for these two quarter-phases of growth are *emergence* and *establishment*, respectively.

In the same way, the peak of application and service in the waning phase is a watershed point dividing it into two parts: a third quarter-phase of *integration* and a fourth quarter-phase of *dissemination.*

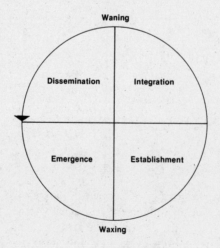

Figure 3. Four quadrants

These quarter-phases are the four "seasons" of your cycles of experience. Like the familiar spring, summer, autumn and winter of our year, they show how all your experiences unfold from seed to plant to flower to fruit and then back to seed again.

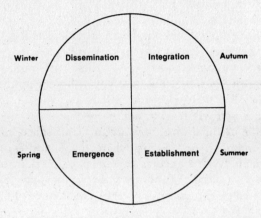

Figure 4. Quadrants and seasons

Each quadrant is further divided into three phases, a beginning, a middle, and an end—a total of twelve phases. This circle, with twelve phases like a clock dial, is the archetype of every complete cycle in astrology.

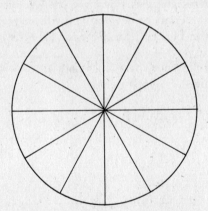

Figure 5. The twelve houses

In the following two exercises you will create a physical model or map in your meditation space of the cycles in your life. You will use this space for the magic of self-transmutation. The first step in any magical operation, we are told, is to draw your magic circle. Then you "charge" it or energize it. Each time you use your meditation space, it becomes more clear to your mind's eye. It becomes more strongly energized for you, like a magnetic field. With practice, you will be able to turn to the inner counterpart of your meditation space, in your mind, and explore it with your inner senses (Appendix 2). In this way, it will become a sanctuary, and a powerful tool, to which you can turn at any time and in any outward circumstances.

In this chapter, you will learn the basic meanings and relationships of the twelve phases of experience, or "houses" as they are called in astrology. You will find your own personal symbols expressing these meanings, drawn from the corresponding areas of your own life, and you will develop their meaning and value in meditation. For this work you will need a loose-leaf notebook with twelve sections (later you will need to add more).

Determine the cardinal directions around your space, north, south, east and west. Use a compass, or observe where the Sun rises and sets, or use landmarks from a map. From the center of your space, mark these directions. The edge of a doorway or a piece of furniture may serve the purpose. If there is no existing mark place an object appropriately, or tape a piece of paper to the wall.

Exercise 1: Sit in the center of your meditation space, facing east. Imagine a river of light and energy flowing from the west into the center of your back, and flowing out again from your heart toward the east. Because the east is the direction of sunrise, it symbolizes *emergence* of new light in your life, *self-expression* out from your center, and *assertion* of your personal ego. See the light emerging in front of you as if there were a movie projector inside you. Behind you, the west symbolizes energies flowing back into your center from other people, bringing you materials to develop and edit in your heart-center as you create the movie of your life. Feel this flow, and the creative process going on within you.

Still in the center of your space, turn and face south, so that the east is on your left side and the west on your right.

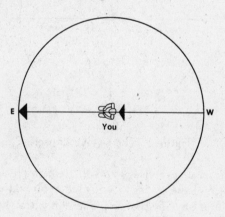

Figure 6. The horizon line

When you were born, the space around you was divided by the horizon line, separating the Earth from the sky. The line from west to east in your meditation space is your symbolic horizon line (figure 6).

At noon, the Sun is directly south of you in the sky, so this direction is "above" your symbolic horizon line (figure 7). Imagine this part of your space as being full of light, out in the open, and visible. If you can, you might even arrange the lighting to produce this effect in your meditation space. The direction south, the point where your circle of houses rises highest above your horizon, symbolizes those experiences that are most intensely public, obvious and "outfront." It is in this part of your circle of houses that you are most involved with your social, political and spiritual *significance* in the world.

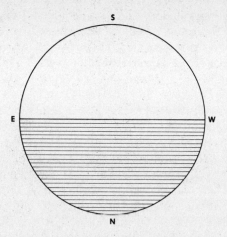

Figure 7. The south-north meridian

Behind you, to the north, is the dark half of your space, the half of your space that is symbolically "underground," below your horizon line. The midnight point of the circle, due north, corresponds to those private, subjective, unconscious or subconsciously-directed experiences in which you express the *roots* of your personality.

Your circle of houses is like a magnetic field structured around the east-west horizon line, surrounding you as you sit in the center. To intensify your awareness of the polarities of this "field" on all levels of your personality, spend some time facing the four directions mulling over the area of experience that each direction symbolizes.

For example, when you face east, think of some experiences you have had while making a new beginning, striking off on your own, asserting yourself, or emerging into a new arena. You may not have realized consciously that you were starting something new at the time, or you may have recognized your first steps only in retrospect.

When you face north, think of your family, your home, things that seem "homey" to you; think of traditions, particularly family traditions.

When you face west, think of your spouse or lover, your partner, or your competitor, those people with thom you are in one-to-one relationships.

When you face south, think of your public image, your reputation, prestige and status, and of your career.

In this way, get some feeling for these four major poles of experience in your life.

Contrast the feelings, qualities and circumstances of the direction you are facing with their opposites in the direction behind your back. Energy projected in one direction always produces a reflex in the opposite direction. This is like Newton's Law, "for every action there is an equal and opposite reaction." For example, when you are feeling rebellious or frustrated, your self-assertion (east) is yoked together with the responses of others (west). When you take a political stance, or embark on a career (south) that either pleases or displeases your family (north), your public identity and your family conditioning have to come to terms with each other.

Which of these directions has the most meaning or interest for you right now? If you wish, walk into the space that you are thinking about. Turn around, and think about its relationship with the other three directions, particularly the opposite side of the circle. Explore fantasies, talk, sing, dance, draw pictures, write—do whatever will capture the flavor of these four basic polarities of experience. By involving all the subtle faculties of your personality, you will understand the four basic polarities of experience with more than just your intellect.

Now that you have some direct knowledge of the major polarities in your circle of experience, you can begin to explore the spaces they define. The east-west horizon line and the north-south meridian divide the circle into four quadrants.

In diagrams of the circle of houses, the cardinal directions are shown differently than on an ordinary geographical map. South is at the top, rather than north. This is because you are oriented to that point in the southern sky where the Sun is at noon, rather than to a compass needle pointing north. In other words, this is a map of the sky, not the earth, and is reversed.

Exercise 2: Sit in the center of your circle. Extend your arms. Point your right arm east and your left arm north. You are now embracing the first quadrant of your circle of experience. It corresponds to the quarter of the heavens that was about to rise above the horizon when you were born. The eastern horizon, where this quadrant begins, is called the Ascendant (figure 8).

The first quadrant symbolizes those experiences of subjective self-expression and assertion through which you establish your ego—your identity as an independent being in the world of ideas and objects. As transiting planets move through your circle of houses, they begin their cycles here, in your

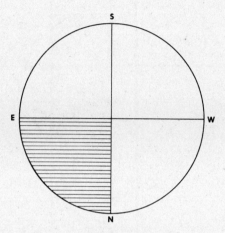

Figure 8. The first quadrant

personal, subjective spring season, bringing new life out of the seeds of the last harvest, bursting into existence with astonishing vitality and freedom.

Now turn counterclockwise to your left, and point your right arm north and your left arm west. You are now embracing the second quadrant (figure 9). The point in the north is called the *Imum Coeli* (Latin for "the lowest point in the heavens"), abbreviated I.C. This quadrant, the subjective summer season of your cycles of experience, begins at that most subjective point where the subconscious roots of your personality draw on the resources of your family, community, culture, and biological endowment, to create both your security and your insecurity. Think of how plants burgeon and flourish in summer, drawing nourishment and support from the Earth, their mother. Or how, in times of drought these same plants harden and clutch the earth with their roots.

Out of this fertile ground of your cultural and biological heritage, your personal creativity draws patterns for you to reweave on the loom of daily life. Think of how improvisations in music, for example in jazz, are based upon traditional musical patterns. In the same way, the improvisations of life are based upon traditional patterns of feeling, thinking and acting.

Contrast your experience of *independence* in the first quadrant with the *dependence* of the second quadrant.

Now turn to the west. This is your Descendant, where other people reflect your image back to you. It is as though your personal impulse goes out to the east by the front door (your Ascendant), then travels around the Earth by a chain of

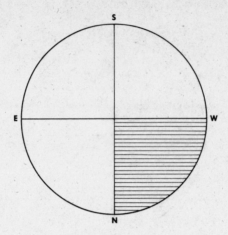

Figure 9. The second quadrant

actions and reactions, being transformed as it changes hands, and finally returns to you through the back door in the west (your Descendant).

Turn counterclockwise again toward your left, and point your right arm west and your left arm south, embracing your third quadrant (figure 10). This autumn season of your cycles of experience symbolizes objective (above the horizon, south) intercourse and encounter with other people (west). This quadrant begins at the outer extreme of the social polarity between self (Ascendant, east) and others (Descendant, west). Here your ego (first quadrant) and its creations (second quadrant) must prove their worth by their *adaptability* to the needs of others, rather than by the self-centered motives with which they started out in the cycle of experience.

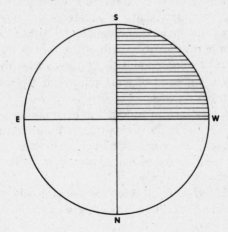

Figure 10. The third quadrant

Contrast the interdependence of this third quadrant with the opposite or complementary independence of the first quadrant. Here in the third quadrant you act *interdependently* with others to reap collectively the karma (consequences) of actions which you *independently* sowed in your first quadrant · and *dependently* cultivated in your second quadrant. In early stages of a cycle you aren't very concerned about what your fellow gardeners are doing, so long as they don't encroach on your private plot, but in the third quadrant of social commitment, they are very much your concern.

Now turn to embrace the fourth and last quadrant of your circle of experience, with your left arm pointing east along the horizon line, and your right arm pointing south along the meridian (figure 11). The fourth quadrant begins with the *Midheaven*, in the south, which is symbolically the apex of your public significance. The fourth quadrant is the realm of objective (above the horizon) self-establishment (east). In this winter season of your cycles of experience you enjoy those fruits that you harvested in the third quadrant, and prepare the seeds from them for the planting of the next cycle.

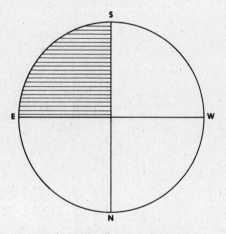

Figure 11. The fourth quadrant

Contrast the public objectivity of the fourth quadrant with the private subjectivity of the second quadrant, on the opposite side of the circle. To experience their relationship, spend a little time moving from one to the other. To the extent that your cycles of experience are successful (that is, to the extent that events flow in the right succession), they enhance your personal *autonomy* here in the fourth quadrant. Independence is the immature first-quadrant illusion that you can operate without any ecological, cultural or social context, as contrasted with autonomy, which literally means being master of one's own domain. You attain autonomy to the extent that you successfully define the boundaries of your domain (first quadrant), master the play of your personal creative resources (second quadrant) and integrate all of this successfully into your social context (third quadrant).

As you sit in the center of your meditation circle, be aware that you are involved simultaneously in all four quadrants in different ways. Later (in Chapter 6) you will see how many simultaneous planetary cycles occur in your life, and how at any time you will probably have at least one cycle focused in each of the four main areas of your life, highlighting them differently as transiting planets pass through the four quadrants of your horoscope.

Here is a summary of the distinctive features of the four quadrants:

Quadrant	Season	Motive	Achievement
First	Spring	Emergence	Independence
Second	Summer	Establishment	Dependence
Third	Autumn	Relationship	Interdependence
Fourth	Winter	Dissemination	Autonomy

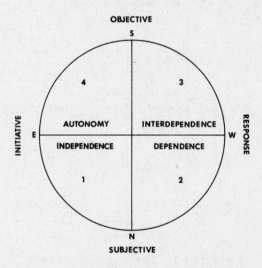

Figure 12. Quadrant keywords

Other suggestions for Exercise 2: You may want to use this exercise as a warm-up, and to put the individual houses in their cyclic context before you do one of the exercises concerned with them, later in this chapter.

Or you may want to use this exercise to reinforce the meanings and polarities of the whole cycle in your consciousness. Feel how your activities and experiences in one quadrant are patterned and influenced by what you have done in the previous quadrant, and how the results of your present activities will be felt in the following quadrant. As you focus your attention into one quadrant, recall the resources of the opposite quadrant, behind you, upon which you can draw for particularly appropriate support. Do those resources appear to be in the control of other people? If so, are they a source of conflict in your social life? Or is there someone ready to help you with the missing pieces of your puzzle, if you only notice and ask? Use your meditation circle in this way to discover ways of solving problems.

You can use this exercise to increase your understanding of some personal entanglement. Locate the major focus of the matter in one of the four quadrants. Then in the other three quadrants look for its antecedents and prospects, its hidden dimensions, its connections with the other affairs of your life. This tool will be made more subtle and more powerful as you learn about the twelve houses that make up the four quadrants.

Now that you have some direct knowledge of the half-phases and quarter-phases of your circle of experience you can begin to explore the three phases of each quadrant, comprising the circle of twelve houses.

Each quadrant has three parts—a beginning, a middle and an end.

The cardinal directions that mark the beginnings of the four quadrants are called the "angles" in astrology. Therefore, the beginning of each quadrant is called its *angular* house (figure 13). It is sometimes called the *active* house, because it represents the initiating impulse which sets the tone and gets things started in that quadrant.

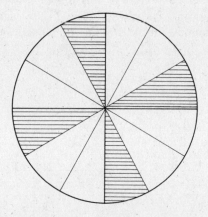

Figure 13. The angular houses

The middle of each quadrant is called the *succedent* house, because it "succeeds" or follows an angular house. It is sometimes called the *reactive* house, because it reacts to and resists the impulse of the preceding angular or active house. Its very resistance imposes form on that impulse. Clay resists the sculptor's tool. If it did not, it would not retain the form which the artist imparts to it. It would merely revert to a smooth surface, like water. The midpoint of the quadrant, which falls in the succedent or reactive house, functions like a pivot or fulcrum, a turning point in the development of the experiences characteristic of the quadrant.

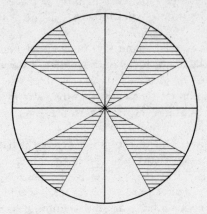

Figure 14. The succedent houses

The end of each quadrant is called the *cadent* or *resultant* house. It *resolves* the contradiction of the first two houses, *adapts* their narrow polarization to a broader context, and thus *prepares* the way for the angular impulse of the next quadrant. The cadent house, like the cadence or *cadenza* of a musical composition, rounds out the rhythm of the quadrant, and completes and fulfills its expression.

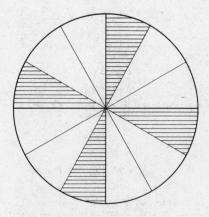

Figure 15. The cadent houses

Like a symphony, a drama or a story, each quadrant or "season" of your cycle of experience has three movements: angular, succedent, cadent—active, reactive, resultant—thesis, antithesis, synthesis—theme, countertheme, resolution—beginning, middle, end.

First House

The first house expresses the quintessential quality of the first quadrant because it is the angular house of the quadrant. Your cycle of experience begins in the first house with independent, subjective, self-initiated assertion of your identity. Your personal identity pushes out from within you like a sprouting seed, making its mark in your physical features, your carriage and mannerisms, your gestures, and in the especially personal characteristics of your actions.

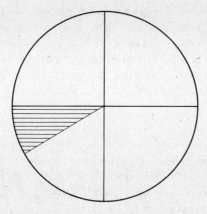

Figure 16. The first house

This is your self-image, which you unconsciously project through your thoughts, words and deeds. The first house shows how you address events, and how you present yourself to the world. It also represents the conditions of your birth and early childhood, insofar as those conditions had a decisive influence in the formation of your character.

Exercise 3: Sit in the first house of your meditation space and meditate on the self-image you present to others.

Suggestions for meditation: A mirror, a photograph or portrait of yourself, a tape-recording of you conversing with someone. What is your characteristic way of doing things—carefully, quickly, deftly, carelessly, with enthusiasm, with anger...? Find objects or remember events that reflect your personal touch. What clues have parents, teachers and peers provided, perhaps inadvertently or unconsciously? For more ideas, review the experiences you discovered in relation to the direction east and the first quadrant in Exercises 1 and 2.

As you discover each facet of your self-image, find a symbol to represent it for your meditation—an object, a souvenir, a snatch of song, a quotation, a descriptive phrase, anything that has meaning and vitality for you as a reflection of yourself. These objects for meditation will anchor you to your chosen topic

(Appendix 2). If an image or object embarrasses you, meditate on it to find out why.

In your meditation, pay particular attention to how you *feel* about these symbols and the qualities associated with them. Their significance and symbolic value may change or deepen from one meditation to another. Record the fruits of your meditations in the first section of your notebook, which should be labelled "First House" and used only for information relating to the first house.

Use your feelings as a compass needle when choosing a focus for your meditation. Don't try to analyze why you are interested in (or perhaps fearful of) one suggestion rather than another. "How" is a more helpful question than "why." Let your meditation show you.

All of the exercises in this book may be repeated and reviewed many times. This exercise in particular will richly reward your efforts after you have meditated on the other houses.

Second House

As your personality is projected outward through your body and your actions, it is reflected first in your personal values, your possessions and your attitudes toward them. The second house concerns those personal resources—energies, money, possessions—that lie definitely within your personal boundaries, where any disturbance is an invasion of privacy.

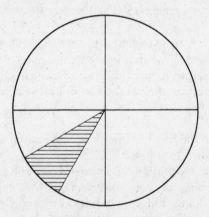

Figure 17. The second house

Exercise 4: Sit in the second house of your space and meditate on your values and resources.

Suggestions for meditation: Money, a checkbook, a catalog of consumer goods; symbols, pictures or other reminders of things you have or would like to have. How do you acquire, use, spend, distribute, give, protect, and otherwise manage your personal resources? How do you distinguish between what is yours, what is not and what is under your stewardship? How do you mark these boundaries for yourself; how do you declare them to others; and how do you respond when they are ignored? How do you respond to losing something you value? Have you ever had a cherished possession stolen? Have you ever experienced the theft or loss of something you valued less highly? Have you ever stolen anything?

How does your first-house image look now, as it is reflected in your possessions, in your values and in your attitudes toward possessions, money and other resources?

Pay particular attention to your *feelings* about these matters. Notice if there are changes when you meditate on them again at a later time. Record the fruits of your meditations in the second-house section of your notebook.

Third House

Just as, in the second house, your personality is expressed in a wider sphere through your personal values, in the third house it is expressed still more broadly through expectations and habitual patterns of thought.

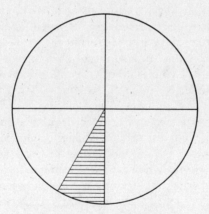

Figure 18. The third house

The third house concerns your personal communications (talk, writings, correspondence) and communicative style. It also concerns your relatives, particularly the appearance and personalities of your brothers and sisters. This is the realm of active, concrete mentality, making connections and finding relationships in the world of direct sensory experience. In this house, your mental patterns are projected onto your environment. Short trips are also included here as excursions into your local environment. (See Appendix 2 for further discussion of the relationship between expectations and perception.)

Exercise 5: Sit in the third-house section of your space and meditate on the ways in which your expectations and habits of thinking are reflected in your perceptions of the world around you.

Suggestions for meditation: An address book, telephone book, telephone, letters, something you have written or are writing, anything to do with your communication with others. How do ideas, words, and images occur to you—in sudden clear flashes, by surprise, in slow organic unfoldment, in logical sequences? How do you communicate your ideas to others? What is your communicative style—are you logical, empathic, dogmatic, adaptable, resistant, defensive, suggestible, aggressive, receptive? Meditate on specific recent ideas and acts of communication to discover the mental habits which underlie them. So that you can characterize these mental patterns in your own terms, derive key words and images for them, and be alert for them in future acts of communication. How are your trains of thought connected—do your mental connections vary in kind, degree or tempo, depending upon your mood, wakefulness, fatigue, type of activity (such as meditation, study, conversation, argument, nonverbal work, daydream, play)? Or do your mental connections depend upon other differences in your state of consciousness?

How do you arrange your possessions to form your personal environment? What does your personal environment communicate about you? How does your environment reflect the furniture and decor of your mind? Is it easy or hard for you to entertain new ideas? Does your openness depend upon your mood, your activity, your state of consciousness or the nature of the new ideas? How is this reflected in your reactions to change in your familiar environment?

Consider your extended environment, with its outlying regions in the homes of friends and relatives, school, shopping places, clubs and so forth. Where and how do you travel around during a typical week? Meditate on car keys, public transportation schedules, tickets or tokens, or other symbols of your means of making short trips. Is there any parallel between these connections in your environment and the connections in your mind? Do you talk with people on the bus? Are you curious about them? Are you wary? Do you ignore them?

Meditate on patterns of communication in your family, among your relatives, and particularly between you and your siblings. Do you communicate with one another openly, guardedly, easily, superficially, often or seldom, expressively or without emotion? Meditate on pictures or other reminders of your siblings. Are your ways of thinking and communicating similar (parallel), opposite (complementary), or incongruent with one another? Is some of this family patterning due to projection on your part? Were your siblings to some extent molded by being part of your environment? How were you affected by being part of their environment?

Record the fruits of your meditations in the third-house section of your notebook, giving particular attention to your changing *feelings* about these matters.

As you pursue these exercises, your subconscious mind will offer you relevant material at odd moments during the day or in your dreams. Particularly likely times are when you first wake up, before falling asleep, or during some routine activity such as eating, cleaning, bathing, washing dishes, garden work, driving and so on. Make a habit of carrying a small notepad in your pocket so you can jot down keywords to develop later and incorporate into your meditations and notebook. This is direct experience of how your subconscious mind constantly processes and integrates the new information and experiences you are taking in.

Fourth House

The fourth house begins the quadrant of dependent experience in the bosom of your family. Your family system is a living organism which expresses itself through the interactions of your family members and will survive, in one form or another, long after you are gone. It has a profound and lasting influence on the conduct and direction of your life. Your childhood conditioning is the wellspring of your personal sense of security and of your ability to nurture and reassure others. It is the matrix out of which your subconscious fears and insecurities arise. In the fourth house your emotional roots push deeply into the fertile soil of personal and collective memory, drawing up strength, vigor and purpose beyond your conscious ken.

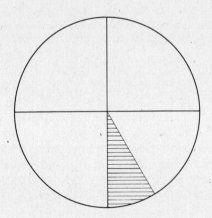

Figure 19. The fourth house

Exercise 6: Sit in the fourth house of your space and meditate on your family roots.

Suggestions for meditation: A picture of your family, your family home or an ancestor; an heirloom; your family tree; mementoes of your childhood; family stories and traditions. Where did your family of origin come from, what values did they bring with them, what expectations, what ideals and fears? How did your parents meet? Of what they each brought to their relationship, what values, expectations and behavior patterns of theirs are incorporated into your personality? As you become aware of family patterns reflected in your personality, note them and monitor them in your daily life. By meditation, learn to use your family patterns without being caught in them blindly.

Meditate on symbols of your present home—photographs, silverware or wedding gifts, a floor plan. (If you do not have a floor plan of your home, draw one from your own measurements.) How did you and your partner or spouse meet, how did you establish your relationship, what did each of you bring to it, and how are your respective values, expectations and patterns of behavior reflected in your home? Whether you are married or single, look for patterns of your family of origin in your present home. Are doors characteristically open or closed in your family? Are different spaces sharply defined or do they flow and blend into one another? How are solitude, privacy, intimacy and social life handled in your home? Look back to the first quadrant: what symbols are there in your home of your purely personal imprint, as distinct from family patterns? Looking ahead to the third quadrant, have other people had a significant impact on your home?

What kinds of experience make you feel secure or insecure? How do you respond to other people's anxiety? How is your response to a person's insecurity related to the degree of intimacy? For example, how do you respond to anxiety in family, friends, acquaintances or strangers? What kinds of people and behavior reassure you when you are anxious?

Describe the fruits of your meditations, and your feelings about them, in the fourth-house section of your notebook.

Fifth House

The first quadrant pivots around the need to embody or reify your personal will (first house) in material form (second house). This quadrant, the second quadrant, pivots around the need to find freedom of *creative expression* for your personal will (fifth house) within the emotional and psychic *forms* you inherited from your family, your community and your ethnic and cultural traditions (fourth house). You cannot help being creative. That is why it is of vital importance to learn what your creative powers are doing, and how to direct them constructively.

The fifth house is the special sphere of personal creativity. Here are the mental, emotional and physical products of your creative powers, including your biological children. Delight and love of fun are never far from the creative process, so the fifth house is also the arena of speculation, amusements, parties, play and love affairs.

The fifth house is also called the house of esoteric or hidden karma. Conflict between your personal creativity (fifth house) and traditional norms (fourth house) is said to be a consequence of your misuse of personal will in the

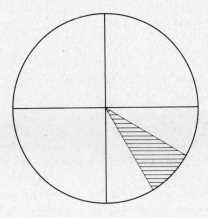

Figure 20. The fifth house

past or in past lives. You may experience this "esoteric or hidden karma" as misbehavior (frustration of your personal will) by your children.

In the fifth house you may make a show of independent creativity, but in fact you depend heavily on your fourth-house roots for emotional and psychic support. One might not guess how much reassurance you need, nor how strongly an audience or a critic can affect you.

Exercise 7: Sit in the fifth house of your space and meditate on your personal creativity.

Suggestions for meditation: Pictures or tokens of your children; drawings, poems, flower arrangements, or other examples of your creative self-expression. What does your mind/body feel like at times of heightened creativity? How do you experience inspiration? How does it come to you, and where does it come from? How do you invite it? What does the image of "courting the Muse" evoke for you? In your creative activities, how much is inspiration, how much is play and how much is work?

Meditate on souvenirs of your childhood, images of playfulness, fun, pleasure, parties, the fun side of a flirtation or love affair—whatever gives you joy and delight. Meditate on the relationship between inspiration and delight. Is your creativity heightened by the delight of a responsive audience? To what extent are your creations and your children creatures of tradition, to what extent are they molded by your personal will, and to what extent do they have a will of their own? Meditate on the nature of "will power." What is the relationship between your personal will and the deeper, transpersonal will of inspiration?

Describe the fruits of your meditations in the fifth-house section of your notebook. If you particularly like or dislike a certain pattern in your life as revealed in your meditation, or if you are embarrassed by a particular pattern, make note of it and of your feelings about it. Be alert for further examples of themes discovered in meditation and watch how your perceptions, emotional reactions and judgments change over time.

Sixth House

In the sixth house you clean up after the fifth-house party is over. As the cycle comes around to the Descendant, you must deal with other people's responses to the behavior of your children. Through an analytical process of sorting, sifting and selecting, you struggle to adapt both your heritage (fourth house) and your personal talents (fifth house) to the needs of your employer. The prime consideration here is practical serviceability, with no frills.

The compromises you have to make in the sixth house to hold a job, or to meet your boss's standards (or your own) can have repercussions on your health. As a consequence, the sixth house also encompasses a concern for health and nutrition, the experience of food as medicine, the desire to keep the body/mind healthy so that it will be dependable.

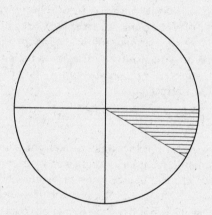

Figure 21. The sixth house

Exercise 8: Sit in the sixth house of your meditation space and meditate on the nature of service.

Suggestions for meditation: Job-related symbols—tools, work clothes, time card, contract, business papers; symbols of your employees or other subordinates. How do you feel about various kinds of service and various conditions of servitude, from slavery, imprisonment and military service through elected office and voluntary philanthropy? How do you serve others? How do you serve your community, your society, your planet? Meditate on the relationship between humility and humiliation, with respect to the pride characteristic of your fifth house.

What are your attitudes toward food and nutrition? Do you choose foods because of taste, appearance, familiarity, nutritional value or other factors?

What factors do you think *should* govern your choice of food? What kinds of experience can "put you off your feed"? How is your health and feeling of well-being related to your diet? Have you ever adopted a special diet, for example to gain or lose weight? How did it affect you?

How is your health related to your work experience? How does criticism affect you physically, mentally and emotionally? How do you analyze or criticize yourself? How do you digest and assimilate experiences arising in your fourth and fifth houses? How do you analyze and criticize others?

Describe the fruits of your meditations, and your feelings about them, in the sixth-house section of your notebook.

Seventh House

In the seventh house you are looking into someone else's first house, through your relationship with that person. In the sequence of houses, this is the first house above the horizon in the realm of conscious, objective activity. The subjective independence of the first quadrant, and the subconscious dependence of the second quadrant, are followed here in the third quadrant by conscious, objective interdependence. The seventh house begins with the extreme of "not-self" symbolized by the Descendant in the west, opposite the self-centered extreme symbolized on the eastern horizon by the Ascendant and first house. The greater consciousness and objectivity of the houses above the horizon are brought into your life through seventh-house encounters, partnerships and other relationships, including marriage. Growth in consciousness comes through relationships because the significant others in your life mirror those aspects of your personality that you cannot see. Hence, as Oscar Wilde noted, one cannot be too careful in one's choice of enemies: They help us find and correct those weaknesses that our friends politely ignore. The seventh house is also the realm of open, avowed adversaries and competitors.

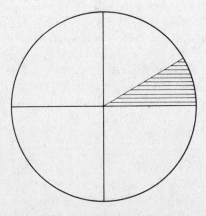

Figure 22. The seventh house

Exercise 9: Sit in the seventh house of your circle and meditate on symbols of otherness in your life.

Suggestions for meditation: Pictures or other tokens of your spouse or lover, of your marriage, of other social or business partnerships, of your adversaries or rivals, of contests or competition, contracts and agreements. In what circumstances and under what conditions do you meet new people? How do you make contact with others—by reaching out, by waiting receptively, by attracting their attention? How do other people introduce themselves to you? How do you feel about strangers? How do you relate to strangers in your home, in public places, and in their homes? Contrast your experiences among strangers with your experiences as a member of an in-group.

What are the bases of the relationships you have? Are they based on intellectual, emotional or empathic exchange, or on a combination of these? Are they founded on social, business or political interactions, or on other shared interests and activities? Do you cultivate any of these activities as pastimes primarily for the sake of the relationships, rather than for their intrinsic pleasure? Have you ever sacrificed an activity for the sake of a relationship, or vice-versa?

What qualities and responses do you like, appreciate or admire in the other people in your life? What qualities and responses do you dislike, resent or abhor in others? How are these value judgments related to your own personality structure, particularly those aspects that you have explored in your first three houses? Meditate on a particular relationship; use it as a mirror reflecting features of your personality you cannot directly see. What features are reflected by more than one relationship in your life? Notice how other people's gestures, expressions, accents, values, attitudes, fears and other features of personality-expression become incorporated into your personal repertoire. In the case of someone you dislike, have you assimilated the polar opposite attitudes, expressions and so on? If so, how did that happen? Were you aware of it?

What are the family roots of your way of relating? How did (and do) your parents make contact and maintain their relationships, both with each other and with others? Are there family enemies? Do they reflect family values, perhaps by embodying the opposite values? What was social life like in your family of origin?

Record the fruits of your meditations in the seventh-house section of your notebook. Be prepared for new insights coming to you through your daily interactions with others, and watch for changes in your feelings and attitudes about these matters.

Eighth House

In the eighth house you are looking into the second house of each person with whom you have a relationship. In general, the eighth house concerns other people's resources; more particularly, it is concerned with legacies, power plays and exchanges of energy, including transpersonal aspects of sexuality. The eighth house takes in certain experiences of the occult such as astral adventures, spiritual regeneration (alchemy) and all sorts of death/rebirth experiences, insofar as they penetrate the mysteries of "otherness."

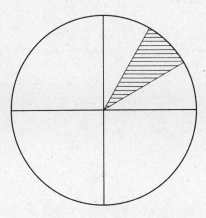

Figure 23. The eighth house

Exercise 10: Sit in the eighth house of your circle of houses and meditate on the resources and values of the people with whom you have seventh-house relationships.

Suggestions for meditation: Bills, receipts, loan agreements, financial reports, your joint tax return. In each partnership and relationship, how do you treat joint property differently from private property? How do you distinguish these three areas of ownership: "yours," "joint," and "theirs"? How do you mark the boundaries? How do you signal when boundaries are transgressed by your partner? By outsiders? Meditate on property issues such as ownership, stewardship, theft, gift, exchange, barter, sale, profit, vandalism, loss and waste. Consider these issues from these four points of view: your own point of view, the point of view of your partner, the point of view of your relationship as a distinct entity and the point of view of outsiders.

What are the aesthetic, moral, legal, religious, philosophical and other values of the people you identified as significant others in your seventh house? Are these values parallel to your own values, or are they divergent, contrary or entirely unrelated to your own values (second house)? What is the relationship of these values to the values of your family and your heritage of traditional values (fourth house)?

What imagery has sexual significance for you? Meditate on the sexual feelings evoked by this imagery, and on your experience of sexuality: How do sexual feelings arise, how do you respond to them, where do they go? In this process, what changes and what remains changeless? Concern yourself here particularly with those aspects of sexuality that come from beyond you and take you out of yourself.

Meditate on symbols of personal transformation. (Some possible sources include Jungian psychology, Eastern religions, esoteric or occult traditions, and personal experiences, either your own or those you know about at second hand.) As you meditate on each symbol, observe carefully how it resonates with your personality. If you do not like the personal values it evokes and reinforces in your consciousness, meditate on those values and on your attitudes toward them, and thus learn what the symbol has to teach you. Or choose a different symbol with more congenial associations, reserving the more challenging symbolism for a later time. For this work I particularly recommend the writings of Paul Foster Case (see the Bibliography).

Relics of death can be especially potent symbols for meditations relating to the eighth house. You might choose something as simple as a dead leaf, a memento of a childhood hobby or a souvenir of some personal attachment you have relinquished (or must presently relinquish) in the process of your growth. Again, consider what changes in these matters, as opposed to what is changeless.

Record your findings in the eighth-house section of your notebook.

Ninth House

In your seventh and eighth houses, your interdependent activities with other people take you "out of yourself." They compel you to take account of those transpersonal or spiritual principles by which you guide your life. Just as in the third house you explore the connections and relationships among things in your environment (thus reaching beyond the narrow egotism of your first and second houses), so too in the ninth house you come out of the immediate personal and social concerns of your seventh and eighth houses to explore and experience a wider world.

The ninth house concerns all sorts of experiences that expand your consciousness, "trips" that take you beyond your routine daily round not only in physical terms, but in mental, emotional and psychic terms as well, such as higher education, philosophy, spiritual disciplines and religion. It is through such experiences that you gain perspective on your actions and reactions, learning to see them as manifestations of universal principles at work in the world; or by orienting your actions to the religious, ethical and legal principles of your society. In the ninth house, you learn to guide your life by higher metaphysical principles rather than by makeshift expedients for day-to-day survival. In this way you assimilate your third-quadrant experiences in preparation for your emergence into the public eye in the fourth quadrant.

Exercise 11: Sit in the ninth house of your circle of houses, and meditate on your philosophy of life.

Suggestions for meditation: Symbols of travel (for example, travel brochures and books, pictures of places you have been or would like to go, maps, a globe, an atlas); symbols of higher education (for example, a college catalog, a

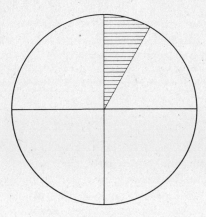

Figure 24. The ninth house

degree, textbooks, an encyclopedia); symbols of organized religion (for example, a Bible or other holy book, a cross, statue, icon or other religious emblem); a text of philosophy or metaphysics, a mandala, mantra, yantra, cabalistic diagram or alchemical illustration; a star map, a diagram of the solar system, astronomical literature and pictures; a horoscope or astrological symbols and writings.

What generalizations have you distilled from your experience to guide your planning, decisions and actions? Do you usually express these as affirmations ("Now I know I can_____if I want to.") or as prohibitions ("Now I know I can't_____.")? In other words, do your guiding principles function by marking blind alleys for you to avoid (the logical or mathematical approach), or do they open doorways for you to explore (the intuitive or aesthetic approach)? Do you make decisions by a process of elimination, or are other processes involved?

What other generalizations can you make about the principles that guide you? Do you derive such principles from the words of people you respect, from the examples such people set, from especially powerful or significant personal experiences, from repeated recognition of a given pattern of experience, or from a combination of these? Are you aware of having modified any of your guiding principles during the last year? Do your *actual* guiding principles differ from your ideals—the principles by which you would like to say you are guided but must admit you are not?

Who or what have been important teachers for you? Meditate on significant learning experiences you have had. How do you characteristically learn—what contexts, what situations, what emotional states, what other factors are generally part of a learning experience for you? How do you characterize your learning style? What things inhibit, distract, frustrate or block you from learning? How do you characterize your most reliable sources of information and guidance? How do you teach others?

Find symbols for meditation in mythology: classical mythology, myths about yourself that you or others may believe, and so on. Explore the power of myth. Find myths that you have created for yourself. Make your personal life-myths strong, powerful and appropriate for you.

Describe your discoveries from your meditations in the ninth-house section of your notebook.

Elements

In addition to the angular, succedent and cadent *modes* which arise from the division of each quadrant into three parts, the cycle of twelve houses is also characterized by four qualities which are symbolized by the alchemical *elements*, Fire, Water, Air and Earth. (The names of the alchemical elements will be capitalized to more clearly distinguish them from their common physical counterparts.)

The alchemical elements are not substances like the chemical elements, they are *qualities*, like hard or soft, which may be observed in all sorts of substances and events. You will learn to recognize the four elements in the circle of houses and in your cycles of experience now, and in later chapters you will deepen and extend this knowledge through other aspects of astrology.

Each element is shared by a group of three houses. These groups of three are called the "triplicities." The ninth house is the last member of the Fiery triplicity, so the element Fire will be introduced here to help you integrate what you have learned about these houses.

The Element Fire: The Personal or Willful △ Houses

The element Fire is angular in the first quadrant (first house), succedent in the second quadrant (fifth house) and cadent in the third quadrant (ninth house). It is absent from the fourth quadrant, as if resting or lying fallow there (figure 25).

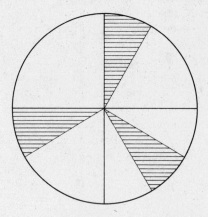

Figure 25. The personal or willful houses

The alchemical element Fire is symbolized by an upward-pointing triangle△; it is associated with the archetypal plane, the sphere of will, ideas and ideals. These three houses are concerned with the exercise of personal will, with inspiration by Divine Will, with the manifestation of ideas, ideals and archetypes.

Exercise 12: Review the material you have gathered through your meditations in your first, fifth and ninth houses, the personal or willful houses, where the element Fire predominates.

Suggestions for meditation: A flame or fire, as of a candle. Archetypal symbols, as of Tarot or Jungian psychology. What is the nature of ideas, ideals, inspiration, vitality, individuality or will?

What generalizations can you draw from your experiences in these three houses? What do they have in common? Express each generalization in a word or phrase, or with a nonverbal symbol that captures your insight, and then meditate on the words or images you have found.

Meditate on the maturation of the element Fire in your cycle of houses, from its childhood in the first quadrant, through its youthful vigor in the second quadrant, to its mature fulfillment in the third quadrant. In the fourth quadrant, think of the Fire element as a kind of "spirit guide," if you will, assisting the other three elements from a disembodied state between its "incarnations." Or, if you prefer, think of it as a retiree who acts as mentor to younger colleagues who are still active in the "business world." Does your personal expression of will, and your grasp of ideas and ideals, become more profound and more mature in the later houses of the Fiery triplicity? If not, what progression do you observe?

Record the fruits of your meditations in a separate section of your notebook, set aside for the element Fire, except where some discovery pertains to one house exclusive of the others.

The fourth quadrant is the outward culmination of the cycle of experience. This is the *objective* (above the horizon), *self-initiated* (east of the meridian) realm of personal *autonomy*. This quadrant corresponds to the winter season, the time to enjoy the benefit of what you planted in the spring, cultivated during the summer and then harvested and put by in the fall. It is a time to enjoy the company of your peers, to benefit from your established position among them and in the world. To continue the metaphor of the seasons, the fourth quadrant is a time to lay plans and prepare seed and equipment for the coming spring.

Tenth House

The tenth house is the angular house of the fourth quadrant. It begins at the high-noon peak of the cycle of experience, at the public extremity of the whole cycle, the opposite pole from the privacy and intimacy of your home and family in the fourth house. The tenth house is the realm of social participation, political power, honor and reputation, socio-economic status, position, career and public significance. As you evolve in consciousness, the tenth house turns out also to be the headquarters of your spiritual identity, your role as an administrator of Divine Will in your personal portion of the world.

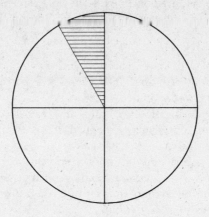

Figure 26. The tenth house

Exercise 13: Sit in the tenth house of your circle of houses and meditate on your worldly significance.

Suggestions for meditation: Diplomas, degrees, licenses, certificates, awards, citations, emblems or badges of office; your resume or curriculum vitae; your pass or I.D. card, membership card, business card, office or desk nameplate; newspaper or magazine articles about you, your work or your business. What is the nature of ambition, of competition, of economic or political power, of success, of organization and organizations, of hierarchies, of commitment (to goals, to organizations and to people)?

How do you feel about authority when you exercise it? When you are subject to it? Think of specific experiences: How do they reflect your attitude toward your honor, reputation, public standing and the other matters enumerated above? What is the nature of honor? of reputation? of status, prestige, popularity, praise, pride, fame; of ridicule, disgrace, humiliation; of insubordination, rebellion, revolt, revolution; of autonomy?

Is your present career truly an expression of your inner *vocation* (literally, your "calling")? What is your definition of success? Mentally review changes you have experienced in your career: Is there a common thread underlying the turning points in your personal history? Has your sense of vocation or calling changed? Has your ambition changed? What motivated these changes? What has remained constant, perhaps as an underlying theme?

The Element Earth: The Practical or Possessive ▽ Houses

The element Earth is angular in the fourth quadrant (tenth house), succedent in the first quadrant (second house), cadent in the second quadrant (sixth house) and absent as if resting or lying fallow in the third quadrant.

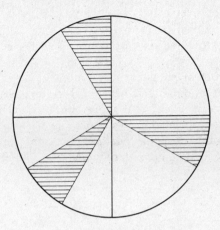

Figure 27. The practical or possessive houses

The alchemical symbol for Earth is a downward-pointing triangle with a cross-bar ▽ . It is associated with the material or physical plane. (There are four states of physical matter: solid, liquid, gas and plasma. The fourth, plasma, corresponds to what is traditionally known as the etheric plane, actually the upper or most subtle stratum of the physical plane. Other, more energy-like states on the energy/matter continuum are not considered to be physical states; they are assigned to higher planes which correspond to the other alchemical elements Air, Water and Fire.) The Earth element symbolizes embodiment, the final stage in the creative process that manifests concrete forms. The houses of the Earthy triplicity are concerned with practical matters, with physical and financial well-being and with the tangible consequences of actions.

Exercise 14: Review the material you have gathered through your meditations in your tenth, second and sixth houses, the practical or possessive houses.

Suggestions for meditation: A brick, symbolizing the physical, material, manifest aspect of things, as distinct from (1) the formative processes and structures of things on chemical, atomic and energy levels (Air element), (2) the forms or patterns that things exemplify (Water element) or (3) the intention or archetype behind the manifestation of things (Fire element).

Meditate on the mechanical, material, billiard-ball-like aspect of some important event in your life, as distinct from the emotional, mental or spiritual aspects of the event.

What is practicality? What does it mean for you to be practical or pragmatic, as opposed to being emotional and romantic, or intellectual and theoretical, or idealistic and inspirational? What is common sense? Meditate on stability, responsibility, being methodical, possessions, ownership, wealth versus poverty, or money. How does it feel to "have both feet on the ground"; to be well-grounded?

What generalizations can you draw from your review of your experiences in these three houses? What do they have in common? Express each generalization in a word or phrase or with a nonverbal symbol that captures or re-evokes your insight, and use these new images as objects of meditation; in this way you will discover a great deal more about the element Earth in your experience than could be printed in this book.

Record the fruits of your meditations in the Earth section of your notebook, unless they have to do with only one of the houses to the exclusion of the others.

Angular Houses

The modes of the houses, which divide the houses into three "quadruplicities" (angular, succedent and cadent), provide another convenient way to review and integrate the relationships among the houses. Since the tenth house is the last of the four angular houses, we will begin here with the angular mode.

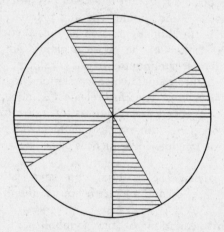

Figure 28. The angular houses

The angular houses symbolize the *emergencies* of your life. Your self-image (first house), home and family (fourth house), relationships and marriage (seventh house) and career (tenth house) are your most vital interfaces with your environment, where you *emerge* into a new quadrant of experience, and where you may be most deeply challenged by your outward circumstances and by the consequences of past actions. Experiences in the angular houses often represent new involvements, and tend to elicit a great deal of intensity and vitality from you.

Exercise 15: Review the material you have gathered in your notebook in your first, fourth, seventh and tenth houses, the angular or active houses.

Suggestions for meditation: What is the nature of causes, of beginnings, of initiation, of emergence, renewal, newness; of emergency, crisis (literally, "a crossroad"), challenge, opportunity?

What generalizations are suggested by your review of your experiences in these four houses? What do these experiences have in common? Find images that capture these generalizations for further meditation.

Record the fruits of your meditations in a separate section of your notebook devoted to the angular mode, unless they pertain to one of the houses exclusively.

Eleventh House

In your eleventh house, your tenth-house ambitions are opposed and shaped by peer pressure and the collective needs of your social milieu; that is, they are molded in the social matrix of your friends, peers, group activities, collective endeavors and the various professional and social organizations to which you may belong. The eleventh house is also the sphere of your personal hopes and fears and your aims; more broadly, it is the sphere of social aims, hopes and fears, as reflected in social reform, progressive politics and activities that foster the awakening of the Aquarian Age, the *Aquarian Conspiracy* as Marilyn Ferguson calls it in her book of that name. (This is because the eleventh house corresponds to the eleventh sign, Aquarius, as we shall see in Chapters 3 and 4.) In the eleventh house you identify with the groups in which you participate.

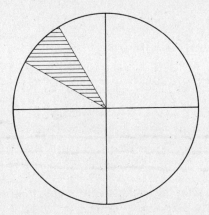

Figure 29. The eleventh house

Whereas the fifth house concerns the personal creativity best exemplified by the artist, it is the scientist who best typifies the collaborative, cooperative creativity of the eleventh house.

The eleventh house concerns *synergy:* that property of systems whereby the whole is greater than the sum of its parts. A social system low in synergy is one whose members experience a conflict between altruism and selfishness, so that they cannot help themselves without hurting their neighbors and they cannot help their neighbors without detriment to themselves. A social system high in synergy is one in which the conflict between selfishness and altruism does not arise, one whose language may lack these very concepts, one in which it is very difficult to hurt others because it is very obvious that such behavior would be injurious to oneself. Anthropologist Ruth Benedict developed this social application of synergy in a series of lectures in 1941 (see the Bibliography). R. Buckminster Fuller sees the miracle of synergy at the root of many of his greatest discoveries. To illustrate the concept of synergy, he offers a paradoxical equation:

$$1 + 2 = 4$$

which he explains as follows (figure 30): One equilateral triangle hinged onto two others can be folded into a three-sided tent (a tetrahedron) whose base is a fourth triangle. The fourth triangle appears unexpectedly, as if by magic, when you move from two dimensions into three dimensions.

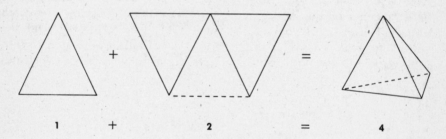

Figure 30. The principle of synergy

There are two clues to the nature of synergy here: expect the unexpected, because the behavior of a system as a whole is not predicted by the behavior of its parts; and the shift from the parts to the whole system requires you, the participating observer, to make a radical shift in perspective.

Exercise 16: Sit in the eleventh house of your circle of houses and meditate on your social matrix of peers and colleagues.

Suggestions for meditation: What role do your friends play in your life? What is the nature of friendship? List your closest friends on a page of your notebook; write a word or two describing or symbolizing some basic characteristics or qualities of each friend, and then other images for the quality of your friendship with each. What kinds of friends and friendships do you have?

What do you and your friends have in common? Do you form friendships easily, cautiously, impulsively or in other ways?

Who are your peers? Your professional colleagues? What is the character of your peer group; what are your collective interests and endeavors? To what clubs or other social or professional organizations do you belong? What are their aims and activities? Are you an active leader, a helper behind the scenes, a rank-and-file member or only a dues-payer? To what extent do you identify with the organizations to which you belong? In what areas of life are you a joiner? A loner? What does loyalty mean to you; what part does it play in your social and political life? To what sorts of peer pressure do you conform? Rebel against? Ignore?

What are your political attitudes? Where did you get them? What do you consider to be humanitarian ideals; how do you feel about them? Review the spectrum of political persuasions (i.e., reactionary, conservative, liberal, progressive, radical, revolutionary and so forth): How do you feel about each? How do you feel about "the masses," *hoi polloi*, the elite, the "better class of people," social privilege, economic exploitation, facism, sexism, ageism, public education, welfare? Add other social and political issues, meditate on them and delineate your own social and political values in your notebook.

Meditate on the Aquarian Age concept of synergy: How can you increase the level of synergy in your life?

The Element Air: The Connective or Synergetic △ Houses

The element Air is angular in the the third quadrant (seventh house), succedent in the fourth quadrant (eleventh house), cadent in the first quadrant (third house) and absent, as if resting or in retirement, in the second quadrant.

The alchemical symbol for Air is an upward-pointing triangle with a cross-bar△. It symbolizes phenomena of the mental plane. The lower strata of the mental plane comprise what is commonly called the astral plane. In addition to the more glamorous phenomena of hallucinations, hypnotic illusions and so on, the astral plane is the realm of the systematic processes and connections behind surface appearances which are studied to some extent in chemistry and physics. The higher strata of the mental plane involve similar but more subtle phenomena such as those studied in the mental and social sciences, including psychology, linguistics, sociology, anthropology and various branches of philosophy.

Houses of the Air triplicity are concerned with those personal mental activities that explore and articulate the ecological interconnections among people and things within larger systems. Social and ecological systems are cybernetic and therefore essentially mental: This is part of the truth behind the ancient Hermetic axiom which states that the universe is mental. (These ideas naturally tend to be articulated in Airy theoretical terms which will appeal most strongly to readers with a strong Air influence in their horoscopes.)

Exercise 17: Review the material you have gathered in your meditations in your seventh, eleventh and third houses, the connective or synergetic houses.

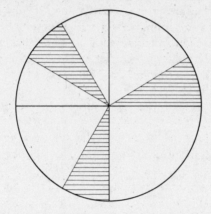

Figure 31. The connective or synergetic houses

Suggestions for meditation: Meditate on the nature and characteristics of air, wind and the atmosphere as a metaphor for mental activity, intellect, adaptation, connection, connectedness, relativity, analogy, correspondences, communication. Meditate on a particular experience of personal significance to you, from the point of view of those mental and psychological processes that are involved behind the outer appearances of the event.

How does it feel when you are caught up in abstractions and theories, preoccupied with verbal descriptions and arguments—on a "head trip" rather than being practical and pragmatic (Earth), or emotional and empathic (Water), or idealistic and inspirational (Fire)?

What generalizations emerge from your review of your experiences in the houses in the Airy triplicity? What do these experiences have in common? Express each generalization in a word or phrase, or with some nonverbal symbol that captures your insight. Use these new images as objects of meditation, to discover more about the element Air in your experience.

Record the fruits of your meditations in the Air section of your notebook, except where they pertain to one of the houses exclusively.

Succedent Houses

In the succedent houses you respond to ongoing activities and energies in your life, and put most of your concern into developing the meaning and lasting value of your involvements. In these houses you check to assure that you are not being pulled off course by some emergent or "emergency" action in the preceding angular houses. Your experiences in these houses elicit the conservative, goal-oriented side of your character, and represent your ability to learn from experience.

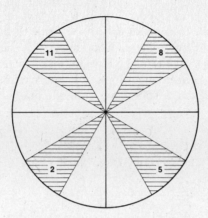

Figure 32. The succedent houses

Exercise 18: Review the material you have gathered in your fifth, eighth, eleventh and second houses, the succedent or reactive houses.

Suggestions for meditation: What is the nature of consequences, karma, results; of effects as opposed to causes? To what extent do you choose experiences in your life consciously, by your responses to events, and to what extent are your experiences conditioned unconsciously by your automatic reactions to events?

Recall some particular experience of importance to you. At the time, how did you evaluate and judge that experience? Did you interpret it according to its relationship to your personal goals: for example, whether it helped you to focus, form and consolidate your aims, or whether it blocked or distracted you? Did your evaluation and judgment seem unrelated to your conscious goals? If so, does this suggest that you may have unconscious aims in addition to those of which you are conscious?

What generalizations can you draw from your review of your experiences in the houses of the succedent triplicity? What do your experiences in these houses have in common? Try to find a word or phrase, or a nonverbal image, that captures your insights for further meditation.

Record the fruits of your meditations in a separate section of your notebook for the succedent mode, except where they pertain to one of the houses exclusively.

Twelfth House

In each quadrant, the issues raised in the angular and succedent houses must be resolved in the final, cadent house. Any unresolved residue forms the seeds of karma in the following quadrant. Thus, karma from the first quadrant is passed along to the second, where it may emerge, for example, as crises in your home life; seeds of karma from the second quadrant sprout up in the third quadrant;

e.g., as a quarrel with your spouse; and karma from the third quadrant affects your experience in the fourth quadrant; for example, through challenges to your reputation or public image. The cadent houses (see below) generally act as clearing-houses for each quadrant. The twelfth house, as the final cadent house of the cycle, is primarily concerned with resolving karma accumulated through the whole cycle, and indeed, accumulated through many turns of the cycle of experience.

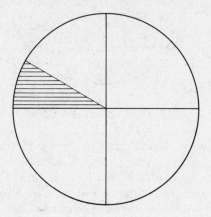

Figure 33. The twelfth house

The antecedents of a particular karmic issue in the twelfth house may even go back to previous lives, it is said. In any case, here you must use your accumulated resources and liabilities to resolve conflicts or imbalances whose origins may be hidden or forgotten. When you do not recognize the antecedent causes of a conflict, it may appear to you in the guise of fate, or of hidden enemies, or of mysteriously unaccountable obstacles, limitations or confinement.

Recognition and resolution of such conflicts often come through serving others unselfishly to alleviate their sufferings and experiences of limitation. When you help someone else to become free of a self-imposed limitation, without immediate concern for your own benefit, you stand to gain in unexpected ways. In order to recognize another person's need, you must have in yourself something corresponding to that need, so you gain in self-knowledge. By learning to recognize yourself in the predicaments of others, you grow beyond the narrow definitions of your own problems, which may, by their very narrowness, have blocked you from resolving them. If you behave with higher synergy, as if you were living in a social world in which benefit to others is indistinguishable from benefit to yourself, and the pain of others is your own pain, then you will find the world of your personal experience becoming more and more easy and rewarding to live in. As you give up your ego's need to be considered first, and allow yourself to be a means for the universe to help its inhabitants, you yourself become more receptive to that assistance.

Exercise 19: Sit in the twelfth house of your circle of houses and meditate on ways to recognize connections between present circumstances and past actions.

Suggestions for meditation: Karma (literally, "the consequences of doing"), consequences, the law of cause and effect. What is the relationship between deception and self-deception: Is it possible to mislead someone without lying to yourself on some level? What personal limitations can you identify in your experience, such as ill health, handicaps (physical, mental or emotional), poverty, obligations to others? As you meditate on a particular limitation, look for its antecedents in the other eleven houses, and consider its consequences as it is carried over into your first house to begin a new cycle. What limitations are experienced by people you know? How might you help them without concern for recognition? In general, what kinds of things have you done indirectly or from behind the scenes?

If you have any affiliation with practical occultism or with any organization devoted to it, meditate on its nature and its role in your life.

Identify a particular karmic issue in one of the other eleven houses, an issue that goes back a number of years in your life, and look in subsequent houses and quadrants for repercussions, until you find a connection with one of your twelfth-house limitations. What is the relationship between the demands your ego makes of the universe, and the constraints the universe appears to impose on you? Can you change an unconditional ego-demand into a preference, one preference among many?

How can you live in each quadrant, or even in each house, in a twelfth-house manner, resolving karma on the spot before it develops any further?

In a very relaxed state, fantasize what your past lives may have been like, and then meditate on these fantasies.

Meditate on the nature of redemption, renewal, selfless love, the mystical aim of atonement ("at-one-ment") and reunion with God.

The Element Water: The Empathic or Subjective △ Houses

The alchemical element Water is angular in the second quadrant (fourth house) succedent in the third quadrant (eighth house), and cadent in the fourth quadrant (twelfth house), and absent from the first quadrant, as if resting or "discarnate" there. (Note that Water is in the "discarnate" role of "adviser" or "teacher" to the other three elements in the first quadrant, at the beginning of the cycle.) Symbolized by a downward-pointing triangle △ Water is associated with the intuitive or Buddhic plane, and with pattern and form, the geometrical basis of all phenomena. These three houses are concerned with psychic sensitivity, empathy, and intuitive or (w)holistic mental processes which depend upon the linkage of all phenomena and all beings in a universal pattern.

When intuitive Watery perceptions of occult (literally "hidden") patterning (Water) are not well-integrated with conscious mental processes of

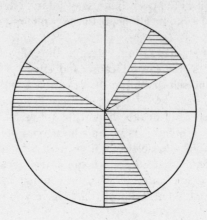

Figure 34. The empathic or subjective houses

observation, reasoning and communication (Air), they crop up inadvertently on the lower mental plane (commonly called the astral plane). This is why, certainly in Western cultures, psychic sensitivity is often associated with emotional instability and with unsettling perceptions of astral-plane phenomena. For this reason, in astrological tradition the element Water is associated with emotional expression, and the houses of the Water triplicity are called subjective as well as empathic houses.

Physical water is an extremely rich metaphor for metaphysical Water. Liquid water is so cohesive that a glassful may be considered to be one continuous, extended molecule. Within liquid water tiny portions of hexagonal crystallization ceaselessly form and dissolve, even when it is heated near the boiling point, as if the substance were continually recalling the geometrical pattern of ice lest it forget.

Since this is the last of the four elements, a comment on the form of the alchemical symbols for the elements is in order here. When the symbol for Fire △ and the symbol for Water ▽ are combined, the result is the six-pointed star, or Shield of David ✡ . This is the origin of the cross-bar in the symbols for the "lower" elements, Air △ and Earth ▽.

Exercise 20: Review material you have gathered in your notebook concerning your fourth, eighth and twelfth houses, the empathic or subjective houses.

Suggestions for meditation: Water in its various states (ice, liquid, steam, vapor). The patterns of snowflakes. Patterns formed by waves.

What is the nature of memory or recall? What is the nature of patterns, of intuition, of psychic perception? What is the nature of wishful thinking, fantasy, daydreaming, dreaming, hallucination, intuition, insight, meditation and other psychic states? How do you distinguish pity, empathy, sympathy and compassion from one another?

What generalizations can you draw from a review of your experiences in the houses of the Watery triplicity? What do they have in common? Express each generalization in a word or phrase, or with some nonverbal symbol that captures your insight. Use these new images as objects of meditation in order to discover more about the element Water in your experience.

Record the fruits of your meditations in the Water section of your notebook, unless they pertain to one or another of the Watery houses exclusively.

Cadent Houses

In the cadent houses, you seek ways to resolve the conflicts and challenges of a quadrant by placing them in a broader context, thereby widening your vision and preparing for the onset of the next quadrant. In the cadent houses you are more impressionable, more perceptive and more adaptable than in the other houses. Your sensitivity is not limited to your personal needs, as in the angular houses, nor to your personal goals and values, as in the succedent houses. Experiences in the cadent houses elicit the harmonious, process-oriented, compromising, adaptive side of your character.

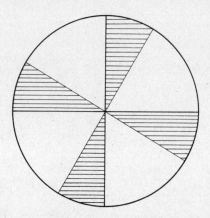

Figure 35. The cadent houses

The cadent mode is in a sense the most mature phase of each triplicity in the cycle of houses. An element in its cadent mode, at the end of a quadrant, must reconcile the angular and succedent expressions of two other elements in the first two houses of the quadrant. For this task of reconciliation it draws on its own prior angular expression (in the opposite quadrant) and succedent expression (in the next preceding quadrant).

For example, cadent Fire (the ninth house) must reconcile the contradiction between angular Air (seventh house) and succedent Water (eighth house). To do so, the Fire element here draws on its experience in the fifth house.

Here in the ninth house, where you are no longer as self-centered as in the first and second quadrants, you can better understand others (seventh house) because you remember your own impulsiveness and your own self-centered behavior (first house). Since pride is no longer as great an impediment in the ninth house as it was in the first and second quadrants, you can now use your personal creativity (fifth house) to help others realize new potential in their personal resources (eighth house).

The cadent mode also plants the seed of the next quadrant. For example, the Fire element in the ninth house plants the seeds that will be brought into manifestation by the Earth element in the tenth house. Cadent Fire here functions as the moderator of a kind of debate between angular Air and succedent Water. Since the Earth element is the only one not represented in this third quadrant, perhaps it is the real topic of their debate.

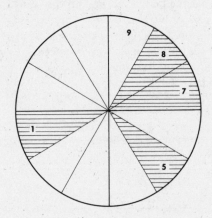

Figure 36. Fire moderating Air-Water "debate" over Earth

Exercise 21: Review the material you have gathered in your notebook concerning your ninth, twelfth, third and sixth houses, the cadent or resultant houses.

Suggestions for meditation: Synthesis, harmony, reconciliation, victory (in the high-synergy sense in which no one loses). What is the nature of eventualities, outcomes and conclusions? What is the nature of whole systems, of holism or "wholism," of ecology, of husbandry? What is the nature of resolution, preparation, readiness, poise, balance, improvisation and adaptation?

Meditate on roles like moderator, ombudsman, arbitrator, midwife, initiator, therapist, facilitator, teacher, catalyst and mediator, in connection with your experiences in your cadent houses.

What generalizations can you draw from the experiences you have associated with the four cadent houses? What do *your* experiences in the cadent quadruplicity have in common? Find words or phrases, or nonverbal images, to capture your insights for further meditation.

Record the fruits of your meditations in a separate section of your notebook for the cadent mode, unless they are relevant to only one of the houses.

By this time, you will have noticed that your experiences are seldom simple expressions of one house or another, but rather usually involve several houses simultaneously in complex ways. I conclude this chapter with a discussion of two of the most important patterns involving more than one house.

Conflicts with Others

In conflicts with others, opposite houses are usually involved. Your interests in one house are opposed by activities in what you perceive as your opposite house. The bone of contention has two ends, one in each of a pair of opposite houses.

Exercise 22: Think of a conflict you have had with another person. What houses were directly involved in the conflict? Determine which house seemed to involve you most intensely. Sit in that house of your meditation space, and imagine the other person sitting in the opposite house, listening. Tell that person what the conflict was about, insofar as it involved the house in which you are sitting. Limit yourself to terms appropriate to that house for the moment. When you have made your case, walk over and sit in the opposite house. Look at the conflict from that point of view. Review the points that you just heard yourself make, and see how they look in the context of the present house. Does your adversary's position really have to do with that house? (Your adversary's experience of the conflict might involve a different pair of houses; this realization would in itself go far toward resolving the conflict.) Once you are certain which pair of houses is involved in your dispute, look for ways in which you can differently manage your affairs in the house occupied by your adversary, to reduce unnecessary pressure on that person. Then return to your first position, in the other house of the opposition, and see how it looks from your original viewpoint now. Respond to your adversary's case. Continue the dialogue back and forth as long as necessary.

Turn to the houses of the same triplicity (Fire, Water, Air or Earth) to find special resources and support to help you clarify and alleviate the conflict. Some of the factors you were projecting onto your adversary may be more easily integrated in terms of these harmoniously-related houses.

When you have some clarity about the role of the house that seemed to involve you most intensely in the conflict, consider another house, whichever one seems most prominent in the conflict now. Your assessment of the conflict is likely to have changed somewhat as a result of your dialogue. Open the same kind of dialogue between this other house and the one opposite it.

Based upon this analysis, how might you have acted differently when the conflict first occurred? What can you learn from this experience for the future?

As you develop facility with this exercise, you will learn to analyze and resolve many interpersonal conflicts as they occur. The relevant astrological symbolism will spontaneously press forward in your mind, when you are receptive to it.

Inner Conflicts

When you experience indecision, doubt, guilt or other forms of conflict within your personality, houses at right angles to each other (90 degrees apart) are generally involved. These are two members of the same quadruplicity, ignoring the opposite house. An example is a conflict between your marriage (seventh house) and your career (tenth house), two angular houses.

An inner conflict is often projected onto another person through the house opposite one of the pair, in an unconscious effort to externalize it and understand it. In the example given above, a challenge to your reputation (tenth house) might make you anxious, defensive, or aggressive about your personal identity (first house, opposite the seventh); or a feeling that your spouse (seventh house) did not adequately support your career efforts (tenth house) might spark a quarrel with your parents (fourth house, opposite the tenth). For this reason, in Exercise 22 you should be alert for possible inner origins of your conflicts with other people.

Exercise 23: Think of a conflict you have experienced within yourself. What house was most directly and strongly involved in the conflict? Sit in that house of your meditation space and describe the conflict as clearly as you can, in terms appropriate to that house. Then walk three houses around the circle, whichever direction seems appropriate to you, to the corresponding house (that is, the house with the same mode, angular, succedent or cadent) in the next quadrant. Meditate for a moment on the characteristics of that house, then re-state your conflict in terms appropriate to that house. Then return to the original house, and look for fresh insight in terms appropriate to the symbolism of that house.

If your first choice does not give you what you need, try walking around your circle of houses in the opposite direction 90 degrees.

Look for ways in which you may be externalizing your conflict by projection onto other people through opposite houses. If you find such channels of conflict with other people, take them to Exercise 22, above.

For each house, look to the pair of houses that share the same element with it. The other two houses of a triplicity can provide special resources and support to help you clarify and alleviate the conflict.

Exercises 22 and 23 are particularly well-adapted to group work. As you learn the meanings of the planets in Chapter 2, and learn to locate the planets of your horoscope in your circle of houses, you will be able to focus these exercises even more sharply, taking roles in each other's horoscopes.

Meanwhile, practice bringing your problems and difficulties into your circle of houses for clarification. This will be your richest source of information about the meanings and relationships of the twelve houses, and the basis for all your subsequent learning. Your notebook will gradually fill with examples of astrological principles at work in your life. No one else could provide better material for you to learn astrology!

In this chapter you have learned about the basic framework of astrology, the foundation of astrological cycles in human experience. In Chapter 2, you will learn to recognize the operation of ten powers and faculties of personality, symbolized by the Sun, Moon and planets. You will explore the distinctive personal qualities of their expression through your circle of houses.

2

The Planets:
Your Powers and Faculties

According to occult tradition, the solar system is a living being, whose pulsing heart is the Sun, and whose other powers and faculties (which correspond to the powers and faculties of our own personalities) are embodied in the planets. You and the solar system are made in the same image. The Sun, our "day-star," is a member of the species we call stars, and that species is different in degree but not in kind from the species we call *homo sapiens*.

The relative strengths, qualities and relationships of the various powers and faculties of personality differ from one human being to another, but we are all influenced alike by the activities and changes of that solar Being in Whom literally "we live and move and have our being," just as we influence one another here on Earth in less pervasive but perhaps more familiar ways.

Astrology is ecology on a cosmic scale. Every part of the universe resonates with every other part, as well as with the whole. Because you are not separable from your environment, in a very real sense the entire cosmos is your body. You are the whole universe *as experienced from your own particular point of view.*

This is the traditional doctrine of macrocosm and microcosm. The macrocosm is the universe and the microcosm is you. The one corresponds to the other. Your personality has the same mental, emotional and physical *pattern* as the solar system, and other larger and smaller systems as well. Your success in managing your personality as part of the universe does indeed help manage the universe at large, because of their mutual resonances. At the same time, the regularity and grace of universal processes can guide you in managing your personality.

To help you understand the patterning and resonance of macrocosm and microcosm, a hologram provides a beautifully apt metaphor. A hologram is a photographic record of the interference pattern produced by laser light coming from two sources. One beam is pure laser light reflected from a mirror onto the film. The second beam, from the same laser, is reflected off an object onto the film, so that the regular "in-step" light waves of the laser beam are distorted in ways that exactly correspond to the surface of the reflecting object. When the two beams of light reach the film, they interfere with one another, producing what is called a *moire pattern* on the film, a "hodgepodge of specks, blobs and whorls" such as you see when you look through two layers of screen mesh overlaid one on another. When you look at the developed film, it makes no sense as a photograph. But just shine a beam of the same laser light through the film, as if in a slide-projector, and you see in mid-air a three-dimensional image of the original object!

The really fascinating part, and the part that makes the hologram such an apt metaphor, is that if you cut off a piece of the film—any piece, taken from any part of the film, regardless of what pattern of light and dark *appears* to be there—and shine the laser beam through it, you see the *same image* there as you would in any other piece of the film! This is because the visual information about the object is stored equally everywhere in the film, since light from every part of the object reached every part of the film. That is why every part of the hologram, however different in superficial appearance, is "made in the same image" as the whole.

However—and this fits the metaphor too—a smaller piece of a hologram presents a more restricted point of view on the object, and gives an image which is generally fuzzier than the image given by a larger piece, because of the "grain" of the film.

If this metaphor has any literal merit, it supports the traditional view of macrocosm and microcosm, the view that every system in the universe—the solar system and your personality, for example—bears the image of the whole. It tells us that when we look at a smaller piece of the universe, such as your personal experiences, we get a more restricted point of view and a fuzzier image. And it tells us to study the patterning of a larger system, such as the solar system, to get a clearer and less restricted view of what is going on. In a nutshell, this is how and why astrology works.

There are indications that the metaphor of the hologram does have considerable merit as literal truth. Karl Pribram, pioneering psychologist and parapsychologist, has been developing a model of cognition that says that the brain stores and processes information the same way a hologram stores the image of an object. Quantum-relativistic physicists believe that the universe itself may be organized like a hologram, and that it may be made up of interference patterns of waves of energy. There is a great deal of excitement about the convergence of modern science with ancient spiritual disciplines.

Now we can see with the eyes of science that the solar system is a vast, shifting field of energy. The physical bodies of the Sun, Moon and planets are the locations where the energy of this field is most intensely concentrated. They are the physical outcroppings of the solar system, somewhat the way islands are the tips of mountains rising from the ocean floor. During times of high sunspot activity the Sun pumps out a pulsating flow of ionized gases, mostly hydrogen.

This "solar wind" provides a vehicle for the Sun's magnetic field, strengthening it, so that it blocks cosmic radiation from penetrating past the orbit of Saturn. In a regular rhythm, sunspot activity subsides again. As the solar wind drops off, the solar system is again open to receive the emanations of other stars and galaxies, while its own emanations are at a low ebb. In this way, the throbbing heart of the solar system links us with other star systems throughout the universe. In the same way, we are told, there is a center of energy in the region of the human heart that links each of us with the Sun and with one another.

The "blood stream" of the Sun is comprised of electromagnetic, magnetic and gravitational fields, and other fields that we know less about. Within this ocean of vibrant energies swim the planets, each with its own fields. Planetary energy fields fluctuate in resonance with local variations of the solar field.

The aurora borealis and aurora australis are striking examples of the interaction of the Sun's emanations with the Earth's ionosphere. These awesome, brilliant curtainlike displays at the poles are the visible hem of Earth's aura, decorating the garment of energy that surrounds and supports planetary life.

Science can now see the planets as the visible outcroppings of the solar system. Like the several tips of a single complex "iceberg," they are the visible physical parts of a single field of vibratory phenomena. In the same way, your physical body is only the most obvious, visible part of you. All over the world, and all through history, people with special gifts of vision have reported perceiving centers or vortices of energy in the human body. In the Sanskrit literature of India, these are called *chakras*, a Sanskrit word meaning wheel or vortex. In the Western tradition, the alchemists, the Western equivalent of yogis, called them "our interior stars."

In resonance with the planets of the solar system, your "interior stars" go through cycles. The major chakras along the spinal column are said to resonate most strongly with particular planets, as shown in figure 37. You may develop awareness of your energy system as a result of the exercises in this book. Even if you do not, you will enrich your intuitive understanding of the planets in astrology by learning more about the chakras and studying their planetary correspondences.

These are the most important energy centers, or chakras. For some years, Dr. Brugh Joy has been teaching ordinary, "non-psychic" people to feel the energies of the chakras with their hands at some distance from another person's body. (See his book, *Joy's Way*, as cited in the Bibliography at the end of this book.)

Uranus is the higher octave of Mercury, so it is somewhat involved with the crown chakra. Similarly, Neptune is the higher octave of the Moon and Pluto is the higher octave of Mars. That is why the adrenal chakra, the brow chakra (or "third eye") and the crown chakra are shown with two planetary correspondences. The higher-octave planet is in parentheses.

The symbols for the planets will be explained further on in this chapter. The major chakras, their basic qualities, and their planetary correspondences, are as follows:

Chakra	Planet	Function	Physical Correlate
Root chakra	Saturn	survival, physical security	sacral plexus, base of spine
Adrenal chakra	Mars (Pluto)	passion; clairsentience (sensitivity to feelings)	prostatic ganglion
Splenic chakra	Pluto	regeneration	spleen
Solar plexus chakra	Jupiter	personal will, social expansion	solar plexus
Heart chakra	Sun	inner identity, purpose	cardiac plexus
Mid-chest chakra	Neptune	enthusiasm, inspiration	thymus
Throat chakra	Venus	clairaudience	pharyngeal plexus
Brow chakra	Moon (Neptune)	clairvoyance	postnasal ganglion
Crown chakra	Mercury (Uranus)	information; telepathy in purest sense	pineal gland
Transpersonal point	Uranus	intuition; non-attachment	about twenty inches above the head

In addition, there are minor chakras at the shoulders, elbows, hands, hips, knees and feet, whose astrological correspondences are not presently known. These chakras are all shown in figure 37.

Some people occasionally feel disorientation, confusion or vertigo. This may be due simply to returning too abruptly to a customary state of consciousness from meditation, or from sleep for that matter; or it may be symptomatic of imbalances in the metabolism of energy in your energy system. If your chakras get out of balance, due to your overemphasizing some functions and neglecting others, there are several visualization techniques that help restore balance. These are given in the Appendix on meditation.

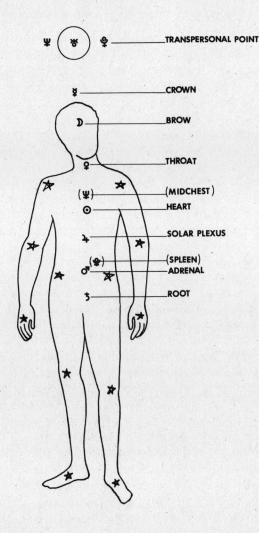

Figure 37. Chakras and planets

Planetary Symbols and Qualities

In addition to the chakras, there are other correspondences to the planets which have proven useful. Many of these derive from the spiritual discipline called alchemy in the West, and yoga in the East.

We are dealing here with qualities, not things. The alchemical elements Fire, Water, Air and Earth are qualities which are exemplified and symbolized by the things we know as fire, water, air and earth. Physical fire is emblematic of the metaphysical element Fire because it has the same "fiery" qualities that we perceive, for example, when we refer to a "fiery" temper. Just so, the Sun and the planets Mars and Pluto have "Fiery" qualities.

The alchemists also speak of specific metals in metaphysical, symbolic ways, intending that the qualities and characteristics of the metals should be taken as hints about the qualities and characteristics of more subtle things, such as the astrological energies of the planets and the chakras.

The planets also have color correspondences. Color is light vibration at specific frequencies. The planetary energies are vibrations many octaves higher in frequency. If you meditate on the color associated with a planet, the higher-octave planetary energy will also begin to vibrate within you, just as the higher-octave strings on a piano will vibrate when you hit a lower note. This well-known principle of resonance is central to an understanding of astrology.

By the same token, there are musical pitches associated with the planets. These are given variously by different authors. We must remember that standard musical pitch is a relatively recent innovation. The pitches given here (from Paul Foster Case, *The Tarot*) take into account the changes in definitions of musical pitches since older books were written.

Finally, there are Tarot associations. The Tarot cards are symbolic pictures which unite and illuminate every branch of esoteric science (yoga or alchemy). They were developed to protect students at times when secular and religious authorities were hostile to practices leading to direct experience ("gnosis" or cognition) of a higher and far superior power. They are especially powerful objects for meditation. (The Tarot images are reproduced here and in Chapter 3 by kind permission of the Builders of the Adytum, Ltd. The B.O.T.A. is the teaching organization founded by Dr. Case.)

In the following list, the planets are in their "alphabetical order." Except for the Moon, this is the order of increasing astronomical distance from the Sun. The Earth is omitted (it comes between Venus and Mars) because it is not one of the planets we are looking at. Rather, it is literally our point of view. The Moon, which orbits quite closely around the Earth, is placed next to the Sun because it is the next-brightest object in Earth's sky, and because its astrological influence is second only to the Sun's.

Science now realizes that everything in the observable universe is composed of vibrations or waves that form patterns of energy, as in a hologram. Sound and light are very clear examples. As you will see in Chapter 3, the twelve tones of the color-wheel are many octaves above the corresponding twelve tones of the Western musical scale, and the twelve signs of the zodiac are also composed of vibrations or waves which are in turn many octaves above the frequency of visible light. Similarly, the energies of the planets correspond to the vibration-frequencies of colors, many octaves higher.

Planet	Glyph	Chakra	Alchemical Element	Alchemical Metal	Color Resonance	Musical Resonance	Tarot Image
The Sun	☉	heart	Fiery (plus Air)	gold	orange	D	19 The Sun
The Moon	☽	brow	Watery	silver	blue	G#	2 The High Priestess
Mercury	☿	crown	Airy	quicksilver	yellow	E	1 The Magician
Venus	♀	throat	Watery (plus Air)	copper	green	F#	3 The Empress
Mars	♂	adrenal	Fiery	Iron, steel	red	C	4 The Emperor
Jupiter	♃	solar plexus	Airy (plus Water)	tin	violet	A#	10 The Wheel of Fortune
Saturn	♄	root	Earthy	lead	indigo	A	21 The World
Uranus	♅	transpersonal	Air		yellow	E	0 The Fool
Neptune	♆	mid-chest	Water		blue	G#	12 The Hanged Man
Pluto	♇	splenic	Fire		red	C	20 The Last Judgement

Figure 38 shows the inner portion of the color wheel. The central circle, which is indigo or deep blue-violet, is surrounded by the three primary colors, red, yellow and blue. These in turn are surrounded by six colors, the three primaries plus the three secondary colors that result from mixing primary pigments. The three secondary colors are orange, green and violet. The symbols or glyphs of the planets are shown where the corresponding colors would go. If you make a large copy of figure 38, color it and meditate on it in relation to the planets, it will teach you a great deal about the planetary energies. I recommend that you refer to this wheel of vibratory relationships as you do the exercises in this book.

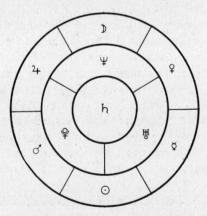

Figure 38. Planetary color wheel

Now we will look at the symbols or glyphs of the planets more closely. They are "words" in the symbol-language of astrology. Each may be translated into various words and phrases in ordinary, linear, verbal language. I recommend that you make a series of flash-cards. Draw each glyph on one side of an index card. On the reverse side, write the name of the planet at the top. Below that, write the correspondences given in the table, above. Leave room for more information as you learn it. Go through these cards at least twice a day, looking at the glyph and remembering what you can, then flipping the card over to check and refresh your memory.

As you draw the glyph of each planet, pay careful attention to how it is made. All of the planetary glyphs are composed of four graphic elements:

○	Circle	Whole, the Cosmic Egg, the No-thing, zero, black hole; spirit
☽	Crescent	Cup, chalice, container, focusing mirror; psyche or soul
|	Vertical line	Wand, staff, scepter, lightning rod, bolt; will or intention
—	Horizontal line	Plane, horizon, ground, realm, field; expression or extension

The vertical line corresponds to the meridian line in your circle of houses, the cusps of the tenth and fourth houses. The horizontal line corresponds to the Ascendant-Descendant axis of your circle of houses, the cusps of the first and seventh houses. Together, they form the "cross of manifestation" or the "cross of matter." This cross signifies synthesis, cyclic unity, the field of manifestation, the observable universe.

The circle corresponds to the perimeter of the circle of houses, that unity "in Whom we live and move and have our being." In the symbol for the Sun, the point in the center represents the innermost identity of a being, and the circle represents the expression of that identity undiscriminatingly outward in all directions. The circle may be taken to represent the perimeter of the solar system and the dot in the center as the Sun itself. The dot is actually a very small circle, since a point in the pure sense of the word has no dimensions and cannot be printed on a page. The point of innermost identity is not part of the universe which it creates and observes. Instead, and paradoxically, the manifested universe is part of it. From this "inside-out" point of view, the circle represents the inner identity of all things which are manifested within it. The dot and the circle are both representations of the One Thing.

The crescent is a half-circle. It corresponds to the waxing phase or to the waning phase of a cycle. Whenever you see a crescent ☽ , you know that there is another crescent that you don't see, oriented in the opposite direction ☾ . Together, the two crescents would complement one another and form a complete circle. Yet we usually see only one at a time, and the other stays out of awareness.

In Exercise 22, for example, you explored a conflict with another person by locating your point of view in one house and discovering your adversary's point of view in the opposite house. By putting your point of view into the same picture with the opposite point of view, you were able to move to a higher perspective and see how they complemented one another to form a unity. From this higher perspective, the resolution of the conflict became obvious. (If you have not yet had this remarkable experience, by all means try Exercise 22 again.)

It is possible to state categorically that whenever you are experiencing a problem in your life, it is because you are seeing only part of the picture. This is what is called the world of dualism, the world of the pairs of opposites.

When you put the cross of manifestation inside the circle, the result $\oplus$ is the symbol for the Earth, our planet. This symbol looks just like the four quadrants of the cycle of houses. Remember how the horizon and meridian lines divided the cycle of houses first into half-cycles, like the waxing and waning phases of the Moon, and then divided each of the half-cycles in two. This represents the world of duality, the world of the pairs of opposites, operating on itself to rediscover unity.

All the other planetary glyphs are combinations of circle, cross and crescent. Mercury is represented by a circle surmounting a cross and crowned with a crescent. Venus is a circle above a cross. Mars was originally represented by the opposite combination, a cross above a circle ♂ , but it has been modified by folding the horizontal line into an arrow point ♂ and directing it to the right at an angle. Jupiter is represented by a crescent above the left arm of a cross, and Saturn is represented by a crescent below a cross; often, Saturn's crescent is recurved like a shepherd's crook. Uranus is represented by two opposed crescents linked by a cross with a circle beneath. Neptune is a crescent penetrated from beneath by a cross, forming a trident. Pluto is represented by a crescent embracing a circle and surmounting a cross.

Meditate on the planetary glyphs as you have drawn them on your index cards. Consider the graphic elements that make up each glyph, as described above, and meditate on their relationships to gain deeper insight into the nature and qualities of each planet. When you draw the glyphs, use the color correspondences given above. (Outline the yellow Mercury symbol and Uranus symbol in black or violet to make them more easily visible.) Include these colors and their relationships in your meditations.

The ten planets correspond to ten powers and faculties of the universe. As a hologram-piece of the universe, your personality also is comprised of these same ten powers and faculties. Make ten more sections in your notebook, one for each of the planets. In these sections you will write your discoveries about the planetary energies in your meditations and in your observations of your daily life. You will discover how the universal energies represented by the planets are filtered, combined and focused in a unique way through the field of your personality to manifest as your personal powers and faculties; you will learn to recognize your unique personal rhythms, the cyclic interplay and modulation of your powers and faculties in resonance with the cycles of the solar system from day to day.

In ancient times, the planets were depicted as gods and goddesses. As you come to love and honor them in all their myriad diminutive, particularized expressions through the various personalities you encounter, your own expression of them will widen and deepen. You will learn to participate consciously in your own evolution, following that vaster and clearer replica of the Divine Image embodied in our solar system.

The Sun ⊙

The heart of our solar system, the Sun, corresponds to your heart chakra. The Sanskrit name of the heart chakra, *anahata*, means "unbeaten." Its alchemical correspondence is the metal gold, and its symbol or glyph is a gold or orange circle with a central point. In your personal consciousness, you experience this power as your sense of life-purpose, your drive for personal significance, and the deepest, purest expressions of will (in the universal sense) in your life. This is the root of your ego, your innermost identity, which your other personal powers and faculties reflect and modulate but cannot obscure.

Exercise 1: Meditate on the question "What do I want?" Write as many sentences as you can beginning with "I want," whether they seem significant or trivial. Put a sign on your wall asking "What do you want?" or affirming "I want..." and leaving a space for you to fill in mentally. These will remind you. See what you can come up with during the course of a week. Then let them rest a week or more before you study your answers and put them in order. One desire may be included within another or may be a step toward a broader and higher aim. One may be precluded by another because it is unnecessary or contrary to another aim which you desire even more. As you find these relationships among your various wants and desires, they will help you to boil down your lists of wants so that you can pinpoint your most essential desires.

When you have a reduced list of your core wants, meditate on these to discover what they have in common. Find the underlying motivation of each coherent group of wants, and state these deeper drives in a simple, clear way. Continue this process until you are able to state clearly and simply your deepest personal motivation in life. You will know when you have this because your subsidiary desires will all be steps to attaining your one deepest desire, or facets of it. Your prime intention is the core of a successful philosophy of life for you.

You must find this for yourself. No one else's aims will work for you. For this reason, be especially clear about distinguishing what you *want* from what you *should* do or have. If your search for motivation evokes feelings of anger or depression, or any feeling other than inspiration and joy, it may be because you have allowed some of the outer conditioning and adaptiveness of the Moon side of your personality to intrude in your list of wants. It may be that some of the "shoulds" of your life are blocking you from truly embracing your innermost life-purpose, and a reminder of this evokes anger, frustration or depression.

Your statement of your inner purpose is likely to evolve as you grow in awareness. Meditate on your closest approximation. Visualize what your life will be like when you attain your aim. If your imagination presents you with images that you don't like, use that feedback to help you refine your aim.

Finally, keep your statement of life-intention to yourself. It is no one's business but your own. It is a lens for accumulating and focusing power. The opinions and judgments of others cloud that lens with doubts and "shoulds." Polish it daily, and it will be an extraordinarily rich source of inspiration and strength. For example, it will enable you to make decisions quickly and easily because you will see immediately whether your choice helps or hinders the manifestation of your heart's desire.

Suggestions for further meditation: Meditate on the glyph for the Sun which you have drawn on an index card in orange or gold. What ideas, feelings and other images does it evoke?

Meditate on Tarot Key 19, The Sun (figure 39). Study the corresponding chapter in Paul Case's *The Tarot* (see the Bibliography).

Figure 39. Tarot Key 19, The Sun

Meditate on the nature of courage; confidence; self-assurance; "hearty" behavior; unconditional love; compassion.

How do you justify what you do and what you refuse to do? As you continue your work in the circle of houses, relate your discoveries about the solar side of your personality to your experiences in your first and fifth houses.

Record your observations in the Sun section of your notebook.

The Moon ☽

Properly speaking, the Moon is a satellite of the Earth and not a planet in the modern sense of the word, but her influence on the Earth is exceeded only by the influence of the Sun. Traditionally, the Sun and Moon are called the "luminaries" or the "lights" of the horoscope. The orbit of the Moon is said to coincide with the perimeter of the Earth's astral body, that is, with the edge of Earth's life-field (like the life-field that biologists are discovering around living creatures). The Moon is associated with astral perceptions, out-of-body experiences and so on, and corresponds to the brow chakra or "third eye" (called *ajna* in Sanskrit, meaning "command"). The alchemical correspondence is the metal silver and a Watery quality; silver and water were both used as mirrors before the day of glass mirrors, and the principle of reflection and duality is central to the symbolism of the Moon. Psychologically, the Moon corresponds to your subconscious mind, memory, the formation and change of habit patterns, the models you try to live up (or down) to, your conditioning, your personal insecurities and your manner of reassuring and nurturing others—in short, to the vast realms of subliminal consciousness below the threshold of conscious attention. (The word "subliminal" comes from Latin *sub* "below" plus *limen* "threshold.")

The lunar aspect of your personality gives form and substance to your solar motivation by resisting it. The relation of solar purpose to lunar expression is analogous to the relation of the succedent houses to the preceding angular houses. The inertia of the Moon provides the stable foundation of your psyche. It represents the fundamental sub-stance (literally "under-standing") out of which your personal character is wrought by your other powers and faculties in accord with your inner life-purpose. Like silver, the substance of the psyche is malleable. However, if your inner purpose is not clearly focused, your lunar self will be shaped by influences from other people in conflicting ways.

Exercise 2: Meditate on the question "What do I need?" Write as many sentences as you can think of in the form "I need_____ to order to_____." or "I need_____for_____." For each want or desire that you identified in Exercise 1, above, there is at least one need. Fill in the blanks, putting your wants in the second blank and the corresponding needs in the first.

Include other things you feel you need. These may be related to what you feel you *should* be and do, or they may disclose deeper desires and motives which you missed in Exercise 1, and now need to consider in your list of wants.

Study and organize this list, and discover its essential core, your deepest needs, as you did with your wants in Exercise 1.

One of the major challenges of life is the integration of your solar *aims* with your lunar *means*. For example, you may not *want* to take some of the steps you need to in order to accomplish what you do consciously want (e.g., practicing a musical instrument, or meditating regularly). Conversely, you may crave something irrelevant, or actively inimical, to wants and needs that are more important to you on a conscious level (e.g., television). These cravings may be simple matters of habit.

Meditate on this statement of your most strongly-felt needs, in relation to your solar motivation. As it evolves and becomes more refined over time, this affirmation will show you how to accomplish your desires and how to remove obstacles from your path.

If you don't take care of your needs, who will? And why should they?

Suggestions for further meditation: Draw the glyph for the Moon ☽ on a card in blue or silver, and meditate on this simple image. What ideas, feelings and other images does it evoke?

Meditate on Tarot Key 2, the High Priestess. Study the corresponding chapter in Paul Case's book.

Figure 40. Tarot Key 2, The High Priestess

Meditate on the nature of memory: How does your memory work? Are your strongest memories verbal, emotional, sensual, visual, auditory, tactile, olfactory, kinesthetic or in some other sensory mode? Do memories affect you differently, depending upon the sensory mode(s) involved? What kinds of experiences make you feel good and secure, or bad and insecure? What memory-association does each of these experiences and feelings evoke? What houses are involved in these experiences and memories?

Meditate on your habits: What are your good, constructive, helpful habits? How did you form them? How do you feel about your "bad" habits, and what do you do about them? How do you change your habit-patterns? How is this related to your style of learning (Chapter 1, Exercise 11, ninth house)?

Meditate on the nature of suggestion, and the power of suggestion: How do you determine which attributions about yourself and about the world pass the gates of your conscious mind and enter your subconscious mind as suggestions?

Meditate on the nature of security: What makes you feel secure or insecure? How do you recognize other people's insecurity? How do you assure people who are distressed? What kinds of distress can you alleviate with reassurance? What kinds of distress do you avoid or ignore? What kinds of distress do you discount as "not serious"? What kinds of distress upset you to such an extent that you need reassurance yourself, before you can help the distressed person? Have you ever had the experience of reassuring another person with the surprising effect of calming and reassuring yourself? Meditate on the life-giving, nurturing aspect of parenting or mothering.

Meditate on the nature of mind: Use the traditional image of a pool of water which reflects like a mirror. As you watch your stream of consciousness, look for the spaces *between* your thoughts. How are your mental images connected or associated? What is the nature of the subtle substance that carries them or reflects them?

As you continue your work in the circle of houses, relate your discoveries about the lunar side of your personality to your experiences in your second and fourth houses.

Record the fruits of your meditations in the Moon section of your notebook.

Mercury ☿

This closest planet to the Sun is symbolically an intermediary communicating the wisdom of the heart to the other powers and faculties of the personality. In mythology, Mercury is the messenger of the gods, carrying information, gossip and mischief among them. In your personality, Mercury corresponds to that monkey-like faculty, the intellect (from the Latin *inter-ligere*, "to discriminate"), and its vehicle, the senses. It corresponds to the crown chakra, called in Sanskit *sahasrara* ("thousand," referring to the many spokes or "petals" of this chakra). Its alchemical correspondence is the metal mercury or quicksilver, the alchemists' universal solvent, which reconciles the pairs of opposites—Sun and Moon, yang and yin, Fire and Water—in the same way that the cadent houses resolve the polarity of the preceding angular and succedent houses. It is associated with the alchemical element Air, and its color correspondence is bright yellow. The symbol for Mercury is a circle surmounting a cross and crowned by a crescent. Although your conscious mind, with its powers of observation, reason, verbalization and manipulation, is a direct reflection of your inner identity (the circle), and is capable of governing and manipulating the four elements of manifestation (the cross below the circle), it can do no more than is allowed by its system of beliefs and disbeliefs rooted in subconscious memory and habit (the crescent above the circle). Only after you have consciously conditioned your subconscious mind (your Moon) to reject any suggestions which contradict your inner life-purpose (your Sun) will the ego-shell of self-limiting patterns be dissolved. Mercury makes this possible.

Exercise 3. Practice concentration on an object which has no particular intrinsic interest for you: a mark on a blank piece of paper, the head of a match, your rhythm of breathing, your heartbeat (block your ears with oil-soaked cotton balls to hear), any simple, persistent focus for your concentration. Set a definite time limit for each sitting, five minutes to start.

Are you able to concentrate, or are you easily distracted? What sorts of things distract you? What does this tell you about your interests and motivations? How does your mind react to this discipline?

Suggestions for further meditation: What is the character of your verbal ability? Are you good at describing or explaining things? Is verbal or nonverbal communication (body language, gestures, emotional tone, etc.) more important for you? What kinds of things are easy or hard for you to describe or explain to someone—feelings, human interactions, mechanical things, abstractions and theories, personal preferences and tastes, experiences in your personal history? Is your mind rigorously logical? flexible and adaptable? fanciful and imaginative, playful? emotionally or aesthetically sensitive? intuitive, with flashes of insight?

Does your mind work quickly or slowly—does it leap ahead of your present situation, or do you evaluate and analyze by hindsight? Does your mind buzz and skip along with energy, or does it plod methodically? If the pace and tempo of your mental process vary, do the variations follow any discernible rhythm? Can you identify causes of variation in your mental functioning?

Meditate on the metal quicksilver or mercury.

Listen to the Mercury section of Holst's orchestral suite *The Planets* and meditate on Mercury.

Meditate on Tarot Key 1, The Magician. Study the corresponding chapter in Case's *The Tarot*.

Figure 41. Tarot Key 1, The Magician

Draw the symbol for Mercury ☿ in yellow on a card, outlined with a thin black or violet line. Meditate on this image and on the way it is composed of crescent, circle and cross. What ideas, feelings and other images does it evoke?

As you continue your work in your circle of houses, relate your discoveries about your Mercurial conscious mental faculties to your experiences in your third and sixth houses.

Record the fruits of your meditations in the Mercury section of your notebook.

Venus ♀

Venus, the other planet between the Earth and the Sun, represents the other side of your personal mentality, the intuitional, holistic side, including your creative imagination, your personal tastes and values and your sense of appreciation. According to one tradition, the symbol represents the goddess Venus's hand mirror. The circle above the cross suggests the raising of the four elements of manifestation (the cross) toward perfection.

Venus resonates with the throat chakra, called *visuddha* ("pure") in Sanskrit, which is linked with the inner sense of hearing, the door to true intuition (in-tuition, inner teaching). The color correspondence is emerald green, and the emerald is sacred to the goddess Venus. The alchemical metal is copper, together with its alloys, brass and bronze.

Venus is closely allied with the Moon. They are the two phases of subconsciousness: Whereas the Moon is passive, receptive and associative, the faculty of memory, Venus is active, productive and deductive, the faculty of imagination. Creative imagination is the result of suggestions being implanted in subconsciousness (the Moon) by an act of conscious attention (Mercury); mix Mercury (yellow) with the Moon (blue) and the result is creative imagination, Venus (green). You pay closest attention to things you most like or dislike, so your imagination develops images that reflect your values and tastes. You express these images through your affections and your personal attractiveness. Venus is, after all, goddess of love as well as of the arts and graces.

Exercise 4: Meditate on the question "What do I like?" Write as many sentences as occur to you beginning with "I like" and "I appreciate." What do you find attractive? If you think of something that you dislike, or that you find repulsive, look for the polar opposite thing that you like and are attracted to. See what you can come up with in the course of a week, then study and organize your answers to discover their essential core, your deepest personal values, the seat of your desires.

Suggestions for further meditation: Review what you discovered about your personal values in your second house. What do you like in your possessions and your physical environment? What kind of environment attracts you? Meditate on the nature of good taste and bad taste.

Review what you discovered about your social values in your seventh house. What do you like in your relationships and in your social environment? What kind of person do you find attractive? What kind of person is attracted to you? What do they find attractive or unattractive in you? How do you express appreciation? Affection? How does it feel to be appreciated? Meditate on the experience of falling in love, of being in love, which may include feelings of possessiveness and jealousy. Meditate on unconditional love, in which possessiveness and jealousy do not arise. What is the role of imagination in the ups and downs of love? Review your experiences in your twelfth house for information about unconditional love.

What is the nature of imagination, fancy, fantasy? How do you experience the relationship between imagination and memory? imagination and observation? imagination and reason? imagination and intuition? Are you aware of your imagination as a distinct faculty to which you may turn at will, or does it operate unconsciously, automatically, in combination with your other powers and faculties? Does your imagination anticipate events, or does it evaluate experiences after the fact? Find ways to play with your imagination, to enjoy it.

Meditate on Tarot Key 3, The Empress, and study the corresponding chapter in Case's *The Tarot*.

Figure 42. Tarot Key 3, The Empress

Listen to the Venus section of Holst's *The Planets* and meditate on Venus.

Meditate on the color green. Meditate on the nature of healing or making whole and the role of the imagination in health. Draw the symbol for Venus ♀ in green on a card. Meditate on this image and the relationship of the cross to the circle. What ideas, feelings and other images does it evoke?

As you continue your work in your circle of houses, relate your discoveries about your subconscious Venusian creativity to your experiences in your second, seventh and twelfth houses.

Record the fruits of your meditation in the Venus section of your notebook.

Mars ♂

Mars is the opposite and complement of Venus. Its orbit is just outside that of the Earth, and Venus's orbit is just within the orbit of the Earth. Anciently, its symbol was a cross above a circle, the imperial globe, symbol of dominion, rule and authority. The modern form of the glyph is familiar to us as a symbol for the male sex in opposition to the Venus symbol, which symbolizes the female sex. Its color resonance is red, the complement of Venus's green.

Mars resonates with the adrenal chakra below the navel, which is called in Sanskrit *svadhisthana* ("abode of the vital force" or "seat of the psyche"). The alchemical metal is iron and its various alloys which are all called steel. It manifests as your aggressiveness, ambitiousness, energy, vitality and muscle tone. It is the vehicle for expressing personal volition.

Exercise 5: What do you *do* about the things you like? What arouses you? What stirs up your adrenalin? Answer the question "What do I go for?" Consider what would threaten or oppose the things you like, which you discovered in connection with Venus. Study and organize your answers, to discover the essence of these things which arouse your aggressiveness.

Suggestions for further meditation: What kind of experience makes you angry? hostile? aggressive? assertive? What situations make you timid or uncertain? Do you prefer to fight verbally, physically, emotionally or not at all? How do you feel about fair fighting and dirty fighting? Do you expect others to fight fair? Do you fight fair when you doubt your ability to win? When do you fight dirty? How do you fight unfairly?

What are you ambitious for? What makes you work hard? What really turns you on? In what way? What turns you off? Does your vitality go through phases, or are you energies constant? How is your muscle tone—firm, flabby or so-so?

How do you react to various kinds of threat? To being limited or thwarted? To someone's mistakes or stupidity? To your own errors? Meditate on the experience of frustration: What is going on in each part of your body, in your emotional responses, and in your mental processes when you are frustrated?

Meditate on Tarot Key 16, The Tower, and study the corresponding chapter in Case's *The Tarot*.

Figure 43. Tarot Key 16, The Tower

Listen to the Mars section of Holst's *The Planets* and meditate on Mars. Meditate on the color red. Meditate on strength, courage and vitality.

Draw the symbol for Mars ♂ in red on a card. Meditate on this simple image. What ideas, feelings and other images does it evoke?

As you continue your work in your circle of houses, relate your discoveries about your Mars energy to your experiences in your first, eighth and tenth houses.

Record the fruits of your meditations in the Mars section of your notebook.

Jupiter ♃

The largest planet in the solar system, a so-called "gas giant" type, Jupiter represents the principle of *expansion.* It is a powerful emitter of radio signals. The correspondence in your personal energy system is the *manipura* chakra. This Sanskrit term means "navel," not because of any direct connection to your physical navel, but because it is the umbilicus of your subtle energy system, the point of emanation for projections of personal will. (See descriptions of these energy-cords, for example, in the books of Carlos Castaneda, and in the autobiography of Elizabeth Haich.) In the physical body, this chakra is associated with the solar plexus, the neural complex in the pit of the stomach, named not for any occult connection with the Sun, but because of its size and corona-like shape. The solar plexus is sometimes called the "abdominal brain" because of its preeminence in the autonomic nervous system, following the lunar rhythms of the pituitary gland. The glyph for Jupiter shows a crescent standing over one arm of the cross of matter, symbolizing the manifestation of subconscious lunar patterns through this principle of growth and incorporation. Jupiter is linked with alchemical tin, and with the color violet. In personal terms, you experience this power as joviality, generosity and optimism, or as overexpansion, overextension, overestimation of your resources and abilities, pride, egotism and other issues of balanced *judgment.*

Exercise 6: Meditate on the nature of opportunity. Answer the question "For what do I hope?" If something you fear occurs to you, think of the polar opposite thing you hope for, in positive terms, and include it in your list. Study and organize your answers, to get a clear statement of your highest hopes. What events or circumstances would help you realize these hopes? How can you recognize these opportunities when they occur?

Suggestions for further meditation: Meditate on the nature of optimism. When are you generous and expansive, or cautious and stingy? Which mood predominates in your experience? Are you generally gregarious and extroverted or moody and introverted? Think of specific experiences that have led you to be one way or the other. Which houses are associated with "Jovial" experiences in your life?

Do you consider yourself lucky or unlucky? What houses have been involved in your "lucky" experiences? Meditate on the nature of luck or fortune.

In which houses are you most apt to overextend yourself? Recall experiences in which you overindulged; in which you overestimated your resources or abilities; in which you gave a gift you could not have afforded for yourself; or in which you acquired all the equipment and trappings for something you wanted to do, without developing the skills to use them. Meditate on these experiences in your circle of houses, making note of the connection with Jupiter for future reference.

Meditate on Tarot Key 10, The Wheel of Fortune, and study the corresponding chapter in Case's *The Tarot.*

Figure 44. Tarot Key 10, The Wheel of Fortune

Listen to the Jupiter section of Holst's *The Planets* and meditate on Jupiter.

Meditate on the color violet. Meditate on synergy (Chapter 1, Exercise 16).

Draw the symbol for Jupiter ♃ , in violet on a card. Meditate on this simple image. What ideas, feelings and other images does it evoke?

As you continue your work in your circle of houses, relate your discoveries about your Jupiterian powers of judgment to your experiences in your fourth, ninth and twelfth houses.

Record the fruits of your meditations in the Jupiter section of your notebook.

Saturn ♄

The glyph for Saturn is a cross surmounting a crescent, the opposite of the symbol for Jupiter. Here, the rhythmic powers of the subconscious mind (the crescent) are overshadowed and channeled by the formal and structural necessities of manifestation (the cross). Saturn represents the principle of contraction, the complement of Jupiter's expansive quality. Saturn resonates with the root chakra at the base of the spine, called *muladhara* in Sanskrit (*mula* "root" plus *adhara* "vital part, support"), which is connected with being grounded (see below), physical survival, elimination of wastes and reproduction (survival of the species). Its metal is the lead which the alchemists transmute to gold. The color resonance is the deep indigo or blue-violet of the night sky, almost black. In the body, Saturn rules the bony structure of the skeleton; in your personality, it manifests as your administrative faculty, your capacity for discipline, organization and responsibility. Saturn is the teacher of cause-and-effect, consequences and necessity, the architect of our karmic lessons.

Exercise 7: Meditate on responsibility; what is the connection between the noun "responsibility" and the verb "to respond"? Answer the question "What do I fear?" or "What must I be prepared for?" Think of all the things that could prevent the fulfillment of your hopes; how can you keep your balance and stay on course in changing circumstances?

Suggestions for further meditation: What is the nature of gravity, of weight? How does the same principle of gravitation that makes a bar of steel sink in water, cause a boat of steel to float on the water?

Meditate on the nature of authority: How do you feel about authorities? What kinds of authority do you believe in? Have you ever been a true believer or a party-liner? What kinds of people do you feel are generally trustworthy, or not trustworthy? How do you decide whether or not to believe someone?

Meditate on the nature of discipline: Are you self-disciplined, or do you need the external structure of a class and teacher to study, or of a boss or supervisor to get a job done? In which houses do things come easily, though perhaps you accomplish less? In which houses do you have to work for everything you get, but you get what you work for? In which houses do you experience frustration or limitation? Meditate on the nature of limitation.

Meditate on the nature of structure and of organization: What structures or organized systems do you use in each house? What organizations or social structures do you belong to or participate in?

Meditate on the nature of administration.

Meditate on Tarot Key 21, The World, and study the corresponding chapter of Case's *The Tarot.*

Figure 45. Tarot Key 21, The World

Listen to the Saturn section of Holst's *The Planets* and meditate on Saturn.

Meditate on the color indigo (blue-violet) and on being centered. (The Alice Bailey books have indigo covers.)

Draw the symbol for Saturn ♄ in indigo or black on a card. Meditate on this simple image. What ideas, feelings and other images does it evoke?

As you continue your work in your circle of houses, relate your discoveries about your Saturnian discipline to your experiences in your seventh, tenth and eleventh houses.

Record the fruits of your meditations in the Saturn section of your notebook.

Uranus ♅

The unexpected planet, Uranus, is sometimes faintly visible to the naked eye. It was not discovered until 1781 because it was well known that Saturn with its rings was the "ring-pass-not" or outer limit of the solar system. Uranus had actually been photographed several times by people looking for other objects, and its discoverer, Sir William Herschel, at first thought it was a comet. For astrologers, Uranus became the new ruler of the sign Aquarian, supplanting Saturn, in anticipation of the Aquarian Age.

Uranus rolls around its orbit with one pole turned perpetually toward the Sun; most irregular and eccentric behavior. It has five moons and five very fine, subtle rings, suggesting a correspondence to the five senses. It is the first planet not shielded by the solar wind from interstellar influences. It is the higher octave of Mercury. As Mercury is intellect, reason and observation, Uranus is *intuition* in its personal expression. We perceive its influence as brilliant flashes of insight when they are "stepped down" to the level of normal consciousness (Mercury).

The glyph for Uranus, originally derived from the initial "H" of Herschel, its discoverer's name, is a pair of opposed crescents linked by a cross, with a small circle suspended below. In an experience of intuition, four things are linked at the heart of the process of manifestation: at the top of the cross is the invisible point of the primal identity or intention which precedes the circle (see the discussion of the point and the circle at the beginning of this chapter, on pp. 56-57).

Uranus corresponds to the alchemical element Air, rather than to a metal. The color resonance is a clear, pale yellow. As the higher octave of Mercury, Uranus connects with the higher, more subtle energies of the crown (or *sahasrara*) chakra in addition to its primary focus in the transpersonal point abut twenty inches above the crown.

Uranian intuition is the first of the transpersonal faculties. If the receiving equipment (Mercury) is poorly focused or cluttered with opinions, the voice of intuition may be heard only sporadically, resulting in sudden, unpredictable flashes of insight and erratic, eccentric behavior. If your conscious attention (Mercury) is strongly influenced by unresolved emotional states retained in the lower chakras, you may be accident-prone when the influence of Uranus throws you off balance.

In general, with Uranus, expect the unexpected.

Exercise 8: Meditate on freedom and spontaneity. Recall times when you experienced great personal freedom; when your spontaneous behavior was right on target; when you intuitively knew what to do and how. What houses were involved? How can you attune yourself to this magical grace of the spirit?

Suggestions for further meditation:　Review your material on Mercury. How receptive is your attention (Mercury) to inner experiences like intuition (Uranus)? Is your attention pre-empted by your expectations, opinions or other emotion-laden concerns?

Review your material on the element Air in the connective houses (Chapter 1, Exercise 17). Meditate on breath as a symbol for spirit. (Note: the word for "spirit" in many languages means literally "breath"—for example, Latin *spiritus*, Greek *pneuma*, Sanskrit *prana* and Hebrew *ruach*.)

Meditate on ambiguity and paradox, for example the seeming paradox of light behaving in some respects like particles and in other respects like waves. Meditate on something in your life that puzzles you; suppose that there is another, equally valid interpretation of your perception, and search for this opposite or complementary interpretation. Meditate on the nature of ambiguity. If you have ever had puns erupt into your awareness, meditate on the nature of punning and other play with ambiguity. Consider puns as holes in the walls of language, through which you may catch an occasional glimpse of something beyond.

Meditate on Tarot Key 0, The Fool, and study the corresponding chapter in Case's *The Tarot*. Read the meditation on Aleph in Case's *The Book of Tokens*.

Listen to the Uranus section of Holst's *The Planets* and meditate on Uranus.

Figure 46. Tarot Key 0, The Fool

Meditate on the color yellow and on the Living Light of consciousness which prevades the universe.

Draw the symbol for Uranus ♅ in clear, pale yellow on a card, outlined with a thin violet line, and meditate on this simple image. What ideas, feelings and other images does it evoke?

As you continue your work in your circle of houses, relate your discoveries about your Uranian intuition and spontaneity to your experiences in your eighth and eleventh houses.

Record the fruits of your meditations in the Uranus section of your notebook.

Neptune ♆

The next "impossible" planet to be discovered was Neptune. It was found by gazing into apparently empty space, in a direction calculated from irregularities in the orbit of Uranus. This took a measure of faith; most astronomers refused to waste their time.

In mythology, Neptune is the god of water and of the sea; the glyph for the planet resembles the trident of the god Neptune. The alchemical correspondence is the element Water, rather than a metal, and Neptune is the higher octave of the Moon. The cross of the glyph pierces the cupped crescent to tap the wellsprings of inspiration.

Neptune is the psychedelic planet. The character of your "trip" depends heavily on your set (predisposition) and setting (circumstances). The Water of the psyche is like a supersaturated solution; anything you drop into it acts like a seed crystal. Any personal attachment or addiction works powerfully through your imagination until it manifests as an experience of something you desire or fear. Neptune is the transpersonal power which dissolves the protective cocoon of the ego that was constructed by Saturn. You may experience this power as empathy, compassion, selfless love, psychism, ESP, glamour, illusion or delusion.

As the higher octave of the Moon, Neptune resonates with the more subtle energies of the brow or *ajna* chakra, as well as with the mid-chest chakra between the throat and heart chakras. Many astrologers consider Neptune to be the higher octave of Venus. This is really due to the close connection of the Moon (and Neptune) to Venus as yin and yang aspects of subconscious (see above, in the section on Venus). Neptune stimulates the imagination even more strongly than the Moon. The color resonance is blue, a paler, clearer shade than that of the Moon.

Exercise 9:   Meditate on the nature of compassion. Choose one of your interpersonal conflicts from Exercise 22 in Chapter 1. Recall the details of the conflict. Sitting in the center of your circle of houses, clearly visualize both parties to the conflict—yourself and the other person. Imagine your point of view rising above your head to the transpersonal point, and ask (as if talking of someone else) what is the compassionate thing for you to have your personality do in this situation. Practice this until you are able to achieve a transpersonal perspective when a conflict is actually happening.

Suggestions for further meditation: Meditate on the nature of deception, and its relationship to self-deception. Can you lie to someone without deceiving yourself in some respect? Can you lie to yourself and be frank with others? Can you be deceived by anyone else if you do not deceive yourself, if you are at one with your inner truth?

Recall any experiences you may have had of a "psychic" nature and meditate on the nature of psychism and ESP. Recall any experiences you may have had of personal glamour or charisma, when you were swept away starry-eyed, and meditate on those qualities that affected you. Recall experiences of disillusionment and meditate on the illusions that came before, and the illusions that replaced them. Recall experiences of disenchantment, and meditate on the process that freed you from enchantment and its illusions. What role does imagination play in all of this?

Meditate on Tarot Key 12, The Hanged Man, and study the corresponding chapter in Case's *The Tarot*.

Figure 47. Tarot Key 12, The Hanged Man

Listen to the Neptune section of Holst's *The Planets* and meditate on Neptune.

Meditate on the color blue and on the concept of the universal mind.

Draw the symbol for Neptune ♆ in pale blue on a card, and meditate on this simple image. What ideas, feelings and other images does it evoke?

As you continue your work in your circle of houses, relate your discoveries about your Neptune empathy to your experiences in your fifth and twelfth houses.

Record the fruits of your meditations in the Neptune section of your notebook.

Pluto ♀

From 1979 to 1999, Pluto's orbit brings it inside the orbit of Neptune, closer to us than it has been since its discovery in 1930 by Clyde Tombaugh, a twenty-four year-old amateur astronomer working at the Lowell Observatory in Flagstaff, Arizona. Contrary to popular history, Percival Lowell's calculations predicting a trans-Neptunian planet did not guide Tombaugh's observations. He was painstakingly comparing recently-taken photographs of the area of sky which happened to be best for seeing at the time. Nonetheless, Pluto turned up just six degrees from the point Lowell had predicted. Coincidence, of course.

The power of Pluto seems to depend on "coincidence" to open new channels of expression. Things just happen to line up so that one "accident" dovetails with another.

Pluto's orbit is also inclined more than that of any other planet (17° from the ecliptic), suggesting the extremes of exaltation and degradation that have come to be associated with the planet, astrologically.

Physically, Pluto is much smaller than had been thought, actually a little smaller than our Moon. Pluto's moon is named Charon, for the ferryman who carried the souls of the dead across the river Styx into Pluto's realm. Charon is relatively huge as a moon, 40 percent of Pluto's diameter, and extremely close, so that the two are virtually a binary planet system. They are probably made of ice. We think of Hades as a fiery place, but the deepest core of Hades in Dante's *Inferno* is frozen solid, while the outer manifestations of Hades involve a lot of fire and brimstone.

Pluto represents the transpersonal power which tears and burns away outworn forms of life-expression whose time as cocoon or scaffold is done; the power of perpetual dying whereby life moves from one stage to another; the power of perpetual rebirth whereby life transforms itself:

> The force that through the green fuse drives the flower
> Drives my green age; that blasts the roots of trees
> Is my destroyer.   —Dylan Thomas

This force is that searing power which ambitious persons seek to wield; as often as not, it wields them, and this is the source of the pain concealed by their pride and pomp.

We experience the influence of Pluto most often as the use and misuse of power, and as hidden, deep-running currents of motivation which address collective needs through experiences of catharsis or death-and-rebirth, purging whatever is unnecessary to life. Its energy manifests by being "stepped down," as it were, to the level of its lower octave, Mars, where it is expressed as the use and misuse of personal aggression.

Pluto corresponds to the alchemical element Fire rather than to a metal, and, like its lower octave Mars, its color is red. It relates to the higher vibration of the adrenal or *svadisthana* chakra as well as the splenic chakra below the ribs on the left side.

Exercise 10: Meditate on the nature of power. Recall occasions when you held power over others, and occasions when you were subject to another's power. Meditate on the saying "power corrupts, and absolute power corrupts absolutely" in connection with these experiences, and with other examples of the use of power, such as: the life of a master, teacher or guru to whom this maxim would seem not to apply (Christ, Buddha, Milarepa and such beings), or the life of someone in a guru, teacher or therapist role whose corruptibility and use of power you may question.

Suggestions for further meditation: Meditate on the nature of a catalyst. Recall occasions when you have had experiences of fundamental transformation and redirection in your life, and occasions when you had a catalytic or powerful influence in the life of another person, triggering such experiences in them.

Meditate on the concept of rebirth, second birth, awakening or enlightenment.

Meditate on Tarot Key 20, Judgement, and study the corresponding chapter in Case's *The Tarot*.

Figure 48. Tarot Key 20, Judgement

Listen to the Mars section of Holst's *The Planets* and meditate on Pluto as it manifests through Mars.

Meditate on the color red and the element Fire.

Draw the symbol for Pluto ♀ in red on a card. Meditate on this simple image. What ideas, feelings and other images does it evoke?

As you continue your work in your circle of houses, relate your discoveries about the transforming power of Pluto to your experiences in your eighth house.

Record the fruits of your meditation in the Pluto section of your notebook.

Other Planets

Some astronomers suspect there may be one or more planets beyond the orbit of Pluto. The discoveries of Uranus, Neptune and Pluto account for many but not all of the irregularities in planetary orbits, particularly since Pluto turns out to be much smaller than astronomers anticipated. There may even be gas giants like Jupiter, undiscovered because of their enormous distance and slow orbital progress among the stars. Transpluto, Bacchus, Psyche and other planets postulated by some astrologers have yet to be confirmed astronomically.

Some astrologers are studying the possible significance of the larger asteroids, notably the recently-discovered "minor planet," Chiron.

There is an old tradition of a small planet within the orbit of Mercury, called Vulcan, as yet unverified.

In the complex energy field of our solar system, there may be planetary focal points that have no visible dense physical form. Astrologers of the Hamburg School claim to have determined the positions and movements of several such planets in their "Uranian astrology." One difficulty is that most of them are described as having circular orbits, whereas all the known planets have elliptical orbits.

I suggest that you get a firm grasp of the fundamentals before attempting to incorporate these less well-attested factors, which are beyond the scope of this book.

In this chapter you have learned about ten powers and faculties of personality, symbolized by the planets. As you explore your own experience of them in each of the twelve houses of your meditation circle, continuing the exercises of Chapter 1, you will recognize more and more clearly the distinctive personal characteristics taken by the energies of the solar system as they operate through the field of your personality.

In Chapter 3, you will learn more about the way these parts of your personality are related to the corresponding parts of the solar system, the planets. The connection is by way of the energy field of the Earth. The planetary field puts the energies of the solar system in a context relevant to life on Earth. It also functions like a transformer in a power line which "steps down" the high voltage of the main power line to a level that is safe and appropriate for the needs of your home. The zodiac is the last thing to be added to your meditation circle before you start to interpret your horoscope in Part II.

3
The Zodiac: Your Planetary Context

The tropical zodiac or zodiac of signs is different from the sidereal zodiac of constellations. It has nothing directly to do with the stars. It is simply that portion of the Sun's energy field that surrounds the Earth. If you like, you can think of it as the "astral body" or "aura" of the Earth (an idea discussed more fully at the close of this chapter).

The twelve signs of the zodiac are the "houses" or cyclic phases of experience for our planet as a whole. In figure 49, the twelve signs are shown lined up with the corresponding houses, as follows:

Aries	first house	Libra	seventh house
Taurus	second house	Scorpio	eighth house
Gemini	third house	Sagittarius	ninth house
Cancer	fourth house	Capricorn	tenth house
Leo	fifth house	Aquarius	eleventh house
Virgo	sixth house	Pisces	twelfth house

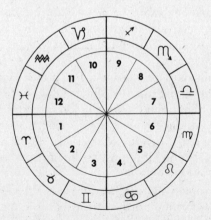

Figure 49. A "natural" horoscope

This is a "natural horoscope." Each sign is lined up with the corresponding house. This alignment happens only once a day, when the sign Aries actually rises over the eastern horizon where you are. About two hours later, Taurus will be rising, and then Gemini, and so on. If the Sun is in Gemini (May-June) it will be sunrise at the time when Gemini is rising, four hours later than the time of this "natural horoscope."

The signs correspond in meaning as well as in form with your houses. As you might imagine, however, their meaning is enormously larger, since they are planetary rather than personal in scope. We get a glimmer when we think in planetary terms—for example, when we are concerned about large-scale pollution, or nuclear proliferation, and the welfare of all life on Earth. Or, think of how one of the millions of cells in your body might experience your activities as a person. This is much like your experience of the phases of planetary life, the signs.

In some ways, you might say that there is always an influence of the sign Aries in your first house, even if Aries is somewhere else in your horoscope, in your tenth house for example. You will see how this works further on in this chapter.

The various parts and attributes of the circle of houses have their correspondences in the zodiac of signs, as follows:

Circle of Houses	Zodiac of Signs
Horizon line	Equinoctical axis
Meridian line	Solstitial axis
Angular houses	Cardinal signs
Succedent houses	Fixed signs
Cadent houses	Mutable signs
Willful (Fire) houses	Fire signs
Empathic (Water) houses	Water signs
Connective (Air) houses	Air signs
Possessive (Earth) houses	Earth signs

The equinoctial axis is an imaginary line drawn between the point where the Sun is located at the vernal equinox, the first day of spring, and the autumnal equinox, the first day of autumn (figure 50). On those two days of the year, the Sun rises due east, passes directly over the equator, and sets due west. The day and night are of equal length (*equi*, "equal"; *nox* "night"). The equinoctial axis defines the cusps of Aries and Libra, just as the horizon line defines the cusps of the first and seventh houses.

In exactly the same way, the solstitial axis is based on the solstices, the points where the Sun is farthest north of the equator in the summer (the summer solstice on June 21), and farthest south of the equator in the winter (the winter solstice on December 21). It defines the cusps of Cancer and Capricorn in the same way that the meridian line (north-south line) defines the cusps of the fourth and tenth houses. These are respectively the longest and the shortest days of the year.

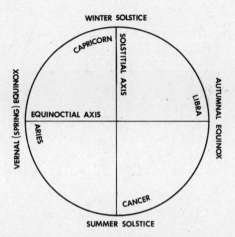

Figure 50. The axes and quadrants of the zodiac

A horoscope is made of two maps of the energies surrounding your birth, one superimposed on the other. The first map is the circle of houses, determined by the horizon and the meridian at your place of birth, and by the rising and setting of the planets at that exact time of day. Superimposed over this is a second map of the energies surrounding the Earth as a whole, the zodiac, determined by the location of the Earth in space relative to all of the planets. Depending on the time of day, your Midheaven (your direction "up" and south) could have been pointing at any of the twelve signs of the zodiac; any of the signs might have been rising over the eastern horizon. It is possible to say that a sign is located in one or another of your houses, and that a planet is located in one or another house.

I will go into this in greater detail in Part II. Some of the exercises in this chapter ask you to determine the house positions of the signs and planets, for those readers who have their horoscopes and know how to do this.

The Cardinal Signs

The cardinal signs, which correspond to the angular houses, begin each quadrant or season of the year. They are called cardinal (from Latin *cardo*, "hinge") because they are at the pivots or turning points of the year, the equinoxes and solstices. They are Aries ♈ , Cancer ♋ , Libra ♎ and Capricorn ♑ .

Aries ♈ : The cardinal Fire sign, analogous to your first house, says: "I am!" The symbol represents the head and horns of a ram, the meaning of the Latin word *aries*. It also resembles the line of nose and eyebrows of a human face:

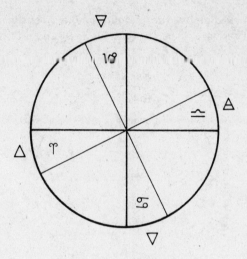

Figure 51. Cardinal Signs

Aries rules the upper part of the head and the eyes. This first phase of Earth's cycle of signs concerns new beginnings among the creatures of our planet: the symbol suggests a new shoot springing up from the earth. This sign is associated with qualities of energy, initiative, courage, originality and activity. The symbol also suggests a fork in the road, and in this opening phase of our planet's cycle of experience, when life is new and its forms of expression are ill-defined, there are many decisions to be made. Decisiveness is another characteristic associated with this sign. It corresponds to Tarot Key 4, The Emperor.

Figure 52. Tarot Key 4, The Emperor

Cancer ♋ : The cardinal Water sign, analogous to your fourth house, says: "I feel!" The symbol represents the shell and claws of a crab, the meaning of the Latin word *cancer*. The crab carries its home with it, a hard shell to protect its soft inner parts, and it walks sideways, not approaching issues directly. This is apt imagery for some of the qualities of the sign. The symbol resembles the breast and stomach, the parts of the body which the sign rules: nurturing and emotional security are all-important in this fourth phase of the cycle of signs, in which the nest and family security must be provided for, and indeed, the symbol also suggests a nest with two eggs in it. The Tarot correspondence is Key 7, The Chariot.

Figure 53. Tarot Key 7, The Chariot

Libra ♎ : The cardinal Air sign, analogous to your seventh house, says: "I balance." The symbol represents a balance or scales, the meaning of the word *libra* in Latin. In the harvest season the produce of the summer is weighed in the balance of social needs.

Figure 54. Tarot Key 11, Justice

Law and justice are keynotes of this seventh phase of the cycle of signs, and the maintenance of social equilibrium. The symbol resembles a yoke, implying teamwork and balanced effort. Libra, like the seventh house, represents the turning point from subjective concerns to objective consciousness, compelled by *interdependence* with other beings. The Tarot correspondence is Key 11, Justice, which is at the center of the series from Key 1 to Key 21. Justice depicts the active aspect of subconscious (Venus) holding the scales in her left hand, and prepared with a sword in her right hand to maintain equilibrium. Libra rules the kidneys, which maintain the balance of the bloodstream by eliminating the unnecessary.

Capricorn ♑ : The cardinal Earth sign, analogous to your tenth house, says: "I use." The symbol resembles in part the curved horn of a goat, though the Latin word *Capricornus*, "goat-horned," could as well refer to the monstrosity depicted in the Tarot Key that corresponds to this sign, Key 15, The Devil. Here in the tenth phase of the cycle of signs, where the Earthy forces of materialism are at their strongest, the Great Adversary holds sway. The Father of Lies (one of the traditional titles of the Devil) is the fundamental lie of separateness which engenders all other error. Until the low-synergy illusion of separation and isolation is cleared up, the tremendous ambition associated with this sign, the profound craving for *manifested* achievement and *demonstrated* power, can experience only the frustration of being hedged about by Earthy limitations which seem to prevent complete fulfillment. Capricorn rules the knees, which one must learn to bend in humility to achieve true greatness as an administrator of Divine Will.

Figure 55. Tarot Key 15, The Devil

Exercise 1: Review your material on your first house, and as you read the description of Aries above, find correspondences with characteristics of the first house. When you find notes you have written about your first house that have nothing corresponding to them in the description of Aries, seek ways to translate them into more universal terms, appropriate for the first-of-spring qualities of Aries.

Where does the sign Aries fall in your circle of houses? Are you especially apt to begin things or to take on challenges in that area of your experience? What other Aries characteristics can you discover in your experience of that house? (Ignore this part of the exercise for now if you do not yet have your horoscope.)

Do the same initial exploration of the correspondences of the sign Cancer and the fourth house. Which house, if any, begins within the sign Cancer in your horoscope? Are you especially protective of yourself and your loved ones in that area of your experience? What other Cancer characteristics can you discover in your experiences of that house?

Do the same exploration of the sign Libra and the seventh house. Which house, if any, begins within the sign Libra in your horoscope? Are you especially sensitive to your relationships with others in that area of your experience? What other Libra characteristics can you discover in your experiences of that house?

Do the same initial exploration of the relationship of the sign Capricorn and the tenth house. Then find which house begins within the sign Capricorn in your horoscope (if any). Are you particularly ambitious, businesslike, or career-oriented in that area of your experience? What other Capricornian characteristics can you discover in your experience of that house?

Fixed Signs

The middle of each season or quadrant of the zodiac is a fixed sign, corresponding to a succedent house.

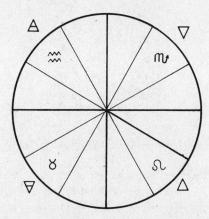

Figure 56. The Fixed Signs

They are called fixed because they "fix" or stabilize the impulse of the preceding cardinal signs. The fixed signs are the resistant, form-crystallizing backbone or keel of the quadrants. They are Taurus $\circ$, Leo Ω , Scorpio $\mathbb{M}$ and Aquarius $\approx$. In Tarot, they are represented by the four creatures in the corners of Keys 10 and 21.

Figure 57. Tarot Key 10, The Wheel of Fortune

Figure 58. Tarot Key 21, The World

Leo Ω **:** The fixed Fire sign, analogous to your fifth house, says: "I will!" This symbol has been likened to the curving tail or sweeping mane of the lion, King of Beasts. Esoterically, it refers to the "serpent power" Kundalini, source of your physical, animal energy. This power may be ruled only from a seat of consciousness in the heart chakra, to which Leo has particular affinity. Courage, heartiness, pride and strong personal will are characteristic of Leo. In this fifth phase of the cycle of signs it is necessary to learn the secret of dominion, not over others but over forces within one's being, which is accomplished by the power of love. This is shown by the Tarot correspondence, Key 8, Strength. Leo rules the heart, the spinal cord and the dorsal region of the spine. According to an old aphorism, Leo rules by divine right and Capricorn by delegated authority. Leo must learn to bend and delegate responsibility, to avoid heart problems.

Figure 59. Tarot Key 8, Strength

Scorpio ♏ : The fixed Water sign, analogous to your eighth house, says: "I (re)generate." This sign is represented by several emblematic animals, which relate to various levels of expression of its energies. The first is the scorpion, the meaning of the Latin word *scorpio*. The arrowhead on the glyph represents the stinging tail of this animal. The second is the eagle. On the Great Seal of the United States the eagle of Scorpio is depicted looking toward the olive branch of peace in its right talon, while holding a bundle of arrows in its left talon.

Figure 60. Tarot Key 13, Death

One commonly-accepted horoscope of the United States has Scorpio on the Ascendant. The third emblematic animal is the phoenix, which was fabled to live in Arabia. When its five-hundred-year life-span was ending, it immolated itself on a flaming pyre, and a new phoenix emerged from the ashes. According to Herodotus it was red and golden and resembled the eagle. (The student of esoteric symbolism will find these rich objects for meditation.) The arrowhead of the symbol, reminiscent of that of Mars, is a reminder of the role of sexual energy in both degeneration and regeneration. Scorpio rules the urino-genital organs, the prostate, and the immediate organs of elimination (bladder, descending colon, etc.). The Tarot correspondence is Key 13, Death, which depicts how life moves from one stage to another.

Aquarius ♒ : The fixed Air sign, analogous to your eleventh house, says "I know." Although it is an Air sign the Latin word *aquarius* means "water-bearer"; but the symbol shows only the flowing water, not the person. This is the Water of Life, the vibrating electromagnetic stuff of which the universe is constituted, which H.P. Blavatsky, the founder of the Theosophical Society, called *fohat*. The high-synergy concepts of resonance, harmony, ecology, holonomy and so forth, are meat and drink to the Aquarian temperament. Radio and television are technological harbingers of the Aquarian Age, broadcasting and receiving information via subtle electromagnetic waves that pass through solid walls. The Tarot correspondence, Key 17, The Star, depicts that revelation of nature which ensues when the mind is stilled in meditation. The reception and dissemination of insight for the betterment of the world is the higher expression of Aquarian energy. Aquarius rules the ankles, the circulatory system and the aura. Meditation effects changes in the circulatory system and in the aura which pervade the whole organism, and allow the reception and propagation of more subtle universal forces.

Figure 61. Tarot Key 17, The Star

Taurus ♉ : The fixed Earth sign, analogous to your second house, says: "I have." The symbol represents the head and horns of a bull (Latin *taurus*), a powerful beast of burden, and a symbol of fertility. It is composed of a bowl-like crescent over a circle, like a wide funnel-mouth on a round, full jar. Like the second house, Taurus has to do with the accumulation of resources. This symbol also resembles a coiled serpent. (The symbols for the four fixed signs may all be interpreted as serpents in various stages of unfoldment.) Taurus rules the neck and throat, and the lower parts of the brain. The creative power of speech is too seldom recognized, though the negative consequences of gossip and slander strike again and again. In this second phase of the cycle of signs, possessiveness will generate negative thoughts and speech and all their karmic consequences, until one learns to trust the universal forces which are the unfailing support of life. This trust follows from listening inwardly, through the Venus chakra located in the throat, to the Voice of the Inner Teacher (intuition) depicted in the corresponding Tarot Key 5, The Hierophant.

Figure 62. Tarot Key 5, The Hierophant

Exercise 2: Review your material on your second house and, as you read the description of Taurus above, find correspondences with characteristics of your second house. When you find notes you have written about your second house that have nothing corresponding to them in the description of Taurus, seek ways to translate them into more universal terms appropriate for the sign Taurus.

Which house in your horoscope, if any, begins within the sign Taurus? do you tend to invest in possessions or equipment related especially to that area of your experience? What other Taurian characteristics can you discover in your experience of that house?

Do the same initial exploration of the correspondences of the sign Leo and the fifth house. Then find which house (if any) begins within the sign Leo in your horoscope. Are you particularly creative, or prideful, or attention-seeking, in that area of your experience? What other Leonine characteristics can you discover in your experience of that house?

Do the same initial exploration of the correspondences of the sign Scorpio and the eighth house. Then find which house (if any) begins within the sign Scorpio in your horoscope. Do you find yourself involved especially with other people's values, energies and resources in that area of your experience? What other Scorpionic characteristics can you discover in your experience of that house?

Do the same initial exploration of the correspondences of the sign Aquarius and the eleventh house. Then find which house (if any) begins within the sign Aquarius in your horoscope. Are you especially involved with friends, peers and collective endeavors in that area of your experience? What other Aquarian characteristics can you discover in your experience of that house?

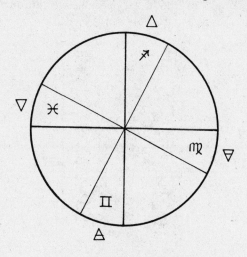

Figure 63. The Mutable Signs

Mutable Signs

Each season or quadrant of the cycle of signs ends with a sign which is called *mutable* because it trans*mutes* the polarity between the preceding pairs of signs (the cardinal and fixed signs of the quadrant) in preparation for the new cardinal impulse of the next quadrant. Then too, people with an emphasis on mutable signs are adaptable and sensitive to the antecedents and context of a situation, rather than opportunistic (cardinal) or dogmatic (fixed). The mutable signs are also called *common* signs because these same people are sensitive to human dynamics of the common man, and to common-sense problems of relationship, rather than getting excited with issues and emergencies (cardinal), or adhering intolerantly to ideals and fixed values (fixed). Like the cadent houses, the mutable or common signs resolve the karma of their quadrant, extract its essential meaning, and dissolve its forms into the sub-stance (under-standing) upon which the following quadrant will draw. In this final segment of a quadrant the opportunity is given to resolve karma rather than create it. The four mutable signs are Gemini ♊ , Virgo ♍ , Sagittarius ♐ , and Pisces ♓ .

Sagittarius ♐ : The mutable Fire sign, analogous to your ninth house, says: "I comprehend." The Latin word *sagittarius* means "archer," from *sagitta* "arrow." The symbol shows the arrow and the central portion of a bow. The bow is held, it is said, by a centaur, a mythical creature with the body of a horse, and with the upper body of a man in place of a horse's head and neck. The arrow points upward, indicating aspiration and high ideals. The disparity between lower and higher natures, between the limitations of the body and the freedom of the mind and spirit, is at the heart of this ninth phase of the cycle of signs. This disparity may manifest in physical terms as intolerance of restriction and love of travel, or in mental and spiritual terms as openness to new ideas and love of learning. "Philosophy" comes from the Greek word meaning love (*philo-*) of wisdom (*sophia*). The Tarot correspondence is Key 14, Temperance, as in tempering a sword. Sagittarius rules the thighs, hips, and sacroilliac region.

Figure 64. Tarot Key 14, Temperance

Pisces ♓ : The mutable Water sign, analogous to your twelfth house, says: "I believe." The symbol here is two fish (Latin *pisces*) tied together but curving in opposite directions, representing again the lower and higher natures: One fish is but the reflection on the under-surface of the water in which the other swims. Abstractly, these are two crescents, like that which symbolizes the Moon, emblem of the subconscious. The Tarot correspondence is Key 18, The Moon, which depicts the path of subjective unfoldment from the familiar to the unexplored, through subconscious processes which transform the organism in its sleep states. The membrane separating inner and outer worlds is very thin and permeable in this twelfth phase of the cycle of signs. Pisces rules the feet. To touch the feet of a great teacher like Christ or Ramakrishna is a Piscean expression of devotion. Christ, Avatar of the Piscean Age, was symbolized by a fish. The dualism of two fish, which we may hope to harmonize as in the Taoist yin-yang symbol, was unified in His at-one-ment.

Figure 65. Tarot Key 18, The Moon

Gemini ♊ : The mutable Air sign, analogous to your third house, says: "I think." The Latin word *gemini* means "twins" and is said to refer to Castor and Pollux of mythology. By a classical tradition, one member of every pair of twins was thought to have been fathered by a god, and thus to be immortal.

Figure 66. Tarot Key 6, The Lovers

Thus, again in a mutable sign the duality of higher and lower natures (cardinal and fixed) must be reconciled. Out of the archetypal polarity of Aries, subject, and Taurus, object, emerges the Gemini relationship between them, the Airy realm of *perception* and *communication*. The Tarot correspondence is to Key 6, The Lovers, which illustrates the maxim "when the two (opposites or complements) are in harmony, a third appears." Proper understanding of this image, through meditation, confers the "sword of discrimination." Gemini rules many body parts that are paired: hands, arms, shoulders, lungs and the metabolism of the subtle energy called in the East *prana*.

Virgo ♍ : The mutable Earth sign, analogous to your sixth house, says: "I perfect." The emblematic figure for this sign is a virgin holding a sheaf of wheat, a grain which grows only in various cultivated forms. The symbol suggests virginity by its self-contained final curve. The loops of the symbol suggest the convolutions of the intestines, which are ruled by Virgo. The "M" of the symbol stands for Mind, whose power of discrimination is heavily taxed, sorting the wheat from the chaff, analyzing the properties of each situation, digesting and assimilating the pure essence of experiences and discarding the rest. The Tarot correspondence is Key 9, The Hermit, depicting the highest goal and end of self-consciousness (Mercury). In comparison with the refined perfection of that guiding light, imperfections of character and circumstances are galling reminders of the inadequacy of things as they appear to be. In this sixth phase, the digestive system of the cycle of signs, one must learn to look for the good uses of all things rather than their imperfections. One must focus on the food that is extracted rather than on the wastes that are expelled. Otherwise, subconscious processes of digestion and assimilation will be confused, and will retain toxins.

Figure 67. Tarot Key 9, The Hermit

Exercise 3: Review your material on your third house. As you read the description of Gemini, above, find correspondences with characteristics of your third house. When you find notes you have written about your third house that have nothing corresponding to them in the description of Gemini, seek ways to translate them into the more universal terms appropriate for the sign Gemini.

Which house in your horoscope, if any, begins within the sign Gemini? Are you especially curious, exploratory, and verbal in connection with the affairs of this house? What other Geminian characteristics can you discover in your experience of that house?

Do the same initial exploration of the correspondences of the sign Virgo and the sixth house. Then find which house (if any) begins within the sign Virgo in your horoscope. Does your employment, or your means of being of service to others, find its focus within this area of your experience? What other Virgoan characteristics can you discover in your experience of that house?

Do the same initial exploration of the correspondences of the sign Sagittarius and the ninth house. Then find which house (if any) begins within the sign Sagittarius in your horoscope. Are you especially concerned to broaden and educate yourself in this area of your experience? What other Sagittarian characteristics can you discover in your experience of that house?

Do the same initial exploration of the correspondences of the sign Pisces and the twelfth house. Then find which house (if any) begins within the sign Pisces in your horoscope. How does the theme of sacrifice, or surrender, strike you as a motif for your affairs in this area of your experience? What other Piscean characteristics can you discover in your experience of that house?

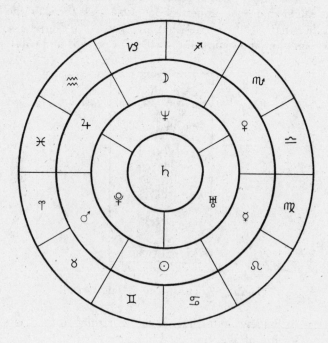

Figure 68. Astrological color-wheel

As was mentioned in Chapter 2, the signs form a twelve-tone scale which corresponds to the twelve-tone scale of music and the twelve-tone color-wheel. The full color wheel is shown in figure 68, including both the planets (as shown previously in figure 38) and the signs (the outermost circle). The implication is that the twelve-tone scale of the zodiac has a vibratory rate many octaves above that of visible light, just as the twelve-tone color-scale in turn is many octaves above the twelve-tone scale of musical sound. Meditating on the color, or on the musical sound, or both, will awaken the corresponding astrological energy in you by resonance, like the resonating strings on a piano, as was explained in Chapter 2.

The color-scale and its zodiacal correspondence is as follows:

Red	♈	Aries	△ Fire
Red-orange	♉	Taurus	▽ Earth
Orange	♊	Gemini	◹ Air
Orange-yellow	♋	Cancer	▽ Water
Yellow	♌	Leo	△ Fire
Yellow-green	♍	Virgo	▽ Earth
Green	♎	Libra	◹ Air
Blue-green	♏	Scorpio	▽ Water
Blue	♐	Sagittarius	△ Fire
Blue-violet (Indigo)	♑	Capricorn	▽ Earth
Violet	♒	Aquarius	◹ Air
Red-violet	♓	Pisces	▽ Water

Note that the Fire signs have primary colors, the Air signs have secondary colors and the Water and Earth signs have tertiary colors, in terms of mixing pigments.

You may want to make your own copy of the color-wheel shown in figure 68 and color it with the colors attributed to the planets and signs. Take care that the colors you use are clear and accurate.

Hang this diagram on the wall or otherwise keep it handy in your meditation space for easy reference. Use it, and the relationships among its colors, as a focus for meditations on the planets, signs and houses throughout this book. It will richly reward your efforts.

If you are uncertain about the meaning of some relationship or attribution, formulate your feeling as a simple, direct question. Your answer will come to you in your meditation, or in your reading, or in conversation—through any of the channels of information you employ. Remember that visual imagery of this sort speaks to the nonverbal, holistic side of your mentality, which must sometimes find indirect means to convey its understanding to your outer, verbal consciousness.

The Sidereal Zodiac

The term *zodiac* is from Greek *zodiakos kyklos*, "circle of little (figures of) animals," which was applied to the zodiac of constellations. It has been clear for a long time that the signs and the constellations are different from one another. Around 120 B.C. Hipparchus wrote about the precession of the equinoxes (the slow, steady movement of the signs of the tropical zodiac backward through the constellations). Nevertheless, the traditional term *zodiac* has been retained for both constellations and signs, resulting in endless confusion.

For example, it is a common misconception that astrology cannot work because the signs no longer line up with the constellations, that the real source of astrological influences is the stars, and that the signs of the tropical zodiac are purely imaginary. (See figure 69.)

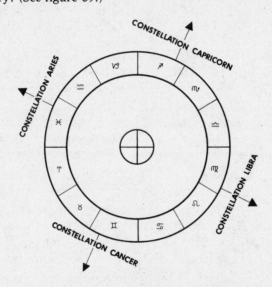

Figure 69. Relation of signs to constellations

Many attempts have been made to establish twelve equal divisions in the zodiac of constellations, to define a *sidereal zodiac*. (*Sidereal* comes from the Latin *sidus, sider*, "star.") These attempts have run into a great many difficulties.

And even when the constellations lined up with the signs around 250 B.C., the alignment was only approximate. One reason is that the constellations vary greatly in size, from about 10 degrees of arc (one-third of a sign) for a small constellation like Aries or Cancer, to over 50 degrees (one and two-thirds signs) for the constellation Virgo. How can any equal division of the circle of constellations be set up if the constellations won't fit? Furthermore, there is no clear starting place for a sidereal zodiac, no cusp which is known so that the others can be measured from it.

But the stars and constellations are part of the same universe with us, so they must have a role in astrology.

It is my belief that sidereal astrology, the astrology of the stars and .constellations, should be studied in heliocentric terms. A heliocentric horoscope has the Sun at the center, and the Earth among the planets around it (figure 70).

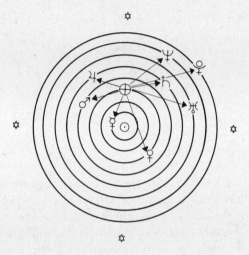

Figure 70: Sidereal, heliocentric situation, showing geocentric point of view

One reason for this suggestion is that heliocentric astrologers find no use for the signs, except as a convenience for locating the planets easily in the horoscope. Another reason is the appropriateness of relating the Sun with other stars in a Sun-centered horoscope.

If you get a heliocentric horoscope for the time of your birth, it will have no house cusps, and the zodiacal signs in it will be merely for convenience. The interpretation is based upon the angular relationships or "aspects" among the planets, which you will study in Chapter 6. A heliocentric horoscope is said to reflect one's inner identity or Higher Self. It might be thought of as an amplified view of the Sun in the corresponding tropical, geocentric horoscope.

Geocentric means Earth-centered. The tropical zodiac is Earth-centered, since it is defined by the relationship between the Earth and the Sun and is an energy field surrounding the Earth. Heliocentric means Sun-centered.

Tropical, geocentric astrology is appropriate for understanding people on the personality level. Sidereal, heliocentric astrology is more spiritual.

This introduction to the zodiac completes Part I of this book. There will be more on the zodiac in Chapters 4 and 5. Check at this point to see if you have learned to recognize all the glyphs (symbols) for the signs and planets. They will become increasingly important and useful to you in Part II.

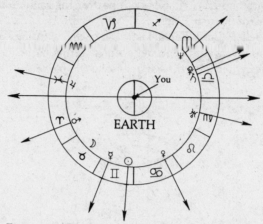

Figure 71. Tropical, geocentric point of view

In Part II, you will integrate the actual patterns of your horoscope into your circle of houses. The twelve-tone spectrum of energies surrounding the Earth, the signs of the zodiac, will show you how your personal cycles of experience fit into the collective experience of life on our planet. In the patterns formed by the planets in your horoscope, you will see how the corresponding human powers and faculties operate in your personality and in your relationships.

You have learned most of the vocabulary of the astrological symbol-language. Now you are ready to deal with its sentences and paragraphs. You are ready for your horoscope to speak to you.

Part II. Your Horoscope: Owner's Manual for Your Personality

In Part I, you learned to interpret your experiences in terms of the basic conceptual categories of astrology, symbolized by the houses, planets and signs.

In Part II, you will learn to interpret the patterns of your horoscope in terms of the patterns of experience you discovered and began to explore in Part I. Through the relationships among the planets, signs and houses, you will learn to recognize deeper and more subtle patterning in your life, patterning that you will now be able to manifest in a variety of ways as a matter of choice rather than unconscious conditioning.

4

The Zodiac Inside Out

In this chapter we explore the connections among the planets, signs and houses. This approach carries your understanding further than would be possible if these elements were to be studied separately. You are taken immediately to the heart of astrological interpretation to develop your fluency in the language of astrological symbolism.

For this chapter you will need a horoscope. If you do not have one, turn to Appendix 3 for instructions on obtaining an accurately-cast natal horoscope.

The Horoscope

Your horoscope shows what is going on in each of your twelve houses, astrologically. The cusp of each house falls within one of the twelve signs, which thereby imparts its characteristics to your experiences in that house. Each of the ten planets falls within one of your houses, indicating the area of experience that the corresponding faculty takes as its primary focus in your life. In this chapter, each combination of planet, sign and house will be woven together. Your subconscious mind is the loom, and your conscious mind the shuttle working back and forth across the threads of astrological symbolism, weaving a unique tapestry of words and images. As you progress, you will see more and more clearly the outlines of your personal history, your character and your personal share of the world.

There are two forms of horoscopes you are likely to encounter: the European style and the American style. The European style of horoscope is in some ways easier to understand, because it shows the relationship between the signs and houses more clearly. In figure 72, a European-style horoscope, the outer circle shows the twelve signs of the zodiac, with 30 degrees marked off for each sign. The house cusps are not pre-printed; instead, the astrologer must line up a ruler with the proper degrees of the signs and draw the cusps by hand.

This style is appropriate when you want to draw up an attractive horoscope for someone. The sign of the Midheaven is drawn in at the top, so that the meridian axis is vertical; then the other signs are drawn in at 30° intervals. The other house cusps are located by placing a ruler across the center of the chart, intersecting the degrees of the signs where they fall.

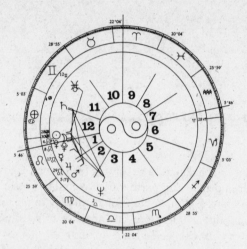

Figure 72. A European-style horoscope

Can you find the Ascendant in figure 72? It is at 6° Leo, written 6 ♌ on the left side of the horoscope. Can you find the Sun? It is above the Ascendant, at 29° Cancer, written 29 ♋ in the twelfth house. This man was born just after sunrise, since the Sun is only 6° above the horizon. It takes about four minutes on the average for 1° of the zodiac to cross the Ascendant, so he was born six times four or about twenty-four minutes after sunrise. He was also born just after the New Moon. Can you see why this is so? The Moon is at 30° Cancer, 1° later in the zodiac than the Sun. Since the Moon travels about 12° in twenty-four hours, or a degree every two hours, the New Moon occurred about two hours prior to the time of this horoscope. That New Moon was also a solar eclipse, as you will come to understand when you learn about the nodes of the Moon later in this chapter.

Look at your own horoscope now. What phase was the Moon in when you were born? That is, was it closest to New Moon (0° from the Sun), First Quarter (90° ahead of the Sun), Full Moon (opposite the Sun) or Third Quarter (270° ahead of the Sun, 90° behind the Sun in the zodiac)? How long before or after the nearest phase of the Moon were you born (figuring about two hours per degree of the zodiac)?

You may have wondered why the horizon line is not horizontal in the horoscope shown in figure 72. The meridian line is always aligned exactly north and south, and so is vertical on the horoscope. The Ascendant-Descendant axis lines up exactly east and west only twice a day, at the moments when the cusp of Libra or Aries is on the Ascendant. In this horoscope, Leo is on the Ascendant, and Leo is one of the summer signs, that is, one of the signs where the Sun is during the summer. The signs in the summer half of the zodiac rise and set further to the north and therefore closer to the fourth-house cusp (the Imum Coeli) at the bottom of the horoscope. The winter signs, from Libra through Capricorn to Aries, all rise and set further to the south and therefore closer to the Midheaven.

That is why the Ascendant, in Leo (a summer sign), is closer to the fourth house cusp, and the Descendant, in Aquarius (the opposite, winter sign), is closer to the tenth-house cusp or Midheaven.

All of this is easy to remember, because the Sun is lower in the southern sky during the winter while the days are shorter, and higher in the sky during the long days of summer.

A horoscope is a two-dimensional map, or projection, of a three-dimensional field in space. More exactly, it is two maps, one superimposed upon the other. The first map is the circle of houses. It is defined by the horizon and the north-south meridian through the Midheaven. To make this map, you need to know the date, time and place of birth; the place, because it is linked with a particular location on the Earth.

The second map is the circle of zodiacal signs, the zodiac. It is defined by the relationship of the Earth to the Sun in space. It defines the locations of the Moon and planets relative to the Earth. To make this second map, you need only know the date and time of birth, since it is not linked to a particular location on the Earth.

When you put them together, you see the connection of the energies of the solar system with the birth of a particular person in a particular time and place.

To see clearly how the two maps are related, it is helpful to look at the spherical fields of energy from which they are projected. The tropical zodiac is not really a belt or band around the Earth, but a spheroidal field around the Earth. The "equator" of the zodiacal sphere lines up with the ecliptic, which is the plane of the Earth's orbit around the Sun (and of the Sun's apparent path through the sky from our viewpoint on Earth), since this field is defined by the relationship of the Earth to the Sun.

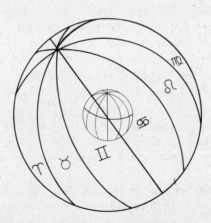

Figure 73. The sphere of the tropical zodiac

Figure 73 shows the sphere of the zodiac, segmented into twelve segments like an orange (the signs), with the Earth at its center. It is seen from a point above the Sun at the time of the summer solstice (when the Sun appears to be at 0° Cancer). The north pole of the Earth is tipped directly toward the viewer.

Similarly, the "circle of houses" is really a sphere surrounding the place of birth. Figure 74 shows the "equator" of the sphere of houses lined up with the surface of the Earth at the birthplace.

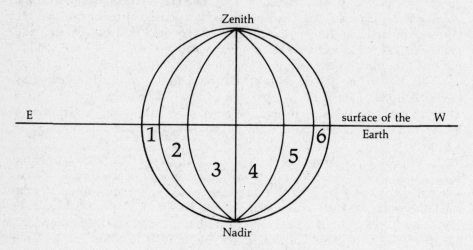

Figure 74. The sphere of houses

There is more disagreement among astrologers about how these two spheres line up with each other than there is on any other topic. Some say the "equator" of the sphere of houses should line up with the horizon around the place of birth, some say it should line up with the equator of the Earth, some say with the east-west meridian passing through the zenith over the place of birth, and so on. Others say the "equator" is not relevant at all, and propose other methods of superimposing the segments of the two spheres to get a composite map.

Whatever method is used, similar issues arise. The "orange-segments" of one do not align with those of the other. Where the "orange-segments" of one are wide, near its equator, those of the other are farther from its equator and therefore narrower.

Look at the horoscope in figure 72 again. This is a cross-section through both spheres together, as though you had sliced the "orange" of the zodiac across its equator. The same slice went at an angle to the equator of the sphere of houses, because of its tilt within the larger sphere of signs. While the sections of the zodiac are all equal, those of the houses are not in figure 72.

The sign Leo is above the "equator" of the sphere of houses, intersecting the "orange-segments" of houses where they get narrower, toward the poles; consequently, the first and second houses are narrow. The opposite sign, Aquarius, is below the "equator" of the sphere of houses, so houses seven and eight are also narrow. The "equator" of the sphere of houses crosses the ecliptic (the "equator" of the sphere of signs) in the signs Taurus and Scorpio, so the fourth and fifth houses are the widest.

Why not line up the sphere of houses with the sphere of signs so that their "equators" match? This is called the "equal-house" system. The difficulty with this system is that, since the Ascendant is usually more or less than 90° from the Midheaven, only one of these two points can be lined up with a house cusp. Usually the Ascendant is chosen as the first house cusp, and the other house cusps are marked off at regular 30° intervals, with the Midheaven falling in either the ninth or the tenth house.

The American-style chart is like a cross-section through the "equator" of the sphere of houses (figure 74). Instead of showing where the cusps of the signs fall (0° Aries, 0° Taurus and so forth), each house cusp is labeled to show the degree of the zodiac where it falls. This style has become popular because it is much easier to draw. You only have to write in the glyphs of the signs and the numbers indicating the positions (in degrees and minutes of arc) of the house cusps within the signs. Unless you think about the meaning of the notations written on the house cusps, it is hard to see the differences in size of the houses.

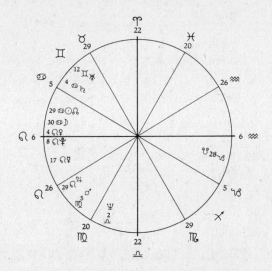

Figure 75. An American-style horoscope

The American-style horoscope is also easier for computers to produce. Figure 76 shows the same horoscope as figures 72 and 75, as printed out by a computer. Your horoscope will look something like this if you obtain it from a computer-horoscope service. It will be easier to read and interpret if you copy it over onto a blank horoscope form. American and European-style horoscope forms are printed in the back of this book, in Appendix 3, for you to photocopy. Forms may be purchased in many bookstores as well.

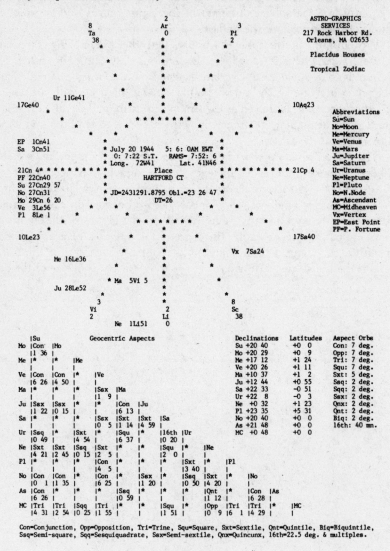

Figure 76. A computer horoscope

Figure 77 shows the computer listing of the zodiacal positions of the planets and house cusps. These are given in degrees and minutes; for example, the

Ascendant is 5° 46' in Leo. Since there are sixty minutes of arc in each degree, I rounded this off to 6° Leo above.

```
                    NATAL HOROSCOPE CALCULATIONS                PAGE 1

                                    JULY 20, 1944
          HARTFORD, CT                LOCAL TIME   5:06 AM
          LATITUDE 41 N 46            EST  4:06
          LONGITUDE 72 W 41           TIME ZONE +5

                    HOUSE DIVISION BY THE PLACIDEAN METHOD
          PLANETS, ASCENDANT, AND MIDHEAVEN LISTED IN STANDARD ORDER

          SUN        IS AT   27 DEG.   31 MIN. OF CANCER     IN HOUSE   1
          MOON       IS AT   29 DEG.    6 MIN. OF CANCER     IN HOUSE   1
          MERCURY    IS AT   16 DEG.   36 MIN. OF LEO        IN HOUSE   2
          VENUS      IS AT    3 DEG.   56 MIN. OF LEO        IN HOUSE   1
          MARS       IS AT    5 DEG.    5 MIN. OF VIRGO      IN HOUSE   3
          JUPITER    IS AT   28 DEG.   52 MIN. OF LEO        IN HOUSE   2
          SATURN     IS AT    3 DEG.   51 MIN. OF CANCER     IN HOUSE  12
          URANUS     IS AT   11 DEG.   41 MIN. OF GEMINI     IN HOUSE  11
          NEPTUNE    IS AT    1 DEG.   51 MIN. OF LIBRA      IN HOUSE   3
          PLUTO      IS AT    8 DEG.    1 MIN. OF LEO        IN HOUSE   1
          ASCENDANT  IS AT   20 DEG.   56 MIN. OF CANCER     IN HOUSE   1
          MIDHEAVEN  IS AT    2 DEG.    1 MIN. OF ARIES      IN HOUSE  10

                    PLANETS AND HOUSE CUSPS SORTED IN ORDER FROM ASCENDANT


          ASCENDANT   IS AT   20 DEG.   55 MIN. OF CANCER
          SUN         IS AT   27 DEG.   31 MIN. OF CANCER
          MOON        IS AT   29 DEG.    6 MIN. OF CANCER
          VENUS       IS AT    3 DEG.   56 MIN. OF LEO
          PLUTO       IS AT    8 DEG.    1 MIN. OF LEO

          2ND HOUSE   IS AT   10 DEG.   24 MIN. OF LEO
          MERCURY     IS AT   16 DEG.   36 MIN. OF LEO
          JUPITER     IS AT   28 DEG.   52 MIN. OF LEO

          3RD HOUSE   IS AT    3 DEG.    5 MIN. OF VIRGO
          MARS        IS AT    5 DEG.    5 MIN. OF VIRGO
          NEPTUNE     IS AT    1 DEG.   51 MIN. OF LIBRA

          4TH HOUSE   IS AT    2 DEG.    1 MIN. OF LIBRA

          5TH HOUSE   IS AT    8 DEG.   41 MIN. OF SCORPIO

          6TH HOUSE   IS AT   17 DEG.   35 MIN. OF SAGITTARIUS

          7TH HOUSE   IS AT   20 DEG.   55 MIN. OF CAPRICORN

          8TH HOUSE   IS AT   10 DEG.   24 MIN. OF AQUARIUS

          9TH HOUSE   IS AT    3 DEG.    5 MIN. OF PISCES

          MIDHEAVEN   IS AT    2 DEG.    1 MIN. OF ARIES

          11TH HOUSE  IS AT    8 DEG.   41 MIN. OF TAURUS
          URANUS      IS AT   11 DEG.   41 MIN. OF GEMINI

          12TH HOUSE  IS AT   17 DEG.   35 MIN. OF GEMINI
          SATURN      IS AT    3 DEG.   51 MIN. OF CANCER

          NATAL CALCULATIONS                                  PAGE 2

                              PLANETARY ASPECTS

          FASTER      ASPECT          SLOWER      ORB OF ASPECT  INTENSITY
          ------      ------          ------      ------------   ---------

          SUN         CONJUNCTION     MOON        1 DEG.  36 MIN.   13.1
          SUN         CONJUNCTION     VENUS       5 DEG.  25 MIN.    1.1
          SUN         SEXTILE         NEPTUNE     4 DEG.  20 MIN.    2.6
          SUN         CONJUNCTION     ASCENDANT   6 DEG.  34 MIN.    0.9
          MOON        CONJUNCTION     VENUS       4 DEG.  50 MIN.    4.0
          MOON        SEXTILE         NEPTUNE     2 DEG.  45 MIN.    4.4
          MERCURY     SEXTILE         URANUS      4 DEG.  55 MIN.    0.1
          VENUS       SEXTILE         NEPTUNE     2 DEG.   4 MIN.    2.9
          VENUS       CONJUNCTION     PLUTO       4 DEG.   5 MIN.    2.3
          MARS        SEXTILE         SATURN      1 DEG.  14 MIN.    1.8
          JUPITER     SEXTILE         SATURN      4 DEG.  58 MIN.    0.1
          SATURN      SQUARE          NEPTUNE     2 DEG.   0 MIN.   11.9
          URANUS      SEXTILE         PLUTO       3 DEG.  39 MIN.    3.6

                    ORBS USED FOR CALCULATING ASPECTS

                    INCONJUNCT  3 DEG.
                    ALL ASPECTS INVOLVING SUN, MOON,
                       OR ASCENDANT  8 DEG.
                    ALL OTHERS  5 DEG.

                    INTENSITY RATING DESCRIBED IN
                    PARA RESEARCH HOROSCOPE CATALOG
```

Figure 77. Computer listing of planets and house cusps

Look at your horoscope now. What sign is on your Ascendant? What sign is your Sun in? What house is it in? Which sign and house is your Moon in? Where are the other planets? In the course of this chapter, you will learn the meanings of each of these combinations of planet, sign and house, and to integrate these meanings in your mind.

Remember that the planets are really beyond the zodiac, even though the horoscope is drawn as though they formed a neat ring within the zodiac. The glyphs of the planets show where a line of sight passes from the Earth, in the center, through the zodiac off in the direction where the planet really is, out in space.

The energy patterns of the solar system influence the Earth through its energy field, the zodiac. The energy patterns of the Earth and the solar system together influence you through your personal energy field, the houses.

Planets
↓
Signs
↓
Houses
↓
You

Planetary Rulerships

Just as the meanings of the signs and houses are closely related, so are the meanings of the signs and the planets—but in a different way.

Each sign derives its fundamental tone or quality from the characteristics of the planet which is said to *rule* it. The rulerships of the seven innermost planets—the Sun, Moon, Mercury, Venus, Mars, Jupiter and Saturn—have been known since ancient times. Since the outer, transpersonal planets, Uranus, Neptune and Pluto, were discovered, they have been included in the traditional system of sign-rulership by making them the new rulers or co-rulers of three of the signs.

The list of the planetary rulerships is as follows:

Sign	Ruler	Co-ruler
Aries	Mars	
Taurus	Venus	
Gemini	Mercury	
Cancer	The Moon	
Leo	The Sun	
Virgo	Mercury	
Libra	Venus	
Scorpio	Mars	Pluto
Sagittarius	Jupiter	
Capricorn	Saturn	
Aquarius	Saturn	Uranus
Pisces	Jupiter	Neptune

A list like this is not easy to learn, unless you happen to like memorizing facts. In list form, the choice of new rulerships or co-rulerships for the outer, transpersonal planets does not seem to follow any logic, and indeed the assignment of traditional rulerships has no immediately obvious pattern.

There is a pattern here, however, which makes the planetary rulerships much easier to remember, and also sheds some light on their interpretation and use in astrology.

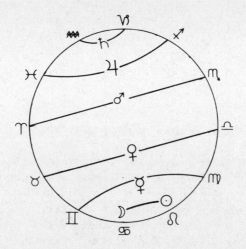

Figure 78. The ladder of traditional rulerships

The rulerships of the inner seven planets follow a simple, ladder-like pattern across the zodiac (figure 78.) The bottom rung of the ladder connects the Sun's rulership of Leo with the Moon's rulership of Cancer. Immediately, there is an implication that one end of a rung is yin and the other yang, since the Sun and Leo are yang, and the Moon and Cancer are yin in gender. The second rung connects the two rulerships of Mercury in Gemini and Virgo. Above that is the Venus rung (connecting Taurus and Libra), the Mars rung (Aries and Scorpio), the Jupiter rung (Sagittarius and Pisces) and the Saturn rung (Capricorn and Aquarius). Note that the "rungs" follow the "alphabetical order" of the planets.

When Uranus was discovered, it took over the rulership of Aquarius from Saturn. Then Neptune took over Pisces from Jupiter and Pluto took over Scorpio from Mars. The new co-rulerships step back down the ladder (figure 79). In relation to Saturn, Uranus is yang in quality, so it takes the yang sign, Aquarius, leaving the yin sign Capricorn to Saturn. Neptune is yin with respect to Jupiter, and Pluto is yin with respect to Mars, so they take over the yin signs on their rungs (Pisces and Scorpio), leaving the corresponding yang signs to the old rulers.

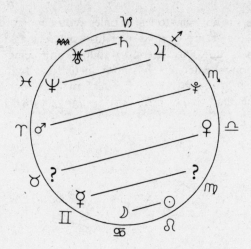

Figure 79. New rulerships on the ladder

Based on this pattern, I am going to indulge in some prediction. I expect two new planets will be discovered. One will become co-ruler of Taurus, because that sign is opposite Pluto's rulership in Scorpio: opposite signs are in general congruent with one another, so it is sensible to expect opposite signs both to have a new ruler. The other will become the co-ruler of Virgo, on the same principle, since it is opposite Neptune's rulership in Pisces. I expect the new ruler of Taurus to be yin with respect to Venus. Psyche, a hypothetical planet that Michael Munkasey and others have been investigating for a number of years, seems to fill the bill. Similarly, I expect the new ruler of Virgo to be yin with respect to Mercury. This is because Taurus and Virgo are the yin signs on their respective rungs of the rulership ladder. (Gender is taken up in greater detail at the end of this chapter.)

Some astrologers surmise that the newly-discovered "minor planet" Chiron shares the rulership of Virgo with the asteroids, collectively. On the other hand, Alice Bailey's *Esoteric Astrology* names the as yet undiscovered planet Vulcan as ruler of both Virgo and Taurus.

Exercise 1: Sit in your circle of houses. For each house in turn, consider the sign on its cusp. The planet that rules the sign on the cusp also rules the house. (For example, if you have Cancer rising, your first house is ruled by the Moon, because the Moon rules Cancer.) In each house place the symbol of the planet that rules the sign on its cusp. If there are two co-rulers, place both symbols there.

For each house in turn, as you review your meditations there, ask yourself how the ruling planet sets the tone or quality of your experiences in that house. How can you turn to this power or faculty for direction and guidance in that part of your life? Are your difficulties there a result of trying to work or act contrary to the nature of the ruling planet? Review your meditations on that planet.

Focus your attention on a particular problem or issue in one of your houses. Consider the ruler of that house; that is, the ruler of the sign on its cusp: Where is that planet actually placed in your horoscope? Are your difficulties connected with some unresolved issue in the house where the ruling planet is located in your horoscope?

Consider any planets that are placed in this house in which you are experiencing difficulty. What houses do they rule? Are your problems here related to your affairs in those houses?

Dispositors

The ruler of a sign is said to be the *dispositor* of any planets located in the sign that it rules. In traditional parlance, it "disposes of" planets in its rulership. For example, if you have Pluto in Leo, the Sun is its dispositor because the Sun rules Leo. If you have the Sun in Cancer, the Moon is its dispositor, because the Moon rules Cancer. The Moon in Gemini is disposed of by Mercury, ruler of Gemini.

In general terms, a planet lends its support to its dispositor. The basic qualities of a sign are laid down by the characteristics of the ruler of the sign, so to speak, so a planet located there tends to behave in ways that are congruent with its dispositor. Any difficulty or ease you are experiencing with a given planet may spread to the planets it disposes; conversely, the difficulty may really be connected with its own dispositor. On the other hand, you may turn to planets disposed of by a stressed planet to help alleviate the difficulty. Usually, you can think of the dispositor of a planet in your horoscope as an advisor to you in your use of the corresponding faculty in your life.

The houses are also said to be ruled by planets. This differs from one horoscope to another, depending upon where the signs fall in the circle of houses.

The dispositor and the ruler of a house serve similar functions in the horoscope. The dispositor of a given planet (the ruler of the sign in which it is located) guides you in your access to the energies represented by that planet. The house-ruler (the ruler of the sign on the cusp of the house) guides you in your application of those energies to your affairs in the house that it rules.

Because the signs usually straddle house cusps, the dispositor and the house-ruler of a given planet may not be the same. For example, in the horoscope you looked at previously (figure 72), Mars is in the second house, which is ruled by the Sun since Leo is on the cusp of the second house, yet Mars is also in the sign Virgo. Therefore, Mars's dispositor is Mercury, while its house-ruler is the Sun. Stimulating ideas (Mercury) open access to this person's vital drive, ambition and assertiveness, but when it comes to applying these manifestations of Mars energy, they must be connected with an inner identity and sense of life purpose (the Sun). In this sense, making money and accumulating possessions (second house) is exciting to him.

Exercise 2: In your meditation circle, sit in that house in which your Sun is placed. Meditate on its dispositor, the ruler of your Sun sign. (If you were born when the Sun was in Leo, continue with the suggestions for further meditation, below.)

How does this planet guide the unfoldment of your innermost identity and your deepest aims in life? How does it influence you in your pursuit of your heart's desire, to the extent that you have discovered it? Review material you have gathered in the Sun section of your notebook. Can you find the influence of the Sun's dispositor in your life?

Next, meditate on the ruler of the house the Sun is in. Whether it is the same planet or a different one, how does it influence the way you express your inner purpose, as represented by the Sun?

Finally, meditate on the placement of the sign Leo in your horoscope. How does the Sun influence the house on whose cusp Leo falls? How about the preceding house: is it influenced in a less prominent way, by virtue of having Leo in its second portion and another sign on its cusp? How about the planets placed in Leo, if any? (If there are no house cusps in Leo, the sign is "intercepted." This will be taken up later in this chapter.)

Suggestions for further meditation: Sit in that house in which the Moon is placed in your horoscope, and meditate on its dispositor. (If you were born when the Moon was in Cancer, move on to the next paragraph of suggestions.) What kind of influence is capable of impressing you deeply? Does the symbolism of the Moon's dispositor help you as you seek answers to this question? Where do you turn to satisfy your emotional needs? Review material in the Moon section of your notebook. What role does the Moon's dispositor have in your experiences of security and insecurity? Does it help you see how your memory works, and how you can form and change habits most effectively? Explore the significance of the ruler of the house in which the Moon is located in your horoscope, as you did for the Sun's house-ruler.

Sit in your meditation circle in that house in which Mercury is placed in your horoscope. Meditate on the dispositor of Mercury, and ask what directs and focuses your attention in one way rather than another? On what basis do you elect to be logical on one occasion and not logical on others? What sort of thing do you characteristically fail to notice, that others do notice? Review the material you have gathered in the Mercury section of your notebook. What role does Mercury's dispositor have in the direction and focus of your senses, both inner and outer? Do you share the commonly-held belief that your rational mind is the seat of all your intelligence, and that your faculty of reason is a free agent in your personality, value-free and "objective"? What are the premises of your logic? What are the character and origin of your assumptions? How do you distinguish between reason and rationalization?

Meditate in like fashion on the other planets and their dispositors in your horoscope. Use your meditations from Part I to formulate questions for meditation like those posed above.

Dispositor Structure

Most or all of the planets in your horoscope are not in the signs they rule. Because of this, the dispositor of one planet in your horoscope will itself have a dispositor, which will be disposed of by a third planet, and so forth, in a definite chain of dispositors.

It is very useful to diagram the *dispositor structure* of your horoscope. This network of dispositors, the "chain of command" among the planets, is different for every horoscope.

To illustrate this, let's look at the horoscope of a client of mine (figure 80). It is shown in the simplified, schematic form called the "flat chart," with the signs doubling as houses, as though 0° Aries were rising and 0° Capricorn were at the Midheaven. This is sufficient to determine the dispositor structure, which is diagrammed in figure 83.

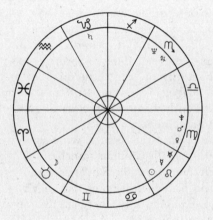

Figure 80. "Flat chart" number one

To determine the dispositor structure, ask first: Are any planets in signs which they rule? Here, the Sun is in Leo and Saturn is in Capricorn. Planets in their own rulerships are placed at the top of the diagram.

Having found a place to start the diagram, the next question is: What planets (if any) do these two planets dispose of? Are there any other planets in Leo (disposed of by the Sun), or in Capricorn or Aquarius (disposed of by Saturn)? The Sun disposes of both Mercury and Uranus, since they are both placed in Leo. Therefore they are connected by branches below the Sun in the diagram.

Saturn remains isolated in the diagram, since there are no planets in either Capricorn or Aquarius. A planet that "disposes of itself" and disposes of no other planets is called an "escape planet." It has a powerful influence, but is somewhat difficult to integrate with the other powers and faculties of the personality because of this lack of connection.

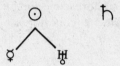

Figure 81. Top of the dispositor structure

The "administrative faculty" (Saturn) goes in and out of focus for this woman. When she takes responsibility for her own experience and brings issues of self-discipline into conscious focus, she can be very self-controlled and may be experienced by others as controlling them. On other occasions she loses patience with herself; her other powers and faculties seem unruly or undisciplined, or she projects these qualities onto others and in that way externalizes her sense of frustration by blaming it on others. At those times, others may see her as attempting to control them, but they experience these attempts as ineffectual at best. Finally, she may project the qualities of Saturn onto some outside authority-figure rather than consciously owning those qualities as part of herself. With Saturn as an escape planet, issues of structure, form and discipline are problematic for this person. It requires conscious attention for her to bring these issues into proper focus and balance.

Returning to the dispositor structure, what sign does Uranus rule? There are no planets in Aquarius, so the Uranian branch of the dispositor structure ends there. The other branch down from the Sun ends with Mercury, ruler of Gemini and Virgo. There are no planets in Gemini, but in Virgo, Mercury disposes of Venus, Mars and Pluto. Consequently, there are three branches below Mercury in the dispositor structure (figure 82).

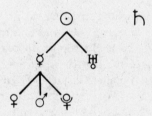

Figure 82. Adding planets under Mercury

What signs does Mars rule? There are no planets in Aries, but both Jupiter and Neptune are in Scorpio. Pluto is the new ruler of Scorpio, so Jupiter and Neptune have two dispositors (figure 83).

The influence of the old ruler is more prominent when the person is behaving in ways that are appropriate for the Piscean Age, which is now coming to an end. The influence of Pluto is stronger when the person is participating in the beginnings of the new age, the Aquarian Age. The discovery of the transpersonal planets Uranus, Neptune and Pluto was a harbinger of the new age. (Incidentally, one might look for a similar fluctuation between two world-views in connection with planets placed in Virgo and Taurus, since they too would have two dispositors if new rulers were discovered for those signs.)

Figure 83 shows the complete dispositor structure. All the planets are included. Except that Saturn is an "escape planet," the *final dispositor* in this horoscope would be the Sun, because it is at the top of the "chain of command." The final dispositor calls the tune for the personality as a whole.

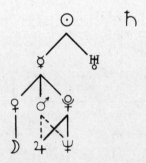

Figure 83. The complete dispositor structure

The immediate tension in the dispositor structure of this horoscope is between the ebullient display and self-dramatization of the Sun in Leo and the sober, restrained orientation to discipline and order symbolized by Saturn in Capricorn. When she projects those Saturnian qualities onto others, she sees people in authority as threats to her pride and self-esteem.

The Sun disposes of Mercury and Uranus, so they serve as employees, or (perhaps more fittingly) as servants of her pride. Her need for attention and her proclivity for self-dramatization and personal display (Sun in Leo) are served by her creative intellectual powers and verbal skills, symbolized by Mercury and Uranus. In turn, her Venusian imagination and esthetic faculty, though critical and tending to go "by the book" (Venus in Virgo), dutifully and thoroughly serves the needs of her intellect, her communications and her manipulations of her environment (Mercury). Finally, her emotional responses, habit patterns, memory and other lunar characteristics are at the disposal of her Venusian creative imagination. The Moon in Taurus grounds the Venus-Mercury branch of the dispositor structure in practicality (Taurus is an Earth sign, and eminently practical in nature).

To summarize what the dispositor structure has shown, this is a willful and rebellious individual at times. One of the major challenges of her life is the problem of integrating her Saturn as inner self-discipline. As she learns humility she will have less need to protect herself from humiliation; her great creative powers will open up. Until then, they will be stifled by self-doubt, which lies not too far beneath the surface of her pride. She tends to rationalize and intellectualize her values, her esthetic sense and her affections (Venus in Virgo, disposed by Mercury). This is a major source of her self-doubt.

I have not included Jupiter and Neptune in this discussion. What can you think of to say about Jupiter's expansiveness and Neptune's empathy being directed by Pluto and Mars? Can you distinguish the new-age and Piscean-age sides of these two planets? Remember that they are themselves the co-rulers of Pisces.

You can diagram the dispositor structure of your own horoscope. It is easy to do. You have probably picked up the idea by following the above discussion. The following flow-chart may help to serve as a kind of check-list to make sure you have done each step correctly.

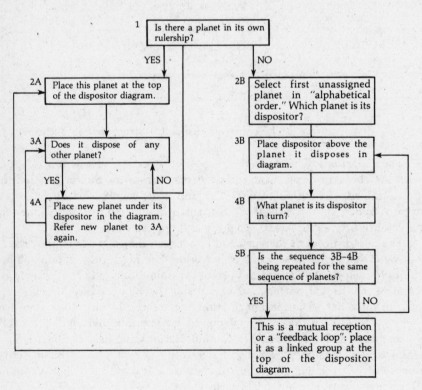

1 Is there a planet in its own rulership?

YES — NO

2A Place this planet at the top of the dispositor diagram.

2B Select first unassigned planet in "alphabetical order." Which planet is its dispositor?

3A Does it dispose of any other planet?

YES — NO

3B Place dispositor above the planet it disposes in diagram.

4A Place new planet under its dispositor in the diagram. Refer new planet to 3A again.

4B What planet is its dispositor in turn?

5B Is the sequence 3B–4B being repeated for the same sequence of planets?

YES — NO

This is a mutual reception or a "feedback loop": place it as a linked group at the top of the dispositor diagram.

Flow-chart: Finding the dispositor structure

A pair of planets, each placed in the sign ruled by the other, is said to be "in mutual reception." This is a special case of what I call a "feedback loop," when several planets are linked in a circular manner in the dispositor structure.

The horoscope shown in figure 84 has both a "mutual reception" and a "feedback loop" involving three planets. We will use it to illustrate how to use the flow-chart, above.

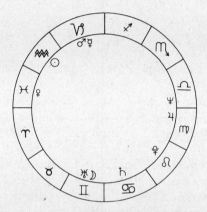

Figure 84. Flat chart number two

In answer to the first question in the flow-chart, there are no planets in their own rulerships in this horoscope. Therefore, we must pick up the track at an arbitrary point (question 2B), starting with the Sun and proceeding (if necessary) through the "alphabetical order" of the planets. The Sun is in Aquarius, so Uranus is its dispositor. Figure 85 shows this part of the dispositor structure, with a secondary link to Saturn, the old ruler of Aquarius.

Figure 85. Dispositors of the Sun

The next question (4B) is: "What planet is its dispositor in turn?" We must ask this question twice, once for Uranus and once for Saturn. Uranus is in Gemini, disposed of by Mercury; and Saturn is in Cancer, disposed of by the Moon (figure 86).

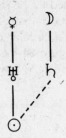

Figure 86. Dispositors of Uranus and Saturn

Question 5B asks: "Is the sequence 3B–4B being repeated for the same sequence of planets?" This question looks for a mutual reception or "feedback loop." The answer at this point is no, so follow the arrow back to 3B and repeat question 4B again.

What is the dispositor of Mercury in Capricorn? Saturn rules Capricorn, but Saturn already has a place in the diagram. The way to "place (Saturn) above (Mercury) in the diagram" (3B) is to move Saturn to a higher position, "stretching" its secondary connection to the Sun (figure 87).

Figure 87. Saturn disposing of Mercury

There are more adjustments in store before this dispositor structure diagram is finished. Look for the dispositor of Saturn. Saturn is disposed of by the Moon, ruler of Cancer. That is why the Moon is above Saturn in figure 87, above.

But now, what is the dispositor of the Moon? The Moon is in Gemini, so it is disposed of by Mercury. Now Mercury must be above the Moon, as well as below Saturn, which is below the Moon! What is going on here?

At this point, the answer to question 5B is "yes," because the Moon, Mercury and Saturn form a "feedback loop." Within a feedback loop, the convention of having a dispositor above the planet(s) it disposes of can no longer be followed; we must begin to use arrows pointing from the "lower" planet to the "higher" one (figure 88).

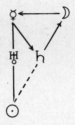

Figure 88. A feedback loop

We are now at the top of the diagram, so we can proceed as if we had found a planet in its own rulership (2A), and look for other planets that are disposed of by the Sun, the Moon, Mercury, Saturn or Uranus. We have to find places for Venus, Mars, Jupiter, Neptune and Pluto. The Sun disposes of Pluto in Leo. There are no other planets in Cancer for the Moon to dispose of, but Mercury disposes of Jupiter in Virgo, Saturn disposes of Mars in Capricorn and the Sun disposes of Pluto in Leo (figure 89).

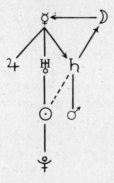

Figure 89. Adding Jupiter, Mars and Pluto

That leaves Venus and Neptune. We have no more leads, so we must return to the beginning and repeat question 2B again. What planet disposes of Venus in Pisces? Jupiter is the old ruler and Neptune is the new ruler of Pisces. We might put Venus under Jupiter (secondary connection), but where does Neptune go? Neptune is in Libra, disposed of by Venus. This is the mutual reception that I mentioned at the outset of this discussion. Its position in the completed dispositor structure is shown in figure 90.

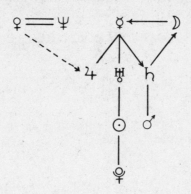

Figure 90. The completed dispositor structure

The three-planet feedback loop functions as a kind of "executive committee" in the place of a single final dispositor. In most such cases it is possible to determine which member of the "committee" functions as the "chairperson." Mercury seems dominant in that it disposes of three planets directly, while Saturn disposes of two planets, and the Moon only one. Furthermore, the three planets that Mercury disposes of (Jupiter, Saturn and Uranus) directly or indirectly dispose of every other planet except the Moon. Finally, Saturn is not strong in Cancer, opposite its rulership in Capricorn.

This means that this person's strong, practical mind (Mercury in Capricorn) is a key to loosening up his Moon-Saturn defenses. He is capable of a poetic gift for disciplined (Saturn) expression (Mercury) of feelings (Moon). This is a relatively easy-to-use arrangement, since Mercury is by its nature the most accessible of the faculties for direct, conscious intervention in the system as a whole.

Because neither Venus nor Neptune disposes of any other planets, the mutual reception is isolated from the rest of the dispositor structure. As a pair, they function rather like an "escape planet," difficult to integrate with the rest of the horoscope. However, they support one another (and Venus gains some direction from Jupiter in the bargain, since Jupiter is co-ruler of Pisces).

Planets in mutual reception generally cooperate in a very closely-integrated way, depending of course on their mutual compatibility. This mutual reception suggests that the inner, transpersonal undercurrent of Neptunian empathy, compassion and possible self-deception in relationships (Neptune in Libra, sign of relationships) is coupled with an urge to serve loved ones, and the need for a selfless or even sacrificial quality in the love life (Venus in Pisces). This combination can be very confusing for this person, coming out of nowhere and leading apparently nowhere, but it also has the power to open doors in relationships that are quite beyond his rather practical, goal-oriented conscious mind (Mercury in Capricorn).

The secondary connection of Venus to Jupiter, the old ruler of Pisces, suggests that traditional values may provide a steadying framework to help integrate the mutual reception into the rest of the dispositor structure. This is not only because Jupiter is the old ruler of Pisces, and therefore associated with values that are passing away with the coming of a new age, but also because Jupiter has a special connection with law, philosophy, religion and traditional values.

Here are two more horoscopes, presented in the same "flat chart" style without the house cusps. Work out their dispositor structures, then check your results in figures 93, 94 and 95 following Exercise 3, below.

The first is the horoscope of Leonardo da Vinci, born about 10 P.M., April 15, 1452 (O.S.), in Florence, Italy. ("O.S." means "old-style," referring to the old-style calendar before the Gregorian calendar reform. The Julian calendar was getting out of step with the seasons, so in 1582 Pope Gregory XIII introduced the device of leap years and suppressed ten days of the calendar. There was resistance to the reform, even riots because people thought the Pope was having God remove ten days from their allotted lifespans. The "old-style" calendar persisted in England and America until 1752, and in Eastern Orthodox countries until the twentieth century.)

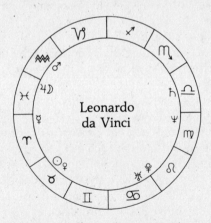

Figure 91. Horoscope of Leonardo da Vinci

The second horoscope for you to work out is that of Albert Einstein, born at 11:30 A.M., March 14, 1879, in Ulm, Germany.

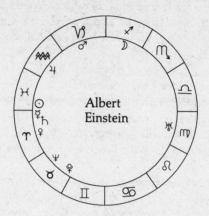

Figure 92. Horoscope of Albert Einstein

You may have to re-draw your diagrams of these dispositor structures several times before they are complete and clear.

(Both horoscopes are from Erlewine, *Circle Book of Charts;* see the Bibliography.)

Exercise 3: Work out the dispositor structure of your own horoscope.

Meditate on the planet or planets at the top of your diagram—the final dispositor, mutual reception, feedback loop, or combination of these. These planets are the strongest in your dispositor structure.

If your dispositor structure has only a single final dispositor, and consequently is not made up of more than one part, what is the role of the final dispositor in your horoscope? Meditate on it in connection with the house and sign in which it is placed.

If your dispositor structure has more than one part—that is, if there is more than one planet that "disposes of itself" in its own rulership, or if there are several "heads," including mutual receptions, feedback loops and rulers—meditate on the constitution of each of these parts. How are the parts of your personality organized? If one of these parts is an "escape planet" or is isolated almost to that extreme, how is that fact reflected in your experience? Review your meditations on the planet or planets involved. How can you connect this part of yourself to the other parts? Consider the house and sign it is in. Do they offer any clues? For example, are there other planets in the same house in the adjacent sign? In the opposite house? Is there a co-ruler?

Suggestions for further meditation: Consider a problem in your life. Which one of your planetary powers and faculties is under particular stress? If this is not immediately obvious, consider the house and sign under stress, look for planets placed there, or the ruler, and see if the corresponding parts of you are not experiencing the distress of your problem. If not, re-think the problem. You may not have it correctly stated.

Identify yourself with the stressed planet, sitting in your meditation circle in the house in which it is placed. Visualize its dispositor as a special friend or guide that can suggest ways to cope with your difficulty, because it has an insider's knowledge of the terrain. Place the symbol of this other planet in the house it occupies in your horoscope.

Start a conversation, as you did in Exercise 22 and 23 (Chapter 1). First, state your problem as clearly as you can, limiting yourself to the point of view of the stressed planet, and speaking directly to its dispositor. Then move to the house in which the dispositor is placed. Think and feel yourself into the point of view of that planet, and re-state the problem as it appears from there, just to be sure you heard it correctly. Ask for clarification where you need it. Then go back to your original position and provide the clarification asked for. Continue the dialog until you have some ideas you want to put to the test of experience and are willing to stop. (This may sound crazy, but it really does work.)

Meditate in the same way on the relationship between a stressed planet and the planet or planets it disposes, to find ways to rechannel the energies of the stressed planet in more desirable forms.

If your dispositor structure has several separate parts, due to several planets being in their own rulerships, or in mutual reception, meditate on the relationships between these parts, to find ways to integrate them. Open a conversation among the heads of each part—the last dispositor, the most prominent member of each mutual reception or "feedback loop," and so on. If you are not clear what is going on in a particular part of your dispositor structure, spend some time in a conversation between its head and the planet(s) it disposes. Bring in your knowledge of the houses in which these planets are placed.

Visualize and feel energy flowing between the chakras corresponding to these planets, in the pattern of your dispositor structure, integrating its several parts (if it has more than one), and reinforcing the relationships that make up your disposition.

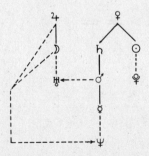

Figure 93. da Vinci's dispositor structure

The dispositor structure of Leonardo da Vinci's horoscope may be drawn as in figure 93.

I have chosen to represent the connections to the transpersonal planets with dotted lines. They had not yet been discovered then. The Aquarian Age, of which they are harbingers, was five hundred years further off in time when da Vinci was born. The consensus of astrologers is that these planets have become more influential in human affairs since their discovery, "coincidental" with the change from the Piscean to the Aquarian Age.

Da Vinci may well have been attuned to them, however. Notice that, without them, the Moon and her dispositor, Jupiter, would be isolated. Today, this structure would be drawn differently, as in figure 94.

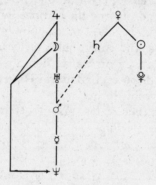

Figure 94. da Vinci today

In this "modern" version, the linking of the two parts of the structure is by way of Saturn, the "old ruler," the planet which makes Aquarius the sign of science as well as of (r)evolution.

The dispositor structure of Albert Einstein's horoscope may be diagrammed as in figure 95.

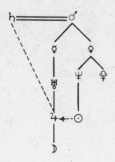

Figure 95. Einstein's dispositor structure

This is a single, unified structure. Note how Einstein's emotional nature was well subordinated to his other powers and faculties, but was by no means suppressed: The Moon is in freedom-loving and wisdom-loving Sagittarius. The Moon's dispositor, Jupiter, is in Aquarius, showing Einstein's innate orientation to the wisdom of the new age. At the top of the diagram the close integration of his Mars energy and Saturn discipline in mutual reception provides a key to his self-discipline, which enabled him to achieve his greatest results with very little external, institutional support. It is well that he was not emotionally dependent upon reassurance by his peers, thanks to the placement of his Moon, though he was emotionally sensitive (Sun in Pisces, Cancer rising).

Detriment

When a planet is in the sign opposite its rulership, like Venus in Aries in Einstein's horoscope, it is said to be *in detriment*. A planet in its detriment does not function well or easily; it is ill-at-ease. The sign opposite its rulership is like Alice's looking-glass world: Things are deceptively familiar but topsy-turvy, full of unexpected reversals. As a consequence, the power or faculty corresponding to a planet in detriment operates in somewhat awkward, off-balance ways, overcompensating and overreacting. It is especially dependent upon guidance from its dispositor, the ruler of the sign it is in, whose nature is in some sense opposite or complementary to its own nature. In Einstein's case, this worked out well. Mars, ruler of Aries, is placed in Capricorn, where it is channeled and focused by the discipline of its dispositor, Saturn. As a consequence, his Venus in Aries did not get out of hand, being disposed by this comparatively sober, restrained Mars energy. His major youthful romance ended when the woman returned to her Eastern European homeland to join the radical underground. After that, he did not seek marriage, but in a very practical way turned Venusian tasks of homemaking, for which he had no patience, over to paid housekeepers.

In general, to understand a planet in its detriment, you can learn much from an examination of the condition of its dispositor in the horoscope.

You may also learn much from your interactions with other people involving the house containing a planet in detriment and the opposite house containing the sign it rules. In such interactions, the planets disposed by a planet in detriment will be placed in or near the opposite house, and will therefore play a role in such interactions with others.

Exercise 4: Is there a planet in detriment in your horoscope? What can you learn from its dispositor, and from the planets it disposes, if any? Review your material on these planets and on the houses and signs in which they are placed. Is the planet in detriment related to any of the problems you have considered in previous exercises? What can you do to draw on the sources of its strength and confidence, in the opposite sign? What can you learn from your interactions with others? Do any of your friends or acquaintances use the energy of this planet, the one you have in detriment, in ways that you might profitably emulate? Where is this planet placed in your parents' horoscopes? How did your childhood experiences with them contribute to your learning how to employ this part of yourself?

Exaltations

A planet is *exalted* in that sign which is most congenial to its nature. In other words, the ruler of that sign fosters the planet's highest and most fulfilled expression. If the ruling planet is the gardener, then the exalted planet is the crop that grows best in the ruling planet's garden.

The natural affinity between the ruler and the exalted planet is suggested by the phrases in the following list:

Sign	Ruler	Exaltation	Suggestions for Meditation
Aries	Mars	Sun	Action opens the heart.
Taurus	Venus	Moon	Harmony fosters security.
Gemini	Mercury		(No traditional exaltation.)
Cancer	Moon	Jupiter	Security fosters growth.
Leo	Sun	Neptune	The heart has no barriers.
Virgo	Mercury	Mercury	The discriminating mind purifies itself.
Libra	Venus	Saturn	Harmony yields stability.
Scorpio	Pluto	Uranus	Power begets insight.
Sagittarius	Jupiter		(No traditional exaltation.)
Capricorn	Saturn	Mars	Discipline focuses energy.
Aquarius	Uranus	Mercury	Insight triggers synthesis.
Pisces	Neptune	Venus	Empathy is the key to harmony.

There is no simple "ladder" diagram for the exaltations as there is for the rulerships, although there are some parallels: The Sun and Moon are exalted in an adjacent pair of signs (Aries and Taurus) just as they rule a pair (Cancer and Leo); directly opposite are the signs in which Saturn and Uranus are exalted (Libra and Scorpio), just as their rulerships in Capricorn and Aquarius are opposite the rulerships of the Sun and Moon (Cancer and Leo).

There is some additional patterning among the exaltations, following the "alphabetical order" of the planets, in that the exaltation of Mercury in Virgo is opposite that of Venus in Pisces, and the exaltation of Mars in Capricorn is opposite that of Jupiter in Cancer.

The exaltations of Mercury in Aquarius and Neptune in Leo are relatively recent, and are not entirely accepted among astrologers. Indeed, the whole subject of rulerships and exaltations is neglected by many contemporary astrologers, who do not know how to use them. As you will see in this chapter and in Chapter 5, they contribute much to the "syntax" of the symbol-language of astrology.

Some astrologers have suggested that both Pluto and Venus are exalted in Pisces, others, that Neptune is exalted in Aquarius and Pluto in Leo. Give some thought to this, on the basis of what you have learned about these planets and signs. Consider which planets might be exalted in Gemini and Sagittarius as well. I will offer some of my own speculations after this exercise.

Exercise 5: Sit in your meditation circle. Think of the twelve houses as the signs of the zodiac, as if 0° Aries were rising. In each sign in turn, place the symbol of the ruling planet, and above it place the symbol of the exalted planet. Meditate on the characteristics of the sign as an expression of the basic qualities of the ruling planet. Meditate on the nature of the exalted planet, and how its greatest potential might find expression if channeled according to the patterns of that sign.

Suggestions for further meditation: For each sign in turn, place the symbol of the ruling planet on top, and under it place the symbol for the planet which is exalted in the opposite sign. When a planet is opposite its exaltation, it is said to be *in fall*. Meditate on the ways in which the energies of each planet are channeled in the sign of its fall. How might the energies of the planet which is exalted there be opposite or complementary in nature? How might one draw upon the exalted planet to assist the one that is in fall? How might one take advantage of the complementarity of these two planets?

Give particular attention to planets that are in exaltation or in fall in your own horoscope.

Pluto, Gemini and Sagittarius

There is no agreed-upon exaltation for Pluto, and no planet is said to be exalted in either Gemini or Sagittarius. One view has it that these two mutable signs have to do with the balancing and harmonizing of all the planetary powers and faculties, so that in fact no planet is exalted above the others when located in Gemini or Sagittarius. As to Pluto, some astrologers have suggested Pisces as its exaltation, others Leo.

I have difficulty with Pluto being exalted in Pisces, because I think the traditional exaltation of Venus there is so apt. Where would Venus be exalted, if not in Pisces? Certainly not in Gemini or Sagittarius; and if in any other sign, where would we assign the planet already considered to be exalted there?

I think those who see Pluto exalted in Leo are a bit short-sighted. Certainly the World War II era was filled with issues of power, Plutonium and atomic energy were discovered and so on, but I doubt that those manifestations represent the highest expression of Pluto's energies. That is yet to come.

Of the two available signs, Sagittarius is the only appropriate one for Pluto's exaltation. It is a Fire sign, fitting Pluto's fiery quality, and Sagittarians do have a tremendous amount of energy and desire to change things that suits

Pluto's symbolism of transformation and regeneration. Under their Jovial surface, they are capable of surprising, explosive demonstrations of power if their freedom is threatened. Finally, Pluto's tenure in Sagittarius will usher in the millenium, and the galactic center is located in Sagittarius. This mythical "central sun," around which our Sun and countless other stars orbit, will peer like a God's eye through the needle's-eye of Pluto's energy field into the heart of our solar system around 2005 to 2010 A.D.: I think we can expect profound changes then.

Turning to Gemini, recall that Mercury, being androgynous, has two exaltations. Its yin, analytic aspect is exalted in Virgo, and its yang, synthesizing aspect is exalted in Aquarius. Should not the same principle apply to Uranus? The yin aspect of Uranus (analytical intuition) is exalted in Scorpio; perhaps the yang aspect (synthesizing intuition) is exalted in Gemini. Since Mercury rules both Gemini and Virgo, the generalization would be that Uranian intuition of both sorts is most facilitated by conscious attention and intellect.

Play with these speculations in your study and your meditations. I have not included them in the discussion of exaltations here, nor in the development and application of exaltations and falls in Chapter 5. Interpolate them for yourself, and put these ideas to the test of your astrological experience. Participate in the process of discovering where Pluto's exaltation lies.

Benefactors

If you are experiencing difficulty in connection with a particular planet in your horoscope, you may turn to the planet that is exalted in the sign where that planet is located.

To express this idea, I have developed the concept of the *benefactor* of a planet, parallel to the traditional concept of dispositor. Just as the ruler of a sign is the dispositor of any planets located there, the exaltation (the exalted planet) is the benefactor of any planets located there.

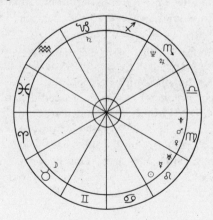

Figure 96. "Flat chart" number one

Take a look at my client's horoscope again (figure 96). Is there a planet in its own exaltation? Yes: the Moon is in Taurus, where it is exalted. Therefore the Moon goes at the top of the benefactor structure diagram. Since there are no other planets in Taurus, the Moon does not benefit any other planets: it will be an "escape" planet.

The Moon is the only planet in its own exaltation. Let's look for "mutual benefits" and feedback loops. Going through the "alphabetical order" of the planets, we find one almost immediately. The Sun is in Leo, with Neptune as benefactor; Neptune is in Scorpio, with Uranus as benefactor; and Uranus is in Leo again, with Neptune as benefactor. Uranus and Neptune are in mutual benefit, each in the other's sign of exaltation. Place this mutual benefit next to the Moon at the top of the benefactor structure (figure 97).

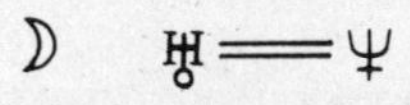

$$ \mathllap{\;\;\;\;\;}\text{☽} \qquad \text{♅} = \text{♆} $$

Figure 97. A "mutual benefactor" structure

The other planet in Scorpio is Jupiter, so Jupiter comes under Uranus in the growing benefactor structure. The planets benefited by Neptune are the Sun and Mercury, since both are located in Leo (figure 98).

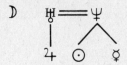

Figure 98. Expanded benefactor structure

Now repeat the question for the Sun, Mercury and Jupiter. There are no planets in Aries or in Cancer, where the Sun and Jupiter are exalted, but Venus, Mars and Pluto are all in Virgo, sign of Mercury's exaltation. There are no planets in Aquarius, Mercury's second exaltation. Place Venus, Mars and Pluto under Mercury in the benefactor structure. The final step is to include Saturn. Saturn is in Capricorn, and since Mars is exalted in Capricorn, Saturn comes under Mars in the dispositor structure (figure 99). Every planet and every benefactor relationship is included, so the benefactor-structure diagram is complete.

Because the Moon is an "escape planet," this woman may be better at receiving care and nourishment than she is at giving it. What other interpretations can you think of for the Moon being so strongly placed, yet poorly integrated in the benefactor structure?

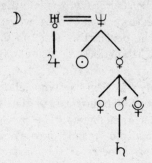

Figure 99. The complete benefactor structure

During the years 1956 to 1962, roughly, Uranus was in Leo and Neptune in Scorpio. In all horoscopes during that period, they were therefore mutual benefactors. In many of these horoscopes, when there were no other planets in either Leo or Scorpio, they were isolated from the rest of the structure; in others, one or both of them benefitted various planets located in Leo or Scorpio. Thus, on one hand, this special relationship of Uranus and Neptune is shared by a great many people born during those years; on the other hand, the shared mutual benefit pattern can have quite a different position and role in the benefactor structures of their horoscopes. Can you see how a whole generation can have some characteristics in common, yet have individual differences in the way in which they manifest those characteristics as individual persons?

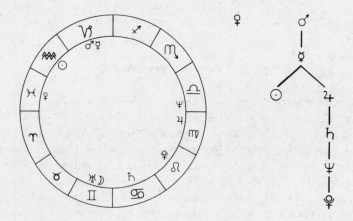

Figure 100. "Flat chart" number two

The second "flat chart" example (figure 100) has a somewhat more complicated benefactor structure. Venus and Mars are the two planets exalted in this horoscope. There are no other planets in Pisces, so Venus is isolated there as an "escape planet." Mars benefits Mercury, located also in Capricorn. Mercury benefits the Sun in Aquarius and Jupiter in Virgo. Jupiter benefits Saturn in Cancer, and Neptune in Libra is in turn the beneficiary of Saturn. Finally, Pluto is located in Leo, sign of Neptune's exaltation. Except for Venus, the "escape planet," Mars is the "final benefactor" in this horoscope.

The Moon and Uranus have been omitted because there is no agreed-upon exaltation in Gemini. What would the dispositor structure look like if you follow the suggestion given earlier concerning the exaltation of Uranus?

Let's look at the relationship of this benefactor structure to the dispositor structure of the same horoscope (figure 90).

In the dispositor structure (figure 90), Mercury was seen as the key to the feedback loop or "executive committee" at the top of the diagram, and thus of the dispositor structure as a whole. In the benefactor structure, Mercury is next to the top, as beneficiary of Mars, the final benefactor. This suggests that whatever sparks this man's Mars energy and turns on his outer motivation will be especially nourishing and healthful for his mentality (Mercury). Conversely, if his assertiveness is stifled and he is stuck doing things that fail to "excite him," he will suffer from mental malnutrition. Because of Mercury's prominence in the dispositor structure, this issue is of crucial importance for this man's well-being as a whole.

Mars is the final benefactor. In the dispositor structure, Mars is disposed of by Saturn. This suggests that the Saturnian discipline and centeredness characteristic of Capricorn are very important values for this person, ensuring that he will always have that Mars energy which is the root of his benefactor structure, and upon which all the other beneficial relationships in it are based.

Venus is isolated in the benefactor structure, just as the mutual reception of Venus and Neptune is isolated in the dispositor structure. However, Saturn is the benefactor of Neptune, and may therefore also be of benefit to Venus, indirectly through the mutual reception. This suggests that a spiritual (Neptune) discipline (Saturn) would not only stabilize this person's psychic life (Neptune), but would also strengthen his personal values and make his love life more stable and secure (Venus).

You might want to look at the benefactor structures of the horoscopes of da Vinci and Einstein and compare them with their dispositor structures.

Exercise 6: Diagram the benefactor structure of your own horoscope. Meditate on the planet or planets in the dominant position(s) of this structure.

If your horoscope has only one final benefactor, what is the role of this planet in your horoscope? Meditate on the house and sign in which it is located.

If your benefactor structure is divided into more than one part, meditate on how each of these parts is made up. What is the dominant planet or group of planets in each (highest benefactor, mutual benefit or feedback loop)? How are the powers and faculties of your personality segregated into factions corresponding to the groups of planets in your benefactor structure?

If any parts of your benefactor structure are isolated, with few or no beneficiaries, how is that fact reflected in your experience? Review your meditations on the planet or planets involved. How can you connect this part of yourself to your other parts? Can you get any ideas from the house and sign it is in?

Suggestions for further meditation: Compare your benefactor structure with your dispositor structure. Give particular attention to the planets in dominant positions in each, and what their roles are in the other structure.

If there are any escape planets or isolated substructures in either your benefactor structure or your dispositor structure, look for ways to integrate them that are not apparent until you compare the two structures.

Identify yourself with a planet that is currently under stress in your life. Visualize its benefactor as a special friend or a source of strength and support that can turn you on to the richest benefits available in that particular sign. Place the symbol of the benefactor in the house position which it occupies in your horoscope. Start a conversation between the two parts of your personality that correspond to these planets, as you did in Exercise 3, above, and in Exercise 22 and 23 in Chapter 1. Continue the dialog between the planet under stress and its benefactor until you have some ideas that you can carry out.

Create a diagram showing the relationships of rulerships and exaltations, as follows: Put the ruling planet of a given sign in the higher position, and the exaltation of that sign in the lower position, for each relationship. (For example, Mars would be placed above the Sun, since Mars rules the sign in which the Sun is exalted.) Draw arrows from exaltation to ruler, where necessary. Meditate on this structure to get further insight into the meanings of the signs of the zodiac.

Gender of Signs and Houses

Every cycle alternates through positive and negative phases, the yang and yin of Taoism. On every level of manifestation the phenomenal universe is pervaded by pairs of opposites. The four alchemical elements are examples of this. The two elements symbolized by upward pointing triangles, Fire and Air, are positive or yang in gender, while the two elements symbolized by downward-pointing triangles, Water and Earth, are receptive, or yin.

The gender of the signs and houses follows from this. As the Sun, Moon and planets move from sign to sign and from house to house, their influence oscillates from yang to yin and back. This is like breathing, in and out.

Psychological tests have shown that people born when the Sun was in a yang sign (that is, in a Fire or Air sign) tend to be more extroverted, and people born with the Sun in yin signs tend to be more introverted.

In general, when a planet is in a yang sign, the corresponding faculty is said to be more outgoing and projective, and when in yin signs it is more reserved and receptive. Mercury in yin signs, for example, corresponds to a more analytical, deductive mentality, while in yang signs it corresponds to a more synthesizing, inductive mentality.

In general, the odd-numbered, yang houses represent expressive, outgoing, centrifugal areas of experience, and the even-numbered, yin houses represent receptive, retiring, centripetal areas of experience.

As the cycle of signs overlays the cycle of houses, their two patterns of alternating yin and yang overlap in the unique configuration of your horoscope. This combination of signs with houses is a powerful factor in the expression of your personality. It shows how your personal existence is integrated with life around you. Look at your own horoscope: The *sign position* of a planet in your horoscope symbolizes how you *gain access* to the energies represented by that planet. The sign shows the direction, form or quality of the corresponding power or faculty in your personality.

The *house position* of a planet in your horoscope shows how you *apply* the energies represented by that planet. The house shows the area of your experience which the corresponding power or faculty is centered in as its point of view or "home base."

Do you have a yang sign rising (Aries, Gemini, Leo, Libra, Sagittarius or Aquarius)? Do the houses in your horoscope in general align with signs of the same gender? Do you feel that the yin-yang oscillation from one phase to the next in your cycles of experience is reinforced by the signs? Do you experience greater extremes of extroverted self-expression versus introverted periods of inward assimilation? How is this influenced by the mode of the sign (Cardinal, Fixed or Mutable) versus that of the house (Angular, Succedent or Cadent)?

If you have a Fire sign rising (Aries, Leo or Sagittarius), you may have signs corresponding to houses of the same element all around your horoscope. Does this result in an expecially direct and uncomplicated quality to your expression of your personality? The extreme in this regard is the Aries-rising personality, where each sign may align with the house that corresponds to it exactly.

Do you have a yin sign rising (Taurus, Cancer, Virgo, Scorpio, Capricorn or Pisces)? Do the houses in your horoscope in general align with signs of opposite gender? Is the yin-yang oscillation of your cycle of houses tempered by the contrary oscillation of the cycle of signs? Are you less inclined to extremes than someone with a yang sign rising? Is there less contrast between your experiences in successive houses?

(If you obtain horoscopes for friends and acquaintances, following the instructions in Appendix 3, or consult one of the published collections of horoscopes of well-known persons, you will be able to make these comparisons.)

Interceptions

At the beginning of this chapter we looked at the zodiac and the field of houses in three dimensions, as spheres with segments like an orange, and we saw how the houses are of unequal size in most horoscopes because the summer signs rise further north and the winter signs rise further south of the east-west axis. Unless you have 0° Aries or 0° Libra rising, the houses of your horoscope will be unequal in size.

You may have found that some signs in your horoscope have two house cusps in them, and others have none. A sign that contains no house cusps, but is itself entirely included within a house, is said to *intercept* that house (from Latin *intercipere* "to interrupt," *inter* "between" plus *capere* "to take, sieze").

Intercepting signs are always found in opposing pairs. Interpretations vary. Do you find that the intercepting signs are more difficult to integrate in the flow of your horoscope? Or do you find that their influences are not tied down to any one house, but rather are suffused throughout the whole cycle of houses in an indirect or even insidious way?

Do you find that the houses that correspond to these intercepting signs (for example, the way Taurus and Scorpio correspond to the second and eighth houses) are in some way hidden or mysterious to you? Normally, your subconscious connection with the cycle of signs (the "houses" of the planet as a whole) is by analogy with your cycle of houses. It may be that you require the direct connection of a given sign with some particular house for you to be able to connect well with that sign at all. As a consequence, the corresponding houses may be less clear to you, lacking the zodiacal analogy in your personal experience.

For example, suppose you have Taurus and Scorpio intercepting your ninth and third houses, respectively. You might find issues of money, resources and values difficult to integrate into the pattern of your life. You might find yourself facing these issues in a diffused manner through all twelve phases of your experience, not focused clearly in any one house. Perhaps you would seek answers especially in education, communication and other affairs of the third and ninth houses. The affairs of the second and eighth houses, corresponding with Taurus and Scorpio, may seem mysterious or veiled, hard to come to grips with, as if this were an area of apprenticeship for you, an area in which you lacked information or experience others seem to have.

If you have intercepted houses in your horoscope, then elsewhere in your horoscope you have two house cusps within one sign, where your houses are smaller than 30° each. If so, do you find the affairs of these houses especially closely linked? Do your experiences in these houses have a lot in common? Is the symbolism of the signs that contain two house cusps especially important in your life?

Exercise 7: If you have intercepted houses in your horoscope, review your meditations on these pairs of opposite houses (in Chapter 2). Explore your experience of these houses for answers to the questions raised above.

Gender of Planets

We have already seen how the Fire and Air signs are yang or masculine in gender and the Water and Earth signs are yin or feminine. The planets have gender too, as follows:

Yang	Androgynous	Yin
Sun ☉		Moon ☽
	Mercury ☿	
Mars ♂		Venus ♀
Saturn ♄		Jupiter ♃
	Uranus ♅	
Pluto ♇		Neptune ♆

The yang planets on the left are the opposites or complements of the yin planets in the corresponding positions on the right. These pairs are the Sun and Moon, Mars and Venus, Saturn and Jupiter, and Pluto and Neptune. The two planets in the middle, Mercury and Uranus, are androgynous (or "gynandrous"), that is, both yang and yin. They are more strongly influenced than the other planets by the gender of the sign in which they are placed. On the other hand, they are more easily compatible with all the signs.

Recall that Pluto is the "higher octave" of Mars, Uranus of Mercury, and Neptune of the Moon (and, in a derived sense, of Venus). Jupiter and Venus, both yin, are traditionally called "benefic" planets, and Mars and Saturn on the other side are traditionally "malefics." The Sun and Saturn both have to do with centeredness and focus; the Moon and Jupiter both have to do with development and growth. In Chinese philosophy, yang manifests as contracted, compact forms and yin manifests as expanded, diffuse forms; these are associated with Saturn and Jupiter, respectively.

Exercise 8: Meditate on the yang planets in your horosocope (the Sun, Mars, Saturn and Pluto). Which ones are in yang signs and which are in yin signs? Do you feel any difference between these two sets of planets?

Meditate on the yin planets in your horoscope (the Moon, Venus, Jupiter and Neptune). Which ones are in yang signs and which are in yin signs? Do you feel any difference between the two sets? Does their manifestation seem more sensitive than that of the yang planets to the gender of the signs they are in, or less sensitive? Can you sense any influence of the gender of the houses they are in?

Suggestions for further meditation: Look at the dispositor structure and benefactor structure of your horoscope. Are the yang planets grouped together, or mixed randomly with the yin planets? What is the gender of the dominant planets? What patterns can you find in terms of gender? How do the yang and yin parts of your personality correspond to the substructures in these diagrams?

Delineation

A delineation (from the Latin word meaning "a sketch") is a brief interpretation of a horoscope. The process of horoscope delineation involves translation from the nonverbal, nonlinear symbol-language of astrology into the linear words and sentences of everyday language.

You have a sense, now, of how the planets, signs and houses are linked together in a complex web of correspondences. In the remainder of this chapter, we will apply these correspondences in the delineation of specific combinations in your horoscope. You will draw on your knowledge of all the elements of astrology—planets, signs and houses, elements, gender and so on—to enrich your understanding of each planet-sign-house combination that you encounter.

Remember that the planets are beyond the zodiac, and that the houses are within the zodiac. It is an old axiom in astrology that the planets tell you what is happening, the signs tell how, and the houses show where in the cycles of your experience.

For example, consider Saturn in Cancer in the eleventh house. What are you talking about? Saturn is the person's administrative faculty, his or her experience and expression of discipline, order and control. How is this faculty manifested? Through emotional restraint, responsibilities having to do with nurturing and family life (the combination of Saturn and Cancer). Where does it manifest in this person's experience? In experiences with friends, peers and groups, through progressive political activities and through development of this person's personal aims and goals in life.

As a first approximation, and a greatly oversimplified one, we can say that the planets function as nouns in the language of astrology, and the signs as adjectives modifying those nouns. The verbs are all the relationships among the planets, including dispositors, benefactors and especially the angular relationships known as aspects, which we will explore in Chapter 6. The houses function as adverbs, showing how the interrelationships of the planets in your horoscope are realized in the actual circumstances of your life.

In practice, of course, the process of translating astrological symbols into words does not follow such a rigid and restrictive schema as this. However, as a rough approximation, it can help to get you started. This is the basic idea behind the old "key-word" systems of interpretation taught by Max Heindel and others.

Let's look at an example. Suppose you have Mars in Gemini in the sixth house, disposing of Venus in Aries in the fourth. Taking our language analogy quite literally, we might come up with something like this:

sixth house (adverb) "where, how"	Gemini (adjective) "what kind"	Mars (noun) "what"	disposes (verb) relationship	fourth house (adverb) "where, how"	Aries (adjective) "what kind"	Venus (noun) "what"
in service in employment concerning health	curious prying nosy perceptive intellectual verbal nervous	energy aggression vitality pushiness drive assertiveness courage	guides directs governs influences facilitates	in a nurturing, caring, emotional, protective, conservative, home-oriented, traditonal way	assertive self-centered courageous aggressive pushy self-assured vital	personal values affections attractiveness magnetism imagination esthetic sense

Turning this table into sentences, we get delineations like the following:

"Your inquisitive energy and nervous aggressiveness manifest in the assertive, self-centered and forthright way you have of expressing your affections and tastes in your home and in your family life."

"You can be quite aggressive about attracting people to you when your curiosity is piqued, or when you find them challenging."

Of course, it is not necessary to pack everything into one sentence, nor even advisable to try. Put the words together for a manageable chunk of the horoscope, meditate on them, and the appropriate images and words will come to you.

Use features and images associated with all the planets, signs and houses involved in a given astrological configuration. In the example, the fundamentally yang aggressiveness of the Mars energy would be expressed in the manner that is characteristic of this yang Air sign, Gemini: questing, exploring with a great deal of mental energy (the dispositor is Mercury). The person might lack perspective or philosophical integrity in the activity because wherever Jupiter is in the horoscope, its influence over Mars is limited, since Jupiter is in its detriment in Gemini. On the other hand, the sixth house is yin, one of the Possessive or Earthy houses, so the paramount issues are practical function, serviceability and self-improvement. This decidedly mental employment of the person's Mars vitality would therefore manifest in experiences and circumstances characterized by subservience to the needs of others (the yin gender of the house).

Not that the yang qualities of Mars and Gemini would get lost in the sixth house. This person would want freedom in his or her work situation to move about, to explore and to exercise a variety of skills. He or she would enjoy and participate in office gossip, and might rebel if the boss tried to stifle extended coffee-break chatter and general nosiness. The boss would do well to overlook these traits, as this person would be basically a good hard worker.

All of this has to do with just the first half of the "sentence" quoted above. Try it now on the second half, Venus in Aries in the fourth house. To understand how the yin qualities of Venus might be expressed in the yang sign Aries, compare instances in your horoscope (or those of people you know) where a yin planet is placed in a yang sign. Recall that Venus rules Libra, the sign opposite Aries, and is in its detriment here. If Venus were in Libra, it would be able to draw on the steadying, centering influence of Saturn (wherever it was placed in the horoscope) because Saturn is exalted in Libra, but in Aries, Venus lacks the steadiness provided by Saturn.

What does this suggest that your experience and expression of personal values would be if you had Venus in Aries? The Sun is exalted in Aries, and the Sun refers everything to one's central core or identity or ego. What would a self-centered expression of affection be like? Mars, the dispositor, is assertive, courageous and impulsive. How would this affect your esthetic judgment? Would you know what you wanted immediately, or only after consideration? Remember that Mars is in Gemini. Would your value judgments tend to be deep-seated opinions or more transient responses? Venus is in the fourth house in this example, directed to issues of home, family, traditional values and personal security. What kind of host or hostess would you be? How would you be likely to react to a person with inhibiting, repressive (Saturnian) values? How could you use this experience to help you get in touch with more valid inner awareness of Saturn's steadiness and centering. Recall that, with Aries in the fourth, you would have Libra in the tenth, a strong place to connect with Saturn wherever it was placed in your horoscope, because Saturn is exalted in Libra, and rules Capricorn, which corresponds to the tenth house.

We have touched lightly on the "verb" in the "sentence" quoted above: Mars *disposes* of Venus. Venus is at the disposal of Mars, so that, even in the home, you would want to "do for" others, following the lead of Mars in the sixth. How would the gossipy mental energy of Mars in Gemini direct your assignment of personal value to the people and things in your environment? In turn, since Mercury is the dispositor of Mars in Gemini, the direction of your Mars energies, and therefore the quality of your value judgments, would depend on how carefully you paid attention to what was going on around you.

Exercise 9: Choose a planet that stands out in some way in the dispositor structure of your horoscope. If you have an "escape planet," save it for a subsequent exercise. A planet involved in a mutual reception or feedback loop might be a good place to start, or a planet with which you feel you are experiencing difficulty.

What is the dispositor of this planet? If you have chosen a planet in its own rulership, pick one of the planets that it disposes of. Turn to the section of your notebook devoted to the disposed planet. Across the top of a blank page, write the format that was used above for Mars in Gemini in the sixth house disposing Venus in Aries in the fourth. Or, if you wish to abbreviate, try something like the following: "where," "what kind," "what" (disposing), "where," "what kind," "what." Under the first "where," put the house that the dispositor is in, followed by the sign under "what kind" and the dispositor itself under "what." Under the second "where" put the house of the disposed planet, followed by its sign under "what kind" and the planet itself under "what."

Now, in each column, list words and phrases appropriate to the house, sign or planet above it, as was done in the example.

Meditate on the relationships of words and ideas in this simple format. Write down the sentences that come to your mind, in terms that emphasize the disposed planet.

Suggestions for further meditation: Turn to the section of your notebook that is devoted to the dispositor, and consider the same relationship as you did in the main part of this exercise. Without consulting the lists of words and phases that you came up with the first time, prepare the same format, and meditate on it in the same way, putting the emphasis this time on the dispositor. Afterward, compare the results of the two sessions.

Do the same for other pairs of planets in your horoscope, as they are related in your dispositor structure and in your benefactor structure.

Go through your results from these sessions and develop your understanding of the relationships of rulership and dispositors on the one hand, and exaltation and benefactors on the other.

Your Ascendant

The eastern horizon of your horoscope, your Ascendant or rising sign and the cusp of your first house, is a point of synthesis and reintegration for all the pairs of opposites in your horoscope. This is the "zero point" of all your cycles of experience, the point where they both end and begin.

Look at your horoscope. What sign is on your Ascendant? This sign, the phase of the zodiac-cycle where your first house begins, symbolizes how you initiate things. It shows your characteristic manner, your personal style of doing all the things that you do. This personal style is developed through all twelve phases of the cycle of houses. Of all the pairs of opposites in your horoscope, the most basic pair is the Sun and Moon. Your rising sign shows how you reconcile your inner motivation (Sun) with your means for putting that motivation into effect and incorporating it into the substance of your life (Moon).

Look at the horoscope in figure 101. The Sun is in Aquarius, in the fifth house. There is a built-in contradiction, since Aquarius corresponds to the eleventh house, which is opposite the fifth. This person's inner life-purpose has to do with far-seeing humanitarian aims, with collective creativity and group activities, and a detached, scientific outlook. However, in the fifth house, it manifests in the area of personal creativity, where the person is not so likely to feel detached and objective about what he is doing, and where his own performance is more important than its long-range objectives. When he has a free hand to develop his new-age ideas in personally creative ways, however, his Aquarian inner identity shines forth brightly.

His Moon is in Gemini in his tenth house. He is very quick, sometimes nervous, in his responses to experiences. His mood-shifts are likewise quick and volatile. This changeability manifests in his public life, career and social

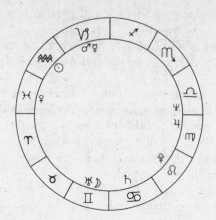

Figure 101. "Flat chart" number two

achievement (tenth house). Because of the Moon's connection with subconsciousness and the collective unconscious mind, he has a natural ability to relate well to the general public, and with his Geminian communication skills he could be a good writer or public speaker.

The Ascendant in Virgo shows how these two sides of his nature are integrated. In themselves, the Sun and Moon in this horoscope indicate a lot of talent. With Virgo rising, however, this person can be too much of a perfectionist to allow his gifts to flower naturally and fully. His picky, critical concern about imperfections and errors in his work (and in that of others) often stifles the creative flow before it has a chance to get properly started. He has to learn to perfect things by focusing on what is already perfect in them, rather than on their faults.

This person experiences a need (Moon) to articulate (Gemini) collective needs and aspirations of the groups he identifies with (Aquarius) in such a way that members of the group consciously assume their share of the collective responsibility. This is done as a service to others (Virgo), through painstaking analysis of the detailed fine texture of group process, discerning the essential and presenting it with care and exactitude.

In a more negative expression, the Gemini Moon might experience anxiety when communication is not flowing well in the group, and might react to this anxiety by trying to "rescue" group members under stress. The Aquarius Sun is capable of using collective aims as a cover for personal egotism, saying "we" when he really means "I," to further his own perhaps unconscious needs and aims. The Virgo Ascendant might integrate these negative traits in a picky, critical way, and become offended if people reject his services, yet resentful of those who accept his repeated invitations to take his services for granted.

What can you say about this combination of Sun, Moon and Ascendant? To stimulate your imagination and open the gate to intuition, list key phrases from the appropriate sections of your notebook devoted to the Sun, Aquarius, the Moon, Gemini, the Ascendant (and first house) and Virgo. Put these in three columns: Sun in Aquarius, Virgo rising, Moon in Gemini. Take an item from each column, let your imagination play with them, and transform them into sentences expressing how the Ascendant might integrate this basic yin-yang polarity of the personality.

Exercise 10: Consider your own rising sign. Turn to the section of your notebook that is devoted to the first house. On a blank page, write your Sun sign, rising sign and Moon sign, in the format suggested above. Review your material on each of these signs and on the Sun and Moon, and glean words and phrases to write in each column. Meditate on these, let your imagination play with them, and write down sentences that occur to you as interpretations showing how your Ascendant might integrate the Sun-Moon polarity in your horoscope.

Suggestions for further meditation: Do the same for other pairs of opposites in your horoscope: Venus and Mars, Jupiter and Saturn, Neptune and Pluto, and any other pairs of planets that are opposed in some way. Meditate on how your Ascendant might bring out their complementarity rather than their conflict.

Enrich these meditations by adding information about the ruler and exaltation, the element, mode and gender and other distinctive features of each sign. Review your material in your notebook on each of these elements, to generate more key phrases.

Can you identify features of your personal style in your rising sign? In your daily life, put some energy into achieving "meta" perspective: step back from being immersed in *content*, where you ask "Why?," to a clear perception of *process*, where you ask "How?" Look at the process (rather than the content) of your life to discover your style, your characteristic manner of doing things. Does the imagery associated with your rising sign help you see your characteristic patterns of behavior more clearly?

Allow yourself to become more aware of differences of style among your friends and acquaintances. As you achieve "meta-perspective" on your interactions with them, watch for indicators of one or another sign on their personal style. Ask yourself, "What is their manner (Ascendant) of implementing (Moon) their intentions (Sun)?" How do your reactions to their style affect your relationship? Do you find your reactions more powerful, or do your reactions overpower you less, when you focus on process rather than content and ask "How?" rather than "Why?"

Consider the ruler of your Ascendant. Where is it in your horoscope? How do you experience the corresponding part of your personality? Does it play a special part in your personal style?

How about the planet that is exalted in your rising sign? Since the ruler of the Ascendant is traditionally the ruler of the horoscope, does it make sense for you to think of this planet as the benefactor of your horoscope as a whole? Does it represent an especially potent resource for your first house? Where is it placed in your horoscope? Is that house easier for you to integrate with the affairs of your first house?

Where is the planet that is in detriment in your rising sign? Could you use more of its particular strengths in your first-house affairs? Where is it placed in your horoscope? Is that house hard for you to integrate with your first house? Is it resistant to your "style," as if the house were somehow "in detriment" as well as the planet that rules it?

Where in your horoscope is the planet which is in fall in your rising sign? How can you improve your access to this resource? Do you have any difficulty relating to the sign and house that it is placed in?

In this chapter, you have learned some of the semantics and syntax of the language of astrology, the connections that link the planets, signs and houses, mirroring the underlying connections that link your experiences of life. Together, they form a unified continuum of meaning. You have begun to read the messages in your horoscope.

In the next chapter, the analysis of signs and planets into their distinctive features is applied in detail to the interpretation of each planet-sign combination that can possibly occur. This is intended as a resource to help you explore your relationships with other people and discover ways of turning sources of potential conflict into occasions for mutual growth and enjoyment. In the process, you will understand your own personality patterns on much deeper levels.

5

Synthesis: Planets in Horoscopes

This chapter is designed to help you integrate all the information that you have gathered about the planets, signs and houses. When learning to interpret horoscopes, it is often helpful to refer to "cookbooks" which provide ready-made delineations of each pair of factors (planet-sign, planet-house and so on) that might be encountered in a horoscope. The "cookbook" provided by this chapter is written in a special analytical format that helps you to see where the information comes from, to create more detailed delineations by drawing on what you have learned, and to integrate one pair of factors with others in the context of the whole horoscope. The last point is especially important; integrating and synthesizing the delineation of a horoscope is extremely difficult with conventional cookbook texts.

    The chapter consists of ten sections, one for each of the planets. Each section begins with a discussion of a planet, supplementing the material given in Chapter 2; this includes a brief summary of "distinctive features" of the planet.

    Following this is a series of twelve subsections devoted to the given planet in each of the twelve signs. These are developed on the framework provided by the analysis of the sign into its distinctive features. Characteristics of the planet-sign combination are attributed to the influence (or lack of influence) of the planets ruling the sign, exalted there, in detriment or in fall.

    The personal characteristics listed for each planet-sign combination are not particularly original or profound; they are part of astrological common knowledge. What is unusual is the way different facets or "distinctive features" of the sign are attributed to other planets, because this implies that the actual relationship of the given planet to those other planets in the horoscope will have an effect on which characteristics will be manifested and in what ways, and it gives clues how to cultivate desired characteristics and offset undesired ones.

    An example will help make this more clear. In subsection number 25, below, Mercury in Aries, you will read the following line:

Mars rules: Quick-thinking, witty, direct and aggressive speaker.

These traits arise from the indirect influence of Mars on Mercury through its rulership of Aries. The idea is that, while people with Mercury in Aries generally exhibit these traits, the traits may be strengthened or weakened, or even concealed entirely, depending upon the placement of Mars in the horoscope and its relationships with other horoscope factors. Your interactions with such a person, furthermore, would depend partly on which houses of your horoscope Mars and Mercury would fall in if they were in those sign positions for you. Thus, if you were experiencing difficulty with the martial quality of such a person's mentality and communicative style, this section will suggest several avenues to explore for increased understanding and more effective responses.

Each subsection ends with a paragraph outlining briefly the kind of interaction one might have with such a person, and suggesting ways to bring out the best in the relationship. You may use this paragraph to "prime the pump" for your own exploration of the symbolism. Use it to enhance your relationships, to see yourself as others may see you (interpreting your own horoscope) or to interpret horoscopes for other people.

The full text of subsection 25 is as follows:

25. Mercury in Aries (Cardinal, yang Fire sign, red color-symbolism.)

Mars rules:	Quick-thinking, witty, direct and aggressive speaker.
Venus exalted:	Frank, self-assertive, decisive, compelling speaker.
Venus in detriment:	Sarcastic, thoughtless, quarrelsome.
Saturn in fall:	Jittery, poor planner, undisciplined mind.

Observe how this person's aggressive style ensures that her point of view is heard—but don't be persuaded too fast. There is no fine print to watch out for, but her impulses are not the most reliable guide to action. Don't get into a quarrel with her, address yourself to her Venus instead, cultivate her sensitivity and her natural desire to see things completed to help her keep her Mars energy on the constructive side rather than the destructive side. How can your responses help her be more centered (Sun and Saturn) without dulling her wit or dampening her natural spark and verve?

Suppose you are looking at a horoscope with Mercury in Aries. First, review the characteristics of Mercury: androgynous (or is it gynandrous?), Airy, resonating with the color yellow. Review your material on Mercury and on the faculty of conscious attention, both when directed outward through the physical senses (the power of observation), when directed inward through the metaphysical senses (the power of reasoning or intellect), and when directed both ways at once (manipulation of the environment and communication).

Then look at the positions of Mars, the Sun, Venus and Saturn in the horoscope. What signs are they in? What houses do they fall in? What houses would those sign-positions fall in in your horoscope? If you would like to strengthen or weaken the part a given characteristic plays in your relationship, or to turn it from a negative to a positive polarity, meditate on the planet to which the characteristic is attributed; consider its placement in the two horoscopes, its relationships to other planets and whether or not it is connected with houses in which you are currently experiencing stress. Meditate on the planet that is its opposite or complement: a change in your relationship to one will affect your relationship to the other.

Consider how your activities and reactions, especially in those houses in which Aries falls in your horoscope, might enhance or inhibit the four facets or faces of Mercury in Aries which are symbolized by the "distinctive feature" planets (Mars, the Sun, Venus and Saturn). How might your use of your own planetary energies, your own personal powers and faculties, amplify, deflect, cancel out or reverse the polarity of each of the character traits associated with these planets?

Observe how this person's mental and verbal aggressiveness affects you by setting up reactions or sympathetic vibrations in your house through the planetary channels noted above. When you have located a house that is under stress in your relationship, look for possible sources of that stress in your other houses, as in Exercises 22 and 23 of Chapter 1.

To explore your relationship with this person further, meditate on those houses in your horoscope in which Aries falls, and on the influence this person with Mercury in Aries has in those areas of your experience. In which houses does Aries fall in this person's horoscope—that is, out of which areas of his or her life does this influence enter your life? In both horoscopes, consider the influence of any other planets placed in these houses, as modified by the condition of the signs and houses they rule. Place the appropriate meditation cards for the planets in these houses in your meditation space to help you focus your meditation on their relationships and influences.

You may want to use the above paragraphs as a guide for exploring other planet-sign combinations, substituting different planets, signs and characteristics where I have referred to Mercury, Aries, Mars and so forth.

Many books are available that will give you more ideas about each planet-sign combination. Analyze these delineations to distinguish the contribution of the sign's different distinctive features; include the sign's mode, element and gender as well as its ruler, exaltation, detriment and fall. This information should be used merely to get your own ideas flowing as you observe people's behavior in relation to their horoscopes. Some of the information from these books may seem wide of the mark—but, if for example a person with Mercury in Aries is not an aggressive speaker, you can expect to find a reason. Mercury, Mars or the Sun may be in the twelfth house, for instance, or subject to the restraining influence of Saturn. The point is to train yourself to think astrologically, and to develop your powers of discrimination so that you can more easily and intelligently learn from what you read and hear.

Start with your own horoscope. Pretend that you are looking at someone else, and try to understand your impact on others. Then, when you continue with other horoscopes you will be able to see your half of your interactions with them.

Work with the horoscopes of family members first, then with those of your friends and associates. Beyond this, there are several books of horoscopes of people with well-documented biographies, for example *The Circle Book of Charts*, by Steven Erlewine (Circle Books, 1972) and *The American Book of Charts* by Lois M. Rodden (Astro Computing Service, 1980, distributed by Para Research).

Levels of Interpretation

Two people can have the identical astrological factor or pattern in their horoscopes, and yet express it in different ways in their lives and their behavior. The analytical approach outlined above accounts for a lot of this sort of variation, but not all. The manifestation of a given astrological factor depends not only on relationships with other factors in the horoscope, but also on the awareness, sensitivity, intelligence and skill of the person. These matters are largely, but not totally, predictable from the horoscope.

Astrology is not totally deterministic or fatalistic. Even if it were, it would not make the task of interpretation easier to say that the client's "evolvement" can be determined from an interpretation of the chart, if the interpretation itself depends upon how well the person is realizing the potential of the horoscope. In practice, direct observation or other feedback puts the interpretation in context.

There are four stages of manifestation, corresponding to the root meanings of the four alchemical elements, Fire, Water, Air and Earth. Any creative process begins with an intention (Fire) and culminates with the embodiment of that intention (Earth); Water and Air symbolize intermediate stages.

A person's awareness will focus now on one level and now on another, but each person typically *prefers* to operate on primarily one level, and this preferred emphasis characterizes his or her level of consciousness or level of personality-focus.

Avoid the evolutionary fallacy; namely the notion that a person whose primary focus is physical and sensual (Earth element) is in some sense less evolved than a person whose primary focus is on one of the higher levels. There is abundant testimony that a person may incarnate with a sensual orientation to make up for omissions from the experiences of prior incarnations. Surely you have experienced very spacey, supposedly "spiritual" people, who were merely incompetent, and who justified their incompetence by an affected distaste for their physical bodies and material circumstances. A highly-evolved person is competent and integrated no matter what level he or she is focused on, having served an apprenticeship as a bumbling beginner. A being may be quite "evolved" and then choose a level where he or she is less competent (and to all appearances an "unevolved soul") precisely in order to further the evolutionary process.

Here are some of the chief characteristics of the four levels:

Fire	Water	Air	Earth
Archetypal plane	Creative plane	Formative plane	Material plane
Will	Pattern	Process	Emodiment
Intention	Recollection	Thought	Action
Idea	Image	Plan	Execution
Adept	Disciple	Politician	"Common man"
Inspiration	Intuition	Intellection	Reaction
Divine Will	Spiritual Guides	Theories	Fate

Fire: If you encounter someone whose awareness is characteristically at the level of will or intention, you probably will not realize it, unless he or she has gone into business as a guru. Generally, adepts do not advertise themselves as such. Theirs is the gift to will that which is Willed. On this level of the Fire element, will is no longer thought of as a personal attribute, it is recognized as a universal property that flows into the field of personality in the form of intention, and out of it in the form of action. On this level will is no longer seen as something which one seeks to strengthen or to prove by exercising it over others—although other people might very well become subject to will through such a person. On this level, will is the one thing to which one is receptive. (The Tarot Key for receptivity-will is Key 7, The Chariot.)

Water: Various sorts of spiritual disciple or aspirant are more frequently met with. The Water level includes not only those who identify themselves as followers of a teacher or guru, but also others who seek to live in harmony with the unfolding pattern of the universe. On this level, the outward circumstances or frustrations of one's life are clearly recognized (re-cognized, recollected) as manifestations of patterns imprinted in one's personality, just as the image on a movie screen is due to the corresponding image on the film in the projector. People who are characteristically focused on this level recognize the source of their outward experiences as being within themselves. They have learned to look at conflicts or frustrations as teachings telling them where they have missed the mark. They seek to make the outer mind, with its thoughts and emotions, calm and receptive, so that they can clearly recognize the right understanding of things. The integrated pattern of the universe makes itself apparent on this level, so that when questions arise in the mind, they arise only to focus the attention on the answers that will soon follow.

Air: Most of the people you will encounter have their primary focus characteristically on the mental-emotional level, the level of social and political process. They typically are caught up in the images, feelings, imaginings and thoughts of the outer mind. They live a fantasy about the world and about themselves. Depending upon the arrangement and relationships of the most personal planets (the Sun, Moon, Mercury, Venus and Mars, and to some extent Jupiter) in their horoscopes, they will express this fantasy life either intellectually, with theories and verbal constructions, or emotionally, with dreams and feeling-reactions. In either case, rationalization is the name of the game—arguing that things should be other than they are (because, because, because), or explaining how they got that way (because, because, because), blaming, placating, justifying, avoiding and always asking "why" (instead of "how").

Earth: On the outermost or "lowest" level, the level of physical conditions and concrete action, people believe that their lives are determined by what they see, hear, feel, taste and touch with their five outer senses. They do not connect these outer experiences with their inner thoughts, feelings, and dreams—the information apprehended by their inner senses. On this level, people are caught up in a sense of predestination, determinism and fate. As astrological clients, they want their fortune told, and the more mysterious and glamorous the process of telling it, the better. They don't want to hear about raising their level of consciousness, they want to hear about a tall, dark stranger with a mole on his cheek, and they want to know how much money he will bring them. This is the condition of the two people pictured in Tarot Key 15, The Devil. It is identical with Key 7, except for the cosmetics. On the Earth-element level, we see only the cosmetics.

When your awareness moves briefly up to a higher (or more "inner") level, you do not lose touch with the level or levels below once you have gained competence there. On the Airy level of *process* you are better able to manage your concerns on the material level of physical cause-and-effect. On the Watery level of *intuition*, the theorizing, planning and politicking of the mental and social process (Air) level of your life is actually easier for you to manage, because a lot of its apparent complexity is just a byproduct of mental agitation when your mental "muscles" are tense and fatigued and fighting one another. The only exception to this principle is for those who are "ungrounded." Many would-be intellectuals and would-be psychics or spiritual teachers drift with no "traction" in the world because they have not grounded themselves thoroughly in the physical plane (Earth-element level). Many of the seemingly harsh or heavy lessons of Saturn have exactly this function. (Recall that Tarot Key 15, The Devil, corresponds to Capricorn, the sign that Saturn rules.)

The materials in this chapter will be an important resource to you as you continue your astrological studies. The process of connecting words with symbol-patterns is more important than the particular delineations given here. Learn to use this process; it is a bridge between the symbol-language of the right hemisphere of your brain and the word-language of the left hemisphere. Refine and strengthen it. The benefits of open communication between the complementary parts of yourself are immeasurably great.

The Sun ☉

The solar system in its entirety, as Michel Gauquelin has observed, could be regarded as being inside the body of the Sun. Even the incandescent mass that we normally call by that name is so much huger than the planets that all of them could disappear within it with scarcely a trace. The total mass of all the planets and their moons amounts to just over two-tenths of one percent of the Sun's mass.

In Chapter 2 we saw how the planets are just the visible, dense "outcroppings" in physical form of a single unified field, the solar system. We saw how the fields of energy surrounding each planet resonate with local eddies and crosscurrents in the vast energy-field of the Sun. Indeed, we are aware of the presence of the planets only by reflected light from the Sun.

In astrological symbolism, the Sun represents a person's inner identity and deepest sense of purpose in life; the intention, if you will, of the current incarnation. All of the other planets reflect and modulate that basic energy.

The Sun represents wholeness. The Sun sign represents the particular way that wholeness is to be manifested in a given personality, the angle of attack or point of view, so to speak. The house the Sun is in represents the area of life where the person can most effectively work out that inner purpose which is represented by the Sun, the arena within which his or her special zodiacal emphasis will be best complemented and completed by the activities of others so as to manifest the original wholeness of the Sun itself.

If you can help a person to act more in accord with his or her inner convictions and life-purpose, or even to become more aware of them, then other difficulties between you will tend to dissolve of their own accord, as dead leaves fall when their time is done.

If you wish to develop the following materials into meditation exercises, you may want to follow a format like that given at the start of this chapter. Review the material on the Sun and on your inner motivation and life-purpose.

Distinctive features of the Sun: Yang or positive, Fiery, orange or gold color-resonance.

1. The Sun in Aries (Cardinal, yang Fire sign, red color-symbolism.)

Mars rules:	Active, impulsive, forceful, assertive, aggressive.
Sun exalted:	Idealistic, courageous, independent, self-starter.
Venus in detriment:	Selfish, insensitive, may not finish what they start, arrogant.
Saturn in fall:	Undisciplined, uncentered, disruptive, impatient, conflict with authority.

Key Phrase: Inner drive for self-assertion.

It is difficult not to be drawn into raw competition with this person. If you choose to be an adversary, you may win her friendship; if you choose to be a follower, she may not notice you (check Leo and her fifth house). Sharing the initiative is generally out of the question—she will interpret that as competition—but by appealing to her idealism and her mental acuteness, and by staying centered in your own inner purpose (Sun), you may be able to share with her the competition to improve the human condition. Discipline can come as a reminder of what she originally intended to do but did not complete; restraint will not work at all.

2. The Sun in Taurus (Fixed, yin Earth sign, red-orange color-symbolism.)

Venus rules:	Resourceful, productive, loves beautiful things.
Moon exalted:	Conservative, practical, motivated by security.
Pluto and Mars in detriment:	Lethargic, self-indulgent, possessive and defensive due to uncertainty of own power.
Uranus in fall:	Stubborn, narrow-minded, intuition in the form of superstition.

Key Phrase: Inner drive for material stability.

Self-analysis would not occur to this person, and does not come naturally to him, though he would benefit greatly from it because his security needs (Moon) and love of harmony (Venus), both subconscious, are such pervasive and powerful determinants of his behavior. Cooperation to him means being nice and friendly, regardless of whether you are even doing anything together. When he seems unreasonable and stubborn, it is because you don't know his reasons. He probably doesn't either, really.

3. The Sun in Gemini (Mutable, yang Air sign, orange color-symbolism.)

Mercury rules:	Communicative, inquisitive, intellectual, doubting.
Jupiter in detriment:	Restless, dilettante, diffuse, inconsistent.
No exaltation or fall:	Adaptable, versatile, changeable, superficial.

Key Phrase: Inner drive for articulation.

The story is told of the monkey who, seeing the Moon reflected in a pool, jumped in to seize it. Amazed and delighted by the myriad flashes of light from the waves on the surface, and, as they died down, dismayed that the Moon was "disappearing," she soon became the weary addict of her own activity, keeping the pool stirred up. How can you persuade the monkey to let the pool (the mind) become quiet (in meditation) so that she can see a clear reflection far more wonderful than all those transient flashes? Perhaps if you just listen to her chatter, without disturbing your own neighboring pool, she will become curious.

4. The Sun in Cancer (Cardinal, yin Water sign, orange-yellow color-symbolism.)

Moon rules:	Protective, nurturing, emotionally sensitive, moody.
Jupiter exalted:	Resourceful, shrewd, generous-hearted, intuitive.
Saturn in detriment:	Undisciplined, inconstant, overemotional.

Mars in fall: Touchy, retiring, defensive, lack of confidence.

Key Phrase: Inner drive for emotional security.

Somewhere under that defensive shell is the generous ebullience and optimism of Jupiter, so if you play up the Jupiter-Sagittarius element in your relationship things will go much more swimmingly. This person craves the dependency of taking care of someone or being taken care of, if only as an ongoing reassurance that insecurities, real or imagined, are being recognized and taken care of. Perhaps there are other ways you can reassure him, perhaps by explicitly referring to the security needs (Moon) involved in your relationship, if you find these dependencies stifling.

5. The Sun in Leo (Fixed, yang Fire sign, yellow color-symbolism.)

Sun rules: Powerful, dignified, natural leader, loves to be the star.

Neptune exalted: Impressive, charismatic, glamorous, noblesse oblige.

Uranus and Saturn in detriment: Snobbish, inflexible, clashes with authority or with those who challenge his authority.

Mercury in fall: Bombastic, boastful.

Key Phrase: Inner drive for self-exemplification.

What this person admires, or what she feels that significant others admire, she pretends to be, with all her innate dramatic flair, and whatever role she puts herself in, that she becomes. Her faults come from not aiming sufficiently high, from admiring what is not sufficiently admirable, and thus betraying her truly great heart. What is your idea of the noblest in humanity? How can you display your admiration for this high ideal so that this person will raise her sights above mere vanity?

6. The Sun in Virgo (Mutable, yin Earth sign, yellow-green color-symbolism.)

Mercury rules and is exalted: Intellectual, discriminating, critical, efficient, methodical, skeptical.

Jupiter in detriment: Worrisome, insecure, mentally myopic, picky.

Neptune in detriment: Interfering, insensitive to other's boundaries.

Venus in fall: Fussy, unloving, hard to love, insecure about values, hypochondriacal.

Key Phrase: Inner drive for self-perfection through service.

This person goes out of his way to help you, makes it plain that he loves it, makes you dependent on him for his reliable services, encourages you to take him for granted—then complains that no one appreciates what he does for them. Just a word or two of thanks and recognition brings a happy, surprised, almost embarrassed smile, and once again the protest that it's no trouble at all; it fits perfectly into his work schedule; etc. His work is his *raison d'etre*. How can you help him accept friends, fun and a little exploration off the beaten track as part of his job description? Watch out! You may prove to him only that you are one of "them"—one of those sloppy, lazy, undisciplined, irresponsible people who keep making messes of things for him to clean up. Your entree to his good graces may be to share some moralizing about "them."

7. The Sun in Libra (Cardinal, yang Air sign, green color-symbolism.)

Venus rules:	Easy-going, friendly, artistic, sensitive, peace-loving.
Saturn exalted:	Organizing, diplomatic, just, idealistic.
Mars in detriment:	Delicate, lazy, hesitant, indecisive.
Sun in fall:	Unconfident, other-directed, dependent, adaptive.

Key Phrase: Inner drive for equilibrium.

Unless this person is one of those rare martial Librans who relish competition, the greatest difficulty you are likely to have with her will be some form of indecision. In either case, your best appeal is through her good taste. If you can show her that your relationship and your mutual aims are an appropriate arena for adjustment according to her fine aesthetic sense, you both will benefit.

8. The Sun in Scorpio (Fixed, yin Water sign, blue-green color-symbolism.)

Mars rules:	Passionate, with great endurance and stamina.
Pluto rules:	Intense, secretive, sexy, much personal power, catalytic.
Uranus exalted:	Intuitive, subject to abrupt transitions, mysterious.
Venus in detriment:	Selfish, unloving, vindictive, jealous, ruthless.
Moon in fall:	Brooding, obstinate, feelings deeply hidden.

Key Phrase: Inner drive for regeneration.

The great vitality and intensity of this person stems from an inner experience with which he is constantly in dialog. Don't expect to be let in on much of the conversation. Even when he seems most intimately involved with you on a one-to-one basis his attention is really divided, looking simultaneously inward to the idiosyncratic or even eccentric (Uranus) values by which he judges the world and holds his course. Don't try to change his mind—you would have to find out what it was first! If you are prepared to suffer loss of pieces of your egotism under the ruthless judgment (Pluto) of his inner vision (Uranus) you will gain his lasting respect. However, your self-esteem (Venus/Moon) must be strong for you to grow so strenuously!

9. The Sun in Sagittarius (Mutable, yang Fire sign, blue color-symbolism.)

Jupiter rules:	Optimistic, enthusiastic, idealistic, frank, philosophical.
Mercury in detriment:	Neglectful, inconsiderate, exaggerating, unorganized.
No exaltation or fall:	Free-ranging, exploring, extravagant, restless, superficial.

Key Phrase: Inner drive for comprehension.

"Man's reach shall e'er exceed his grasp; else what's a 'meta' for?" This person's enthusiastic quest for *more*—more knowledge, more experience, more freedom to explore—outruns her ability to process completely all that she takes in. Whatever she undertakes, she goes into deeply. She may check out every book the library has on astrology, if that is her current passion, and struggle to read them all, but it is too much for her to inwardly organize and assimilate all that she ingests. Literally, she's forgotten more than you may ever know, but still she retains an astonishing breadth of knowledge and even wisdom, and her good will counts far more than any bibliography. If you can appeal to her to make haste in somewhat less of a rush, without appearing to threaten her precious freedom, you and she will go far. She would benefit enormously from regularly focusing her mind (Mercury) in meditation.

10. The Sun in Capricorn (Cardinal, yin Earth sign, blue-violet color-symbolism.)

Saturn rules:	Practical, calculating, reserved, responsible, serious.
Moon in detriment:	Inhibited, slow, depressive, insensitive to feelings.
Jupiter in fall:	Selfish, worrisome, pessimistic, suspicious.

Key Phrase: Inner drive for self-establishment.

This person knows how to parlay a series of safe risks step by step into a bastion of power. He knows how to take orders when his position calls for it, and he expects as his due that subordinates will obey him without regard for their personal needs or feelings. If his definition of his ambition overlooks his own needs (Moon) and doesn't allow him to grow (Jupiter), he can become mean and stingy, but with success he generally enjoys making generous gestures and lavish charities, if only to vindicate himself and demonstrate that he "has made it." Look to the location of his Moon and Jupiter in your horoscope to find ways to nourish his positive qualities. He needs a broad philosophical foundation to get and enjoy the stability he so deeply craves.

11. The Sun in Aquarius (Fixed, yang Air sign, violet color-symbolism.)

Saturn rules:　　　　Impersonal, idealistic, principled, determined.

Uranus rules:　　　　Independent, unconventional, reforming, idealistic, intuitive.

Mercury exalted:　　　Scientific, intellectual, detached, clear-sighted.

Sun in detriment:　　　Erratic, rebellious, other-directed, cool.

Neptune in fall:　　　　Impersonal, unsympathetic, indulges in being "misunderstood."

Key Phrase: Inner drive for synergy.

Pay particular attention to the location of this person's Saturn and Uranus in your horoscope, and learn the effect of your own behavior on these two sides of her character. For example: how can you evoke the Saturnian self-discipline in your Aquarian friend rather than provoke a fight by imposing your own restraints (Saturn) on her wild-card, off-the-wall but so right-on (Uranian) creativity? If you confess your concern for the direction or viability of a group you both are involved with, she may share some real eye-opening perceptions. Be sure you don't lose track of what it all means in concrete terms to each of the individuals in the group, because she may. When she is functioning as a representative or ombudsman for others she is at her best, but also at her most egotistical. Don't let her get away with saying "we" when she means "I," even when it's for your own good. Humility may be humiliating at first, even to a great humanitarian.

12. The Sun in Pisces (Mutable, yin Water sign, red-violet color-symbolism.)

Jupiter rules:　　　　Gregarious, optimistic, generous, aspiring, kindly.

Neptune rules:　　　　Sympathetic, impressionable, moody, psychic, inspired, sacrificing, compassionate.

Venus exalted:　　　　Devoted, considerate, artistic, creative imagination.

Mercury in detriment and fall:　　Impractical, suggestible, unclear thinker, deceitful.

Key Phrase: Inner drive for absolution.

While the outer, yang Jupiter-ruled phase of this personality may try to adapt to commercial models of success, if he betrays that "still, small voice" in his heart, he suffers for it. When he learns to let the expectations of others flow past him without snagging on his ego anywhere, and when he has forgotten how to worry, then he will be free to live merely, which means purely. He will be free to comply with the world in all its fullness rather than in the narrow caricature most of us take for reality. "Let go and let God" is a Piscean motto. Pay particular attention to the location in your horoscope of his Jupiter and Neptune, and of Neptune's lower octave, the Moon. Encourage him to keep and regularly retreat to a protected sanctuary where he can withdraw and meditate within himself when the world is too much with him.

The Moon ☽

The Moon sign discloses subconscious patterns underlying a person's reactions, emotional responses and habitual behavior. If you can present to people the kind of mental-emotional *context* which harmonizes with their lunar patterns, and thus reassures them, they will flow and mesh with you instead of thwarting you and resisting you unreasonably.

The Moon represents a part of the person that needs to be part of a larger gestalt to be whole; it is not whole in and of itself. If you provide a context that complements the lunar needs of a person, it can be a vehicle for awakening both of you. The differences between you are differences in point of view, not substance.

The only complement to the Moon that will result in wholeness, however, is the part of the person represented by the Sun. If you succeed in complementing a person, it is because you mirror his or her solar qualities. To be whole, people must recognize and accept both the solar and lunar aspects of themselves and bring them together. This is the alchemical wedding that results in a person becoming fully human, a new being.

If you wish to develop the following materials into meditation exercises, follow a format like the example given at the start of this chapter. Review your material on the Moon and on your subliminal patterning.

Distinctive features: Yin or receptive, Watery, blue or silver color-resonance.

13. **The Moon in Aries** (Cardinal, yang, Fire sign, red color-symbolism.)

Mars rules:	Quick reactions, hair-trigger emotions, impulsive, aggressive.
Sun exalted:	Enthusiastic, excitable, self-reliant, courageous.
Venus in detriment:	Intolerant, unloving, makes snap judgments, selfish.
Saturn in fall:	Impatient, unsettled, resents authority, uncentered.

Key Phrase: Need to act.

Perhaps, despite appearances, this person is quite strong and forceful. "Don't just stand there, do something!" If you don't, she will move you unceremoniously out of the way and do it herself. She may be working to center the polarity of Mars and Venus herself, and you can help her by your own responses (Moon/Venus). Aries rules the head, and you may be able to help her develop her role as an intellectual pioneer.

14. The Moon in Taurus (Fixed, yin Earth sign, red-orange color-symbolism.)

Venus rules:	Sympathetic, emotionally warm, upset by disharmony.
Moon exalted:	Supportive, cautious, reserved, strong emotions.
Pluto and Mars in detriment:	Unresponsive, possessive, defensive, slow-reacting.
Uranus in fall:	Stubborn, creature of habit, unoriginal.

Key Phrase: Need for material security.

This person is one of the insurance company's favorite customers. Although he could accomplish much out of his native resourcefulness and plain physical savvy, he generally prefers to lay back and enjoy his comfortable high level of self-esteem, that is, smug self-satisfaction, and indulge in pleasant fantasies of all that he could do (and he could!) if he wanted to badly enough. (He is lazy!) If you want more than a charming companion with whom to waste time pleasantly, look for ways to help this person to be always mindful of what is symbolized by the Sun in his horoscope. Sleep is pleasant but scarcely as rewarding as the infinite varieties of wakefulness.

15. The Moon in Gemini (Mutable, yang Air sign, orange color-symbolism.)

Mercury rules:	Curious, clever, intellectual, verbally adept, eager to communicate.
Jupiter in detriment:	Worrisome, ungenerous, shallow, superficial.
No planet exalted or in fall:	Inconsistent, two-faced, unpredictable, versatile.

Key Phrase: Need to articulate.

This person will sacrifice truth to make her tale better in the telling. Although an abundance of information is important to her, and over an incredibly broad range, her coverage is spotty—what she would call the high spots. She is an anecdotalist rather than a novelist, and philosophy to her is love of sophistry rather than love of wisdom. Look to her Jupiter and Saturn to help her place truth before wit. How can you, in your own behavior, model for her how to look below superficial appearance, and how to laugh at her own embroidering of facts? She is a natural, unconscious mimic, and has a lovely sense of the ridiculous. Use these traits for your mutual growth and enjoyment.

16. The Moon in Cancer (Cardinal, yin Water sign, orange-yellow color-symbolism.)

Moon rules:	Sensitive, domestic, nurturing, emotionally responsive, sentimental.
Jupiter exalted:	Sociable, orthodox, emotionally generous.
Saturn in detriment:	Unstable, over-emotional, easily influenced.
Mars in fall:	Clannish, resentful, selfish, passive, easily threatened.

Key Phrase: Need for emotional security.

A big challenge for this person is learning to distinguish between his own feelings and his emotional responses to the feelings of others. He is very receptive to the emotional environment. His intuitions are very strong and convincing, even when they are quite wide of the mark due to an unreckoned emotional bias. For example, he will take misfortunes as a personal attack. Within his shell is a baby who never left home, and who must be protected. Indeed, individuation from his family of origin is unfinished business he keeps putting at the end of his psychological agenda. He feels that he hasn't the strength (Mars/Saturn). How can you help him realize that he does?

17. The Moon in Leo (Fixed, yang Fire sign, yellow color-symbolism.)

Sun rules:	Cheerful, self-confident, dignified, noble, proud, craves recognition.
Neptune exalted:	Impressive, charismatic, dramatic.
Saturn in detriment:	Ostentatious, bridles at discipline.
Uranus in detriment:	Snobbish, opinionated.
Mercury in fall:	Self-satisfied, uncurious.

Key Phrase: Need for recognition.

Neptune is the higher octave of the Moon and its exaltation in Leo is shown by the glamorous, fantasy-heroic model this person is trying to live up to. Her pride is sensitive because it is so strong, and yet there is always of necessity a disparity between the inner image and the outer accomplishment. She wants whatever will help enact that image on the stage of her life, and she goes after it in a straightforward manner. She needs to prune that self-model to eliminate dead "shoulds" and shape it more after her true inner identity. Look to her Sun and her Mercury in particular to find ways to support her in letting go of aspects of her lunar model that don't fit. Your relationship will be a lot more rewarding as a result.

18. The Moon in Virgo (Mutable, yin Earth sign, yellow-green color-symbolism.)

Mercury rules and is exalted:	Meticulous, critical, quietly intelligent, analyzed feelings, studious.

Jupiter in detriment:	Nervous, timid, reserved, insecure, feels inadequate, worrisome.
Venus in fall:	Fastidious, modest, perfectionist, rationalized tastes.

Key Phrase: Need for perfection.

Lacking confidence in his own tastes and values, this person tries very hard to substitute rational guidelines and intellectual processes. If he could take responsibility for his own likes and dislikes, pure and simple, he might be able to let others do likewise, but because he is not ready, and because perfecting the details of his act is his main preoccupation, he delights in pointing out the loose ends in other people's acts. To him, pointing out flaws is a service, the desire to correct them is taken for granted. He also serves by running the detailwork of someone else's business for them, where the standards are explicit and objective. Look to this person's Venus and Jupiter to find ways to help him expand his rational principles and grow more sensitive to and accepting of his own intuitive sense of appreciation.

19. The Moon in Libra (Cardinal, yang Air sign, green color-symbolism.)

Venus rules:	Compromising, courteous, charming, graceful.
Saturn exalted:	Diplomatic, patient, tolerant of just authority.
Mars in detriment:	Evasive, indirect, unresponsive, slow to react.
Sun in fall:	Fickle, capricious, unenthusiastic, other-directed.

Key Phrase: Need for harmony.

This person needs to be in touch with her Mars energy to have the courage to be true to her self (Sun). When she was a child she was very sensitive to other people's responses to her, and her sympathy and understanding will be true instincts for her to follow all her life, but she must learn to see herself in the center as an administrator of equilibrium (Saturn), rather than throwing herself into one of the pans of the balance as a sacrifice to her gods of harmony. She needs to learn that with her natural refinement, gentility and gentleness she will not offend even when she holds her own. Appeasement will only give her a stomach ache.

20. The Moon in Scorpio (Fixed, yin Water sign, blue-green color-symbolism.)

Mars rules:	Impulsive, passionate, emotionally charged.
Pluto rules:	Reserved, deep, intense, hidden motivations, extremist.
Uranus exalted:	Unpredictable emotional changes and responses, intuitive.
Venus in detriment:	Unsympathetic, jealous, unloving.

Moon in fall:	Moody, possessive, resentful, bottles up feelings.

Key Phrase: Need for personal regeneration.

This person is very powerful and aggressive. His subconscious self-model is especially crucial, because his personal power will bring it into actuality. If like most of us he does not take responsibility for his condition in life, and blames others for his circumstances, then his experience is a continual tape loop of injury and revenge. Distortions of power in his relationship with his mother play a part here. If his self-image includes wisdom and the power to grow, then his power (Pluto) is channeled from vain retribution to inner regeneration, and there is literally no limit to what he can do. Be very sure of your own values (Venus).

21. The Moon in Sagittarius (Mutable, yang Fire sign, blue color-symbolism.)

Jupiter rules:	Sincere, cheerful, optimistic, generous, high ideals.
Mercury in detriment:	Careless, impractical, off-hand manner.
No planet in exaltation or fall:	Eclectic, restless, alert, unsettled.

Key Phrase: Need for freedom.

This person loves to identify herself with grand principles and high ideals. Her aims are high but she may have trouble with the intermediate steps (Mercury) on the way to realizing her good intentions. This may be an evasion of responsibility, and if so alcoholism would be a pitfall to be watched. She is very friendly and outgoing, but she needs to make sure her mind is engaged before putting her mouth in motion. Perhaps you can model for her the trick of paying attention (Mercury) to immediacies. Although the journey may be long, the next step is always just a step away. "Obvious" means literally "on the path" (Latin *ob via*). Demonstrate for her how to honor the obvious.

22. The Moon in Capricorn (Cardinal, yin Earth sign, indigo color-symbolism.)

Saturn rules:	Prudent, cautious, reserved, respectable, disciplined.
Mars exalted:	Ambitious, discontented, hard-working, forceful.
Moon in detriment:	Suspicious, apprehensive, cold, depressive.
Jupiter in fall:	Pessimistic, ungenerous.

Key Phrase: Need for power and success.

This person will not be content until he is in a position of authority. It is hard to say whether that would make him happy—perhaps his Venus would allow it—but he would feel secure. He is a hard person, to whom the competition game is as important as love is to another. His parents are a lasting influence in his life-pattern, for good or ill. He needs to learn to expand beyond the hard shell of his ego. If you undertake to exercise your sensitivity (Moon) and expansiveness (Jupiter) in the hope that he will pick some up by osmosis, be sure to keep all your practicality (Saturn) and shrewdness at hand—if it makes competitive sense he may take you for a sucker. If helping you is a token of his success and authority, he is an excellent ally to have.

23. The Moon in Aquarius (Fixed, yang Air sign, violet color-symbolism.)

Saturn rules:	Detached, dispassionate, courteous.
Uranus rules:	Imaginative, intuitive, unpredictable, erratic.
Mercury exalted:	Intellectual, poetic, imaginative, guided by mental principles.
Sun in detriment:	Other-directed, cool, detached emotions.
Neptune in fall:	Aloof, indifferent, unempathic.

Key Phrase: Need for social synergy.

Social, friendly, if this person is not a social worker professionally, she is one by avocation. She espouses social change and new-age organizations with humanitarian aims. She may come from an unconventional family, and appreciates the unusual or eccentric (Uranus). On the Saturnian side, she may not be very warm and giving in one-to-one encounters and in intimate relationships. Her strong will and lack of empathy (Neptune) manifest as a kind of selfishness which ill suits her Aquarian ideals, and this can make her quite unhappy with herself if she becomes aware of it. The problem is, she tends to "hear what she wants to hear and disregard the rest." Her own Sun sign is the way to open her heart (Sun) as wide as her mind (Mercury/Uranus).

24. The Moon in Pisces (Mutable, yin Water sign, red-violet color-symbolism.)

Jupiter rules:	Kindly, outgoing, gregarious, high ideals, self-indulgent.
Neptune rules:	Receptive, psychic, touchy, moody, withdrawn.
Venus exalted:	Artistic, musical, imaginative, amiable, receptive, lazy.
Mercury in detriment and in fall:	Restless, indecisive, emotions cloud thoughts.

Key Phrase: Need for absolution.

This gentle, sensitive soul incidentally has material and financial needs, but they are of concern only as the necessary context for his inner evolution of a personal understanding of the world and himself in it. He will rationalize either material plenty or poverty rather than behave counter to his inner truth, as he currently grasps it. For this reason it is a mystery to his more obviously goal-oriented associates why someone with his refinement and talent doesn't capitalize on his gifts and *make* something of himself in the world, while inwardly he is trying to see what to make of himself *and* the world.

Mercury ☿

As the seat of personal consciousness, Mercury has a central role in whatever you do. The planet Mercury is never more than one sign (28°) away from the Sun, suggesting that the head may contrast with the heart, but may never challenge (90°) or oppose (180°) your heart's desire utterly.

In yin signs (epitomized by Virgo), Mercury emphasizes analysis: It identifies with the receptive, yin, contemplative aspect of conscious awareness; the yang aspect it wields as the sword of discrimination, picking and choosing among the givens of experience.

In yang signs (epitomized by Aquarius), Mercury emphasizes synthesis: It identifies with the yang, projective, manipulative aspect of conscious awareness, pinpoints the object of its concentration and then wields the chalice of receptivity to capture its essence.

The god Mercury (Hermes) is the initiator; esoterically, Mercury rules Aries, and an initiation is literally a beginning. The true beginning of anything is from its heart or center outward in a widening spiral. A spiral is a harmonious combination of yang, centrifugal forces and yin, centripetal forces—of analysis and synthesis. Mercury must be androgynous to perform its function as mediator between the pairs of opposites and initator of new unities combining those opposites.

Reason postulates a cause for every effect, an agent for every activity. The process of thinking itself generates the image of a thinker, an agent, someone who is "doing" the process. It can be alarming to realize that the agent responsible for thinking is the same agent responsible for ocean waves, light waves and astrological "influences." Yet mental processes are not separate from other phases of the ecology, which are also cybernetic or mental.

Each activity generates its own self-image or ego whose function is to preserve and perpetuate the activity from which it sprang. Subjectively, this is interpreted as a survival instinct, fear of death, resistance to change and all the other manifestations of egotism.

Yet to surrender the diminutive mannikin of the "thinker" as an artifact of thinking, and to identify instead with something much vaster which is the agent not only of thinking but of ocean waves and so forth, is the key to meditation and to enlightenment. This surrender, symbolized in Tarot by the Hanged Man, allows the personality to be moved to the center of its own proper activity, instead of straining off to one side as its own pretended agent.

The sign in which Mercury is placed shows that phase of the universal process with which a person identifies as an observer.

If you wish to develop the following materials into meditation exercises, follow a format like that given at the start of this chapter. Review your material on Mercury and on your conscious mental faculties. No "key phrases" are given; you may want to create some to help crystallize your understanding of Mercury in each of the signs.

Distinctive features of Mercury: Androgynous (or gynandrous), Airy, clear yellow color-resonance.

25. Mercury in Aries (Cardinal, yang Fire sign, red color-symbolism.)

Mars rules:	Quick-thinking, witty, direct and aggressive speaker.
Sun exalted:	Frank, self-assertive, decisive, compelling speaker.
Venus in detriment:	Sarcastic, thoughtless, quarrelsome.
Saturn in fall:	Jittery, poor planner, undisciplined mind.

Observe how this person's aggressive style ensures that her point of view is heard—but don't be persuaded too fast. There is no fine print to watch out for, but her impulses are not the most reliable guide to action. Don't get into a quarrel with her, address yourself to her Venus instead: cultivate her sensitivity and her natural desire to see things completed as a way of keeping her Mars energy on the constructive side rather than the destructive side. How can your responses help her be more centered (Sun and Saturn) without dulling her wit or dampening her natural spark and verve?

26. Mercury in Taurus (Fixed, yin Earth sign, red-orange color-symbolism.)

Venus rules:	Sensible, thorough, considerate, diplomatic, follows through.
Moon exalted:	Realistic, practical, deliberate, slow but retentive.
Pluto and Mars in detriment:	Stodgy, brooding, phlegmatic, mental inertia.
Uranus in fall:	Prejudiced, slow-thinking, methodical, doctrinaire.

Here is a reliable friend, but perhaps a bit of a bore. You can always talk about the prices and values of things, and you will get sound advice but nothing very racy or exciting. Find out what he values most highly (Venus) and what is most important to his sense of security (the Moon); you may be able to get him fired up about something. How can you help him to follow his insights (Uranus) without losing his emotional groundedness (the Moon) and sense of proportion (Venus)?

27. Mercury in Gemini (Mutable, yang Air sign, orange color-symbolism.)

Mercury rules:	Alert, inquisitive, fluent, inventive, logical.

Jupiter in detriment:	Gossipy, nervously excitable, fretful, superficial.
No planet exalted or in fall:	Clever, imitative, versatile, needs focus.

This person can talk circles around you—and herself!—so watch out for verbal tangles and logical knots. Her life may sound like a soap opera, but she probably makes it that way to keep it "interesting." You can be interested in her doings (and they are interesting) without getting your self tangled up to the extent that she does; it is really very similar to the loving, patient relationship you develop with your own mind in meditation (see the Introduction and the Appendix on meditation). Just keep re-focusing on things that matter to you and involve you both. Watch for ways to broaden and deepen the perspective of your relationship (Jupiter).

28. Mercury in Cancer (Cardinal, yin Water sign, yellow-orange color-symbolism.)

Moon rules:	Sympathetic, intuitive, emotionally impressionable, good memory.
Jupiter exalted:	Judicious, imaginative, gushy.
Saturn in detriment:	Capricious, irrational, easily swayed.
Mars in fall:	Narrow-minded, defensive, passive mentality.

This person may pretend to be super-rational, even to the extent of believing he is speaking in a calm, rational tone when he is reacting in a strongly emotional way; or he may be unabashedly sentimental and "subjective" in his thinking and speech. This depends largely on the condition of the Moon and Saturn in his chart. Don't argue with this person, or get swept up into emotional exchanges. Appeal to his sympathies and his desire to be cared for without throwing him off-balance or seeming to attack him, and you may draw him out of his shell and share his perceptions.

29. Mercury in Leo (Fixed, yang Fire sign, yellow color-symbolism.)

Sun rules:	Outspoken, optimistic, creative, mentally ambitious.
Neptune exalted:	Broad-minded, empathic, dramatic.
Saturn in detriment:	Conceited, mentally lazy, resents discipline.
Uranus in detriment:	Prejudiced, dogmatic, rigid thinking.
Mercury in fall:	Rude, thoughtless, not objective.

This person may seem to be uninterested in much beyond herself and her rather fixed opinions, but she does need an audience for her thoughts. If she feels adequately appreciated (that is, if she appreciates herself adequately—look to the relationship of Sun and Saturn) she can be quite appreciative of others, and a pleasant companion. Depending upon the position of Neptune, she may be capable of considerable empathy. How can you resonate (Neptune) with her inner identity (the Sun), the higher Self behind and above her personality, instead of clashing wills with her?

30. Mercury in Virgo (Mutable, yin Earth sign, yellow-green color-symbolism.)

Mercury rules and is exalted:	Shrewd, discerning, analytical, assimilative.
Jupiter in detriment:	Worrisome, poor perspective, negative thinking.
Neptune in detriment:	Unempathic, sarcastic, unimaginative.
Venus in fall:	Hypercritical, relies on method instead of taste.

The esoteric ruler of Virgo has not been discovered; Mercury is serving as the regent or steward. The analytical words and categories of the intellect must serve rather than rule this person's perceptions and actions. Too often people "recognize" things before they properly perceive them as they are. This kind of familiarity *is* contempt, and it breeds boredom and a carping, sullen kind of anger. How can you encourage this person's uncertain, doubtful steps to broaden (Jupiter) his cognitive maps?

31. Mercury in Libra (Cardinal, yang Air sign, green color-symbolism.)

Venus rules:	Balanced, thoughtful, appreciative, peacemaker.
Saturn exalted:	Disciplined, reasoning, intelligent, scholarly, steady nerves, good planner.
Mars in detriment:	Indirect, deliberate, weak-willed, slow to "get the point."
Sun in fall:	Indecisive, evasive, adaptive, shallow, vain.

Generally, this person is thoughtful and mentally disciplined (more or less, depending upon Saturn), and you may be surprised as a consequence when you learn that she is subject to inner vacillation and indecisiveness. If you are impatient with her pace or disappointed with her indecisiveness, what does that tell you about your own personality? She has rather snobbish sensory standards, and is somewhat of a perfectionist, so polish up your own Venus side when you relate to her. Her own sense of values (Venus) may have been adopted from the opinions of others at an early age, so she may need encouragement to connect herself (Sun) more deeply with them.

32. Mercury in Scorpio (Fixed, yin Water sign, blue-green color-symbolism.)

Mars rules:	Aggressive speaker, sensuous, preoccupied with sex.
Pluto rules:	Perceptive, penetrating mind, understands power, secretive.
Uranus exalted:	Subtle, intuitive, insightful, quick mind.
Venus in detriment:	Sarcastic, inconsiderate, critical, sensuous.
Moon in fall:	Suspicious, resentful, preoccupied with financial security.

This person has an almost uncanny ability to see below the surface to the motives underlying what is said and done (Pluto and Uranus). Without more appreciation (Venus) for human shenanigans, however, he may be so cool and detached that his observations may seem almost inhuman. What will give him the reassurance he needs (Moon and Venus) to warm up and steer away from outright cruelty? Don't try to manipulate him—seek truth with him.

33. Mercury in Sagittarius (Mutable, yang Fire sign, blue color-symbolism.)

Jupiter rules:	Frank, foresighted, open-minded, optimistic, sincere.
Mercury in detriment:	Nervous, dishonest, impatient, poor concentration.
No planet in exaltation or in fall:	Versatile, open-minded, unstable.

Where Mercury in Virgo suffers from mental myopia, Mercury in Sagittarius suffers from the opposite, mental hyperopia, a preoccupation with faraway abstractions that interferes with attention in the here-and-now. This person needs to keep mindful of the more obvious steps that intervene between her and her high ideas. How can you help her be mentally still and focused in the practical details of the present long enough for her better judgment (Jupiter) to come through? She makes her promises and sets her goals sincerely enough; look for mutually beneficial ways to respond when she fails to deliver on time. There may be help in the house in which Jupiter is placed.

34. Mercury in Capricorn (Cardinal, yin Earth sign, indigo color-symbolism.)

Saturn rules:	Rational, serious, deliberate, exacting, procrastinating.
Mars exalted:	Practical, hardworking mind, technical, ambitious.
Moon in detriment:	Cautious, inhibited, concerned with material security.
Jupiter in fall:	Narrow-minded, humorless, pessimistic, skeptical.

If you want to get down to brass tacks, this person is already there. He is simply and directly aware of just what *is*, without moral or esthetic judgments intervening. However, his conception of what is and what is not real is very conventional. How does his sobriety and mental discipline affect you? How can you foster his optimism and faith (Jupiter), and help him find security (the Moon) in more than superficial material terms? Look for ways to *share* a good belly-laugh when his narrow seriousness becomes just too preposterous and incongruous.

35. Mercury in Aquarius (Fixed, yang Air sign, violet color-symbolism.)

Saturn rules:	Scientific, rational, exacting, studious, good concentration.
Uranus rules:	Intuitive, original, inventive, brilliant, abrupt.
Mercury exalted:	Inquisitive, abstract thinker, gift for synthesizing.
Sun in detriment:	Eccentric, contrary, impersonal, objective.
Neptune in fall:	Inconsiderate, detached, insensitive to feelings.

There are two phases to this person's mentality, the electrifying Uranus phase and the super-reasonable Saturnian phase. Which phase predominates, and when, depends upon the condition of those two planets in her horoscope. You may have a tendency to evoke one or the other due to the position of these planets in your own horoscope. Watch carefully to see which of your own powers and faculties respond to her company, and look for ways to draw out her humane warmth (Sun) and empathy (Neptune).

36. Mercury in Pisces (Mutable, yin Water sign, red-violet color-symbolism.)

Jupiter rules:	Open-minded, inspirational, good sense of humor.
Neptune rules:	Impressionable, intuitive, not objective, psychic, poetic.
Venus exalted:	Creative imagination, artistic, musical, poetic.
Mercury in detriment and in fall:	Irrational, gullible, absent-minded, indecisive, illogical, not ruled by intellect.

This person's attention (Mercury) is mostly turned inward, to his own emotions and psychic responses. If through meditation or therapy he can clarify these, so that they give him truer "readings" of what is happening in his outer world, he will be much better able to cope. The initiative has to come from his conscious attention (Mercury), to educate his subtle, refined, but naive inner responses (Venus, Neptune). A good grounding in applied metaphysics (Jupiter) or practical occultism would help. How can you encourage more objectivity in his communication and other mental processes, without thwarting his creativity and receptivity?

Venus ♀

Of the inner two planets, Venus is the closest to the Earth. The only astrological body that is physically closer is the Moon. It is symbolically appropriate that Venus, representing the active, creative phase of subconsciousness that works out the more inward, passive processes of the Moon in creative imagination, should be one step closer to the Sun. It is as though to reassure us, to paraphrase Blake, that imagination is the gateway to truth.

Venus can never be more than about 48° from the Sun, or about one-and-a-half signs. This suggests a symbolic meaning that your personal values can never deviate far from your heart's desire. On the other hand, the further Venus or Mercury is from the Sun, the greater the independence and clarity of function of the corresponding faculty in your personality. If any planet is too close to the Sun, the corresponding faculty may become enmeshed so closely with your identity that you have difficulty distinguishing it as a separate resource within you to which you may turn at need, and it may function through you more or less unconsciously or automatically.

Venus is associated with love and desire, not because these are central to its symbolism, but because the imagination is the agency for developing seed images of desire into full-blown fantasies and the fulfillment of these fantasies in physical terms. You know from your work with your wants and desires in connection with the Sun in Chapter 2 how remote from your innermost purpose some of your desires can seem—yet, if you truly desire something, it has some bearing on your heart's desire, your deepest purpose in life. Venus is like that. A lingering look at something or someone with a tinge of nostalgia or longing is sufficient to implant an image in your lunar subconsciousness. From there, the active Venus part of your subconscious mind develops the image in a variety of ways and presents you with its imagery in your dreams and fantasies and, yes, in your perceptions of other people and things.

Imagination can lead you where you want to go, if you learn how to read it right. Get acquainted with Venus. Tell her what you want and she will show you how to get it.

If you wish to develop the following materials into meditation exercises, follow the example given at the start of this chapter. Review your material on Venus and your creative imagination. To focus your understanding of each of the sign positions of Venus, you may want to create "key phrases" like those given for the Sun and Moon.

Distinctive features of Venus: Yin or receptive, Watery (with some Air characteristics), green color-resonance.

37. Venus in Aries (Cardinal, yang Fire sign, red color-symbolism.)

Mars rules:	Ardent, demonstrative, erotic, unsentimental, sure of values.
Sun exalted:	Popular, outgoing, persuasive, self-assured.
Venus in detriment:	Selfish, self-seeking, hard to love, ungentle.
Saturn in fall:	Inconsistent, fickle, impatient in love.

If this person likes or dislikes you, you will know it right away. Values are not really a matter of judgment for her, if judgment implies time and care spent weighing alternatives. They are "obvious." If compelled to stop and think about her values and desires, she probably would not be so sure—but challenge her at your own risk! How can you help her put these matters in perspective, with the lessons of context and consequences that Saturn teaches?

38. Venus in Taurus (Fixed, yin Earth sign, red-orange color-symbolism.)

Venus rules:	Affectionate, artistic, attractive, sensual.
Moon exalted:	Sociable, domestic, strong emotions, indulgent.
Pluto and Mars in detriment:	Indolent, possessive, grasping, jealous.
Uranus in fall:	Stubborn, lacking insight, facile, conventional.

The gift of some lovely object will go far toward cementing good relations with this person—but do you want to be cemented? He is too uncertain of his own power to relax into the ebb and flow of human relationships that are now closer, now more distant, depending on mood and transient needs. If he is insecure enough (Moon), he may regard his friends and lovers as possessions, rather like furniture. How can you help him appreciate beauty and harmony on the intangible level of human relationships, as well as in physical objects?

39. Venus in Gemini (Mutable, yang Air sign, orange color-symbolism.)

Mercury rules:	Witty, lighthearted, charming, good-humored, verbalized love.
Jupiter in detriment:	Inconstant, superficial, shallow values and relationships.
No planet in exaltation or fall:	Playful, flirtatious, fickle, complex affairs.

Enjoy, enjoy, by all means enjoy this person's lively company. But don't get so caught up that you betray your own values, or so confused that you lose touch with your own desires. By staying centered, you may help this person get in touch with deeper issues that really are important to her—all in fun of course. Connect with Jupiter in her horoscope to help her educate her Venusian values.

40. Venus in Cancer (Cardinal, yin Water sign, orange-yellow color-symbolism.)

Moon rules:	Loyal, tender, sympathetic, sentimental, loves home.
Jupiter exalted:	Romantic, generous, sentimental.
Saturn in detriment:	Gullible, easily flattered, inconstant.
Mars in fall:	Shy, timid, possessive, gentle.

This person's affections and sense of values are guided by considerations of emotional security. His real likes and dislikes are easily swayed by emotional sympathy or antipathy. He probably knows that his tastes incline to the sentimental; if his Sun is in Cancer too, he may be a bit touchy and defensive about it. Reassurance plays an important role in his relationships. How can you help him feel centered (Saturn) and secure (Moon) in his strength (Mars)?

41. Venus in Leo (Fixed, yang Fire sign, yellow color-symbolism.)

Sun rules:	Warm-hearted, creative, sincere, loyal.
Neptune exalted:	Artistic, empathic, compassionate, romantic, dramatizes feelings.
Saturn in detriment:	Conceit, lack of detachment, ostentation.
Uranus in detriment:	Conventional, patronizing, guided by other's recognition rather than intuition.
Mercury in fall:	Lacks objectivity, feelings out of touch with reason, jealous.

This person has a way of announcing her value-judgments that seems the very soul of self-assurance. She feels she must display her likes and dislikes to best advantage to get a good audience response. A poor reception won't make her change her feelings, however—Leo is a fixed sign. She will seek a better audience, or if her self-esteem is very low, will hide her likes and dislikes and feel "wrong" or "bad" for having them. Remember what it feels like to be "on-stage"? Does it do any harm to give this person the response she desires? How can you help her be more centered (Saturn), spontaneous (Uranus) and objective (Mercury) and less concerned with how she is being received?

42. Venus in Virgo (Mutable, yin Earth sign, yellow-green color-symbolism.)

Mercury rules and is exalted:	Cool, refined, modest, neat, analyzes love, feelings and values.
Neptune in detriment:	Shy, socially awkward, lacks empathy.
Venus in fall:	Fussy, perfectionist, hobbles imagination.

From demonstrations of affection to aesthetic tastes, this person prefers to go by the book with all of the affective functions of Venus. Propriety is the watchword. When genuine, spontaneous evaluations come to his consciousness, he subjects them to critical review and editing before letting them out. How can you look for the real Venusian feeling-responses behind the carefully revised Mercury edition? How can you help him to connect his "rule book" of propriety with his Jovial sense of humor and sense of *possibility* (Jupiter)? To allow his feelings to guess answers that are not in the book?

43. Venus in Libra (Cardinal, yang Air sign, green color-symbolism.)

Venus rules:	Gentle, lovable, unselfish, charming, companionable.
Saturn in exaltation:	Clear, consistent values, makes commitments.
Mars in detriment:	Untidy, sentimental, undemonstrative.
Sun in fall:	Frivolous, discontented, retiring, unimposing, detached.

If everyone had Venus in Libra, relationships would be all clear and pure like the music of Mozart, combining sincerity and impartiality. Passion, assertiveness and anger (Mars) or commitment and real heart-to-heart intimacy (Sun) may be a bit much for her, however. How can you connect with both yang and yin sides of her, both the Fiery Sun and Mars and the Watery Venus and Moon sides of her nature? The full strength of Venus, as ruler of Libra, can be sapped like a flowering tree in a desert of impartiality unless it is integrated with the rest of her chart. The bridge to that integration may be by means of her relationships.

44.   Venus in Scorpio (Fixed, yin Water sign, blue-green color-symbolism.)

Mars rules:	Magnetic charm, aggressive, selfish, passionate, dominating.
Pluto rules:	Deep feelings, powerful sex drive, passionate, subversive, secret love affairs, uses sex for emotional regeneration.
Uranus exalted:	Sudden relationships, abrupt changes in values and affections.
Venus in detriment:	Jealous, hurtful, hateful, sado-masochism.
Moon in fall:	Amoral or immoral, sullen, feelings hidden.

Are you ready for such intensity? When this person is moved to like or dislike, all the power of Mars and Pluto stand behind the feelings he experiences. And with Uranus involved, the turn-on (or turn-off) can be so swift and complete as to leave you in a state of shock. Nonetheless, if you can connect with the yin side of his nature, through his Moon primarily, he may soften up a bit. What would help him feel loved and appreciated? What would help him feel more secure? Watch out for kinks in his Moon patterning.

45.   Venus in Sagittarius: (Mutable, yang Fire sign, blue color-symbolism.)

Jupiter rules:	Ardent, idealistic, demonstrative, intuitive.
Mercury in detriment:	Inconsiderate, licentious, breezy.
No planet in exaltation or fall:	Flirtatious, fickle, freewheeling.

Easy come, easy go, or so it seems. This person does not care to be tied down, even with someone or something she likes. How can you improve the cooperation of Venus and Jupiter in your own horoscope? Some of it might rub off. Conversely, do you find yourself losing touch with your own sense of priorities (as you perceive them through your Mercury intellect and Jupiter judgment) when you are in this person's company? She will object to limitation or unfair treatment of others, particularly children and animals. If her breezy style seems unfair to you, let her know it, without demanding that she pin herself down. She might see it differently in that light.

46. Venus in Capricorn (Cardinal, yin Earth sign, blue-violet color-symbolism.)
    Saturn rules: Deliberate in affections, faithful, stern, modest.
    Mars exalted: Self-seeking, hard to love, ungraceful, spiteful.
    Moon in detriment: Unfeeling, indifferent, reserved, timid, fearful.
    Jupiter in fall: Conservative tastes, cautious in affections.

    This person's likes and dislikes are quite stable, but he does not express them or act on them lightly. If someone else's feelings are expressed first, he will communicate his own more easily, and may be quite surprised to find out what a lot he has to say about his affections, dislikes and values. For him, declaring a liking for something or someone is tantamount to making a commitment for life, and he does not invest himself without careful consideration. Look in your own horoscope for the places where Venus is at home (Taurus, Libra and Pisces) to find ways to lighten and brighten your relationship with this person.

47. Venus in Aquarius (Fixed, yang Air sign, violet color-symbolism.)
    Saturn rules: Coolly affectionate, quiet, uncompromising,
                             idealistic.
    Uranus rules: Unconventional desires, sudden affections,
                             intuitive.
    Mercury exalted: Friendly, platonic love, intellectualizing.
    Sun in detriment: Cool, opportunistic, detached, indifferent.
    Neptune in fall: Lacks empathy, touchy, indifferent, needs to
                             respect partner.

    To cultivate this person's friendship you have to draw on Mercury in your own horoscope to engage her verbally and mentally in interesting ways. If you want a deeper friendship, address her through the house in which Uranus falls. She may have experienced disappointment at the hands of friends in the past, but she herself is quite faithful and reliable, despite her sometimes avante-garde views. For a real heart-to-heart connection you have to be centered enough in your inner identity (Sun) so that you can both open yourselves to Neptunian vulnerability.

48. Venus in Pisces (Mutable, yin Water sign, red-violet color-symbolism.)
    Jupiter rules: Easy-going, generous, sociable.
    Neptune rules: Sensitive, compassionate, artistic, musical,
                             devotional.
    Venus exalted: Artistic, loving, submissive, too soft,
                             unselfish love.
    Mercury in detriment
    and in fall: Confused values, sentimental, not alert, lacks
                             discrimination in love.

    Foresight in relationships and in choice of emotional environments is needed to help this person stay on an even emotional keel. He very easily takes on the value-systems of those around him, and needs to give some attention

(Mercury) to exactly what his own likes and dislikes are. He is capable of subordinating his own tastes to those of his partner, at worst out of weakness or uncertainty, at best as a way of deepening the level of affection between them. How do you respond to his capacity for compassion and selfless love (Neptune), and his willingness to grow by means of the suffering (literally "allowing," the letting-go of ego) such love entails? How can you help him integrate Mercury with Jupiter and Venus to cultivate some much-needed detachment and clarity in his values and affections?

Mars ♂

Mars is the first planet outside the orbit of the Earth. This suits its symbolism of an energy that projects outward beyond the personal realm into the social realm represented by Jupiter and Saturn. It is the first planet that can be on the opposite side of the Earth from the Sun (other than the Moon, of course). Mars energy can really get you "beside yourself" with anger, and it can force your definition of yourself to break open and grow, like a hatching bird cracking open its eggshell. At such times, the impulses associated with Mars can seem diametrically opposed to one's inner purpose in life.

In mythology, Mars was not only the god of war but the protector of fields. The month of March was named for him, the month that "comes in like a lion and goes out like a lamb" with the change from winter to spring.

Mars and Venus have a special relationship in mythology. They were said to be involved in a torrid love affair, somewhat like Lancelot and Guinevere in the Arthurian legend. In astrology, the projective, aggressive energy of Mars and the receptive, attractive energy of Venus are complementary. Their symbols are associated with sexuality, and in sexual expression both partners need to engage both the assertiveness of Mars and the magnetism of Venus to experience fulfillment. The same is true of any creative act. One must not only sense what one desires, or imagine how one would like things to be (Venus), but one must also act on that desire and take steps to make it happen.

If you wish to develop the following materials into meditation exercises, follow a format like that given at the start of this chapter. No "key phrases" are given; you may want to create some to help crystallize your understanding of Mars in each of the signs. Review your material on Mars and on your aggressive energy.

Distinctive features of Mars: Yang or projective, Fiery, red color-resonance.

49.   Mars in Aries (Cardinal, yang Fire sign, red color-symbolism.)
       Mars rules: Energetic, aggressive, decisive, initiative.
       Sun exalted: Self-willed, passionate, noble, independent,
                              courageous.

Venus in detriment: Quick-tempered, violent, not affectionate, lacks sympathy, takes offense.

Saturn in fall: Impulsive, reckless, abrupt, impatient.

How can you stay centered (Saturn) around such aggressive (Mars) energy? Can you escalate your own Mars energies in a companionable rather than competitive way? What resources of fortitude can you draw from the houses in your horoscope influenced by Saturn, without setting yourself up as an obstacle for this person to fight against?

50. Mars in Taurus (Fixed, yin Earth sign, red-orange color-symbolism.)

Venus rules: Industrious, tenacious, persevering.

Moon exalted: Practical, purposeful, conservative actions.

Mars and Pluto in detriment: Sensuous, bad tempered, violent.

Uranus in fall: Extremely obstinate, overmaterialistic, unadaptable.

How can your comportment help calm his security needs (Moon) so that subconscious static ceases to block intuition (Uranus)? Calling on Venus in your own horoscope, what can you genuinely appreciate in this person? What can you attribute to his environment that he will appreciate (Venus), and how does enhancement of harmony in his life affect his management of his Mars energy?

51. Mars in Gemini (Mutable, yang Air sign, orange color-symbolism.)

Mercury rules: Lively, mechanically-minded, alert, witty, sarcastic.

Jupiter in detriment: Diffuse interests, indiscreet, crafty, overexcited.

No exaltation or fall: Varied talents, scattered interests, indecisive, lacking in concentration.

Do you find yourself drawn into this person's exuberant, energy-squandering ways? How can you cultivate a good relationship of Saturn to either Mercury or Jupiter in your own horoscope to model for this person the kind of focus she lacks? Does this help her learn to follow through on some of the things she starts?

52. Mars in Cancer (Cardinal, yin Water sign, orange-yellow color-symbolism.)

Moon rules: Sensuous, tenacious, defensive, highly emotional.

Jupiter exalted: Ambitious, overreactive, defensive of convictions.

Saturn in detriment: Undisciplined, loses perspective, selfish.

Mars in fall: Irritable, indirect in actions, overpossessive.

How good are you at bringing your own subconscious programming

(Moon) to consciousness for revision? Can you model this growth process for a person with Mars in Cancer? How can you help him do likewise while neither attacking his defenses nor merely commiserating with his exaggerated personal troubles and insecurities? Where is Jupiter in this relationship?

53. Mars in Leo (Fixed, yang Fire sign, yellow color-symbolism.)

Sun rules:	Enthusiastic, ambitious, passionate, egocentric.
Neptune exalted:	Dramatic, animal magnetism.
Saturn in detriment:	Arrogant, inflexible.
Mercury in fall:	Melodramatic, uncritical, impulsive.

Much depends upon the condition of the Sun and Saturn in this horoscope: the inner and outer aspects of the ego. Remember that egotism is only the defensiveness of an imaginary creature (the ego) against imaginary threats. If you stay centered and communicate heart-to-heart, the obstacles of egotism will melt away in the sunshine.

54. Mars in Virgo (Mutable, yin Earth sign, yellow-green color-symbolism.)

Mercury rules and is exalted:	Practical, industrious, ingenious.
Jupiter in detriment:	Narrow effort, can't see the forest for the trees, surreptitious.
Neptune in detriment:	Interfering, offensive, doesn't know how to surrender in sexual expression.
Venus in fall:	Emotionally frustrated, feels sexually inadequate, modest.

This person is obsessed with the details of his life. He needs help from Jupiter and Venus to put his house in order, and then to recognize when he has done so, so that he can move on to more rewarding applications of his cleverness. He is a fantastic worker, he needs to learn to be a better manager. How can you demonstrate this in your own conduct?

55. Mars in Libra (Cardinal, yang Air sign, green color-symbolism.)

Venus rules:	Ardent affections, gentle passion, desire for harmony.
Saturn exalted:	Persuasive, persistent, balanced action.
Mars in detriment:	Disputatious, coercive, aggression out of balance.
Sun in fall:	Vulgar, opportunistic, approval-seeking.

This person may be the author of double messages as she swings wildly from surrender to assertiveness, from aggression to acquiescence. She is particularly vulnerable to being psychically "swallowed up" by others, and instinctively strikes out to protect this vulnerability. Where are the Sun and Saturn in her horoscope? What can you do to foster her awareness of her real inner strengths, and that part of her being that can never be engulfed by another?

56. Mars in Scorpio (Fixed, yin Water sign, blue-green color-symbolism.)

Mars rules:	Passionate, courageous, magnetic, determined, willfull.
Pluto rules:	Strongly sexed, strong power drive, catalytic actions, resourceful, probing, relentless.
Uranus exalted:	Volatile energies, quick to anger, perceptive, shrewd.
Venus in detriment:	Aggressive, brutal, ruthless, vengeful, sensuous.
Moon in fall:	Sensuous, secretive, strong resentments, unsociable.

A hidden dynamo generates an incredibly strong field about this person giving him the unconscious, instinctive power to do almost anything except be at ease. He has tremendous influence on others. If he attributes more power to others, and has a low valuation of himself, he may appear weak and vacillating, quarrelsome and escapist, and those around him will become unconscious accomplices in confirming his self-image. Naturally, he may have the same unconscious allies affirming a more positive image of himself. His vocation is reform, in this peculiar sense. It begins at home. How can you help him foster his Venusian sense of his own values and resources? Where is his Moon?

57. Mars in Sagittarius (Mutable, yang Fire sign, blue color-symbolism.)

Jupiter rules:	Sportive, spirited, independent, high aspirations.
Mercury in detriment:	Boisterous, rude, sarcastic, impatient with detail.
No planet in exaltation or in fall:	Explorative, uncontrolled, needs direction.

If there is an occasion for adventure or sport, this person will rise to it—but what commitments or responsibilities is she dropping when she does so? Where is Saturn in her horoscope? How can you help her see what she has to do as an adventure, not as a prison; as a laboratory, not a purgatory, so that her renewed enthusiasm takes the place of the stability, endurance and staying power she lacks? Look to the house in which Jupiter is placed for ideas that will appeal to her.

58. Mars in Capricorn (Cardinal, yin Earth sign, indigo color-symbolism.)

Saturn rules:	Ambitious, authoritative, controlled, practical.
Mars exalted:	Industrious, self-reliant, restless, ambitious.
Moon in detriment:	Irritable, disagreeable, unfeeling.
Jupiter in fall:	Calculating, malicious, stingy, narrow focus.

This person has tremendous control of his energies. Spontaneity and fun are harder for him to master, partly because he takes what he does so seriously.

Where is Jupiter in his horoscope? How can you help him to enjoy the joyful, Jovial, expansive and receptive side of his nature, even if it is a little "wasteful" of energy? Perhaps if he sees you practice humility without being humiliated he can learn to relax the vigilance of his pride. Perhaps for starters he will have to set aside a portion of his energy "budget" for a "rainy day," so that when he experiences unexpected setbacks he can "afford" to relax and dance with the changes in a spirit of fun.

59. Mars in Aquarius (Fixed, yang Air sign, violet color-symbolism.)

Saturn rules:	Resolute, disciplined, principled, group leader.
Uranus rules:	Independent, progressive, idealistic, free spirit.
Mercury exalted:	Enterprising, contentious, high-strung.
Sun in detriment:	Perverse, rebellious, other-directed, erratic.
Neptune in fall:	Impatient, easily influenced, unempathic.

This person's vitality operates in the social realm. Her weakness arises when she is too self-centered. Any setback turns her back to introspective brooding, which reduces her vitality, resulting in further setbacks. To help her avoid this negative tailspin, how can you remind her of those progressive, humanitarian aspirations which inspire her? Where is her Sun? How may the symbolism of its sign and house be expressed in social, humanitarian terms? How can you exemplify for her a connection between feeling and doing, between personal empathy (Neptune) and idealistic humanitarianism (Uranus)?

60. Mars in Pisces (Mutable, yin Water sign, red-violet color-symbolism.)

Jupiter rules:	Generous, over-gushing, expansive actions.
Neptune rules:	Temperamental, indirect or sacrificial actions, addictive personality.
Venus exalted:	Intensely emotional, sensuous, affectionate, warm, strong imagination.
Mercury in detriment and in fall:	Unstable, restless, unfocused, indecisive.

This person is like a small sailboat in a world of speedboats and power yachts. He depends more than most on the ebb and flow of his energies. He must learn to move when current and wind are right, and then be content to rest and inwardly shape his course on unconscious levels, below decks as it were, when his vitality is low. Where is his Mercury? It does not engage well with his Mars on the content level, where his energies are applied to things and events. He must learn to focus his attention on the next higher level, the process level, where the decision whether to work or to rest is made. There he can keep his long-term aims in view while he waits through the changing of the tide, and not get sucked into brooding and depression.

Jupiter ♃

Jupiter is the largest of the planets, over three hundred times as massive as the Earth. Its cycle through the zodiac takes about twelve years, spending about a year in each sign. Despite its huge size, it is composed almost entirely of gasses and liquids.

The huge, diffuse nature of the physical planet suits its expansive, breezy astrological symbolism. Jupiter represents the principle of expansion and growth, and all those genial, ebullient characteristics that we call "jovial," after the Roman god who was called "Jove" as well as "Jupiter." An expansive, generous, jovial person will have a strong influence of Jupiter in his or her horoscope.

It requires good judgment to choose those things that foster growth and well-being. And to judge well, one must have "the long view," the kind of perspective that reaches to distant horizons and puts immediate events into a larger context. Jupiter is associated with issues of good (or bad) judgment, and with education, travel and other experiences that take one out of the daily round and expand one's horizons. It is such experiences, needless to say, that most improve one's judgment.

Jupiter does not represent a faculty of judgment—that is a Mercury function—but rather a capacity to grow in ways that elevate Mercury's functioning from discrimination to real judgment. Jupiter has rather more affinity to the Moon and Venus than it does to Mercury.

Whereas the Moon has to do with the incorporation of information and influence within the person, Jupiter has to do with the integration of the individual person into the world, particularly the social world. As such, it has much to do with philosophy, religion and law, as well as education and travel. Like the Moon, Jupiter is not in itself innovative; it operates within the received values and concepts of society.

If you wish to develop any of the following paragraphs into meditation exercises, follow the example given at the start of this chapter. Try also developing suggestions for interacting with people you know, based upon the placement of Jupiter in their horoscopes, in addition to the observations provided here. What sorts of opportunity does each person recognize? In what ways are they apt to overindulge or overexpand? Are they in touch with the generosity of the universe? Do you need help in that area? Use the rulership, exaltation, detriment and fall to guide your thoughts. Review your material on Jupiter and on your Jovial expansiveness, generosity, optimism and philosophy of life.

Distinctive features: Yin or receptive/expansive, Airy with some Water characteristics, violet color-resonance.

61. Jupiter in Aries (Cardinal, yang Fire sign, red color-symbolism.)
    Mars rules: High-spirited, freedom-loving, energetic.
    Sun exalted: Generous, self-sufficient, open-hearted, hearty.
    Venus in detriment: Bullying, boastful, inconsiderate, egotistic.
    Saturn in fall: Extravagant, overoptimistic, poor judgment.

Self-image is crucial to anyone's success, but especially for this person, whose judgment and perception of opportunity depend heavily upon his ego strength and self-assurance. Consider the location and relationships of his Sun and Mars, as well as the house position of Jupiter, to see what is recognizable to this person as an opportunity. Remember that he is not particularly sensitive to context. Look to his Venus for ways to enhance (or make up for) his awareness of the social and esthetic contexts of his choices, and to Saturn for the political and functional contexts. How can you help him connect these contexts with his self image?

62. Jupiter in Taurus (Fixed, yin Earth sign, red-orange color-symbolism.)

Venus rules:	Sound judgment, good hearted, integration of spiritual and material realms.
Moon exalted:	Reliable, conservative, security-oriented, sympathetic.
Pluto and Mars in detriment:	Self-indulgent, exploitative, fails to follow through.
Uranus in fall:	Opinionated, dislikes surprises, materialistic.

This person recognizes opportunities in events which bear on her security and emotional well-being. All her life, automatically through the unconscious operations of Venus and the Moon, she has been building herself a shock-proof niche in life. She may have inherited one. Consciously, opportunities are ways to elaborate and enhance what she has, rather than openings into new territory. Daring and adventure may have their place in her life (depending upon where Mars and Uranus are placed), but they are seen as risks, not as opportunities for growth and life-enrichment. How does this person relate to power (Pluto)? What would arouse a really passionate response in her? Might she want something she does not already know about?

63. Jupiter in Gemini (Mutable, yang Air sign, orange color-symbolism.)

Mercury rules:	Highly intelligent, broad-minded, charming.
Jupiter in detriment:	Diffuse interests, indiscreet, crafty, impractical.
No planet exalted or in fall:	Varied talents, scattered interests.

The gain or loss of money or property is incidental to this person. To him, opportunities are those experiences that offer novelty, change, adventure or just news. His judgment is not founded on any profound values or ideals, his explorations are not motivated by a desire for growth or wisdom, rather, they reflect an insatiable thirst for experience. What *kind* of experience may be suggested by the position and relationships of his Mercury. What is going on in Sagittarius, and in his ninth house?

64. Jupiter in Cancer (Cardinal, yin Water sign, orange-yellow color-symbolism.)

Moon rules:	Kindly, protective, security-oriented, expansive emotions.
Jupiter exalted:	Charitable, generous, open-handed, Jovial, family.
Saturn in detriment:	Too conscientious, overcautious, overemotional.
Mars in fall:	Extremely touchy, defensive, overprotective, vulnerable.

This person has large wants. Security, luxury and personal enhancement are her criteria for judging what is an opportunity. Depending upon where Saturn is, she probably lacks that sense of "not enough to go around" that might stint her generosity. On the contrary, she assumes others have the same needs for a soft-feathered nest, and as often as not she is right. Opportunities for aggressive advancement of her ambition pass her by unnoticed, unless that ambition centers on a well-appointed home. The polarity of the fourth and tenth houses is particularly important for this person.

65. Jupiter in Leo (Fixed, yang Fire sign, yellow color-symbolism.)

Sun rules:	Big-hearted, dignified, big ego, desire to impress.
Neptune exalted:	Compassionate, generous, charismatic.
Saturn in detriment:	Extravagant, overbearing, unrestrained.
Uranus in detriment:	Intolerant, rigid, steady, conventional.
Mercury in fall:	Self-appraising, self-justifying, imprecise.

For this person, opportunity is an occasion for others to glamorize him. Appreciation, approval and publicity are his ways of growth and expansion, with self-justification hidden not far below the surface. He could do with a stronger sense of practical goals and constraints. Where is Saturn in his horoscope? How can you help him connect his perception of opportunities with the mental detachment of Mercury, and with the impersonal experience of truth or revelation through its higher octave, Uranus? Where are these planets in his horoscope and in yours?

66. Jupiter in Virgo (Mutable, yin Earth sign, yellow-green color-symbolism.)

Mercury rules and is exalted:	Intellectual, practical, scientific, investigative, discriminating, conscientious.
Jupiter in detriment:	Haughty, cautious, insecure, petty, narrow.
Neptune in detriment:	Judgmental, petty, materialistic.
Venus in fall:	Cynical, critical, irritable, fault-finding, hypochondriac.

For this person, opportunity is a chance to remove some imperfection that has come under her diligent scrutiny, and a vehicle for communicating her standards and judgments to others. She goes by the best rule book she can find, because she doesn't like to have her standards challenged. She confuses idealism with perfectionism. If she can find ways to connect her standards with her inner wellsprings of imagination (Venus) and inspiration (Neptune), she will know the difference. Does she know what she wants, or only what she does not want? How can you help her shift her gardening efforts from weeds to crops?

67. Jupiter in Libra (Cardinal yang Air sign, green color-symbolism.)

Venus rules:	Sympathetic, hospitable, good listener, cooperative.
Saturn exalted:	Just, charitable, good perspective, diplomatic.
Mars in detriment:	Lazy, lacking initiative, stuck in a rut.
Sun in fall:	Conceited, other-directed, dependent.

This person is over-responsive to environment and context. Look to his Venus for indications of how he responds to his social and esthetic environment, and look to his Saturn regarding his estimation of his political and functional contexts. He sees opportunity from any point of view, it seems, but his own. He would do well to be more in touch with his own motivations, his own personal desires, and the aims of his own ego. Exercises 1 and 5 in Chapter 3 would be especially helpful for this person, except he is probably too lazy to follow through on them. Where are his Sun and Mars? How can you help him connect them to his perception of opportunity and his capacity for growth?

68. Jupiter in Scorpio (Fixed, yin Water sign, blue-green color-symbolism.)

Mars rules:	Ambitious, aggressive, welcomes challenges.
Pluto rules:	Shrewd, proud, secretive, wants power, a healer.
Uranus exalted:	Keen judgment, subtle, interested in the occult.
Venus in detriment:	Self-indulgent, conceited, self-centered.
Moon in fall:	Possessive, dissatisfied, restless, wanderlust.

Since opportunity for this person is an occasion to express her power, strength, daring and keen insight, she has the knack somehow of always being (or seeming) exactly the right person for the job. She is not inhibited by issues of personal security. However, since much of her aggrandizement draws on the resources of others, it would be well for you (and in the long run, for her) if you could find ways to help her connect her lunar sympathies and Venusian sensibilities with her experiences of opportunity.

69. Jupiter in Sagittarius (Mutable, yang Fire sign, blue color-symbolism.)

Jupiter rules:	Optimistic, philosophical, Jovial, liberal-minded.
Mercury in detriment:	Extravagant, boastful, lawless, impractical.

> *No planet exalted*
> *or in fall:*   Restless, inconstant, impartial.

Here is a person with high ideals, but little sense of the intervening steps necessary to realize them. For him, opportunities bring knowledge, wisdom and growth in philosophical understanding. He has trouble relating his opportunities to his immediate circumstances and practical needs. Where is his Mercury? He can learn to see his high principles enacted before his eyes, if only he would look, in his mundane interactions with others around him. He will need all his powers of attention, directed both inward and outward, to realize this connection.

70. Jupiter in Capricorn (Cardinal, yin Earth sign, indigo color-symbolism.)
> *Saturn rules:*   Responsible, conscientious, organizer,
>   administrator.
> *Mars exalted:*   Productive, resourceful, ambitious, great
>   endurance.
> *Moon in detriment:*   Strong inhibitions, reserved, mean.
> *Jupiter in fall:*   Self-righteous, austere, bigoted, miserly.

Opportunity is for this person a reliable guide to very practical ambitions. Anything that strengthens an authoritative self-image, particularly in a political or organizational context, is seen by her as a guide to success. She is not greatly swayed by a desire for luxury, nor by her emotional and physical needs in general, depending, of course, upon where her Moon and Venus are placed. She could learn much from someone with Jupiter in Taurus. Can you find ways to evoke her sympathy and generosity toward others?

71. Jupiter in Aquarius (Fixed, yang Air sign, violet color-symbolism.)
> *Saturn rules:*   Philosophical, impartial, organization-minded.
> *Uranus rules:*   Humanitarian, tolerant, abrupt growth
>   experiences.
> *Mercury exalted:*   Broad-minded, outgoing, expansive talker.
> *Sun in detriment:*   Indecisive, lack of focus, doctrinaire.
> *Neptune in fall:*   Tactless, unempathic, scattered energies.

This person characteristically fails to connect his own personal wants and needs, along with those of others around him, with the rather impersonal humanitarian principles about which he waxes so enthusiastic; consequently, he often fails to organize and maintain loyal support for his grand schemes and world-embracing aims. Where is his Sun? Can you find ways to demonstrate the need for real, immediate compassion, especially for those who do not share one's progressive goals, although they stand most to benefit from them? Is this a path with heart?

72. Jupiter in Pisces (Mutable, yin Water sign, red-violet color-symbolism.)
> *Jupiter rules:*   Benevolent, humorous, idealistic, spiritual
>   philosophy.
> *Neptune rules:*   Compassionate, psychic, mystical interests.

Venus exalted: Genial, receptive, creative talents.
Mercury in
detriment and fall: Unreliable, over-imaginative, extravagant, self-
               deceptive.

This person sees opportunity in terms of her very private, subjective value system. To others, her judgments may seem whimsical, and indeed it is difficult to determine if the cause-and-effect relations on which they are based are marvellously subtle or merely fanciful. Her acceptance or rejection of opportunities is not based on any objective assessment of consequences. Because her Mercury is not strongly connected with Pisces, she should put extra effort into communicating her values and judgments to others. Then she might notice that what is of benefit to others cannot fail eventually to be of benefit to herself.

Saturn ♄

Saturn is twice as far from the Sun as Jupiter is, and takes more than twice as long to complete a circuit of the zodiac (about twenty-nine years).

Jupiter, Saturn, Uranus and Neptune are all "gas giants," called by astronomers the "Jovial" planets. Saturn is the only planet whose density is actually less than that of water. The symbolism of firmness, strictness and limitation associated with the planet astrologically is not borne out by the hardness or compactness of the planet, but by its famous rings, and by the fact that until the discovery of Uranus it was always known to be the outer limit of the solar system.

Now, as we are learning that limitations are not imposed from outside, but from within, we have discovered the transpersonal planets beyond Saturn, symbolizing our higher potential. In fact, even Saturn's rings have turned out not to be unique; rings have been observed around Jupiter, Uranus and Neptune, and may in fact exist in some form around all the planets.

Symbolically, in Piscean-age terms, Saturn is the Lord of Karma, the teacher of cause-and-effect. Part of the new-age consciousness is the discovery (by each person in due time) that events may be mutually both causes and effects of each other. This is what the Buddhists call "interdependent originations." When we understand cause-and-effect in interdependent, ecological, systemic terms, and when our understanding reaches to the roots of our subconscious habits and reactions, we will no longer be subject to Saturn in the old sense of limitation and discipline. We will have learned the lesson Saturn has been teaching us so patiently and for so long.

Whereas Jupiter represents the integration of the individual into the social realm, the reconciliation of the personal subconscious with the collective subconscious of society, Saturn represents the integration of personal subconsciousness (the Moon) with that collective subconscious of living creatures that determines the concensus reality of all life on Earth. It is difficult for many people to grasp the fact that the "laws of nature" (Saturn's laws) are something one has agreed to on a very deep level of being, and that they can be transcended.

Ultimately, Saturn teaches the uses of limitation. One cannot accomplish anything without determining what one is going to do, and that means eliminating the infinite variety of other options that are available. This choice has been compared with the act of accepting the rules of a game. Without the limitations of Saturn, we are in the position of little Alice trying to play croquet with a flamingo, watching the wickets and croquet balls leave their posts and walk away in looking-glass land. When we have created a cage of circumstances, however, we need to remember that "we are equal beings, and the universe is our relations with each other" (Thaddeus Golas, *The Lazy Man's Guide to Enlightenment*).

If you wish to develop the following paragraphs into meditation exercises, follow the format offered in the introduction to this chapter. Try developing ways to anticipate conflict, to identify its sources and to cultivate the strengths of people with Saturn in the various signs. Use your understanding of the rulership, detriment, exaltation and fall of each sign. Review your material on Saturn and on your administrative faculty, your Saturnian qualities of self-control, restraint, discipline, gravity, sobriety and responsibility.

Distinctive features: Yang or contractive/assertive, Earthy, indigo color-resonance (dark blue-violet, near black).

73. Saturn in Aries (Cardinal, yang Fire sign, red color-symbolism.)

Mars rules:	Persistent, practical, mechanically ingenious.
Sun exalted:	Ambitious, self-reliant, sincere, self-disciplined.
Venus in detriment:	Destructive, cruel, tactless, indiscriminate.
Saturn in fall:	Autocratic, judgmental, irresponsible, bad timing.

This person likes best to feel he is at the center of things. However, things are not always arranged so, and the adversities against which he defends himself often arise when his behavior is incongruous with its context. The position and relationships of Venus in his horoscope will indicate aspects of the social and esthetic context that may escape his consideration. His tenth house may indicate his Saturnian context.

74. Saturn in Taurus (Fixed, yin Earth sign, red-orange color-symbolism.)

Venus rules:	Methodical, constructive, patient, rigid values.
Moon exalted:	Stable, enduring, materialistic, stubborn, reserved.
Mars and Pluto in detriment:	Dour, avaricious, hard to pacify.
Uranus in fall:	Materialistic, inflexible, not playful.

Possessions form a natural defensive shell around this person, for whom self-preservation is largely a matter of physical security and comfort. Indeed, if all is well in her second house, she is quite easygoing and open. Her nest egg need not be large, but it must be, or seem to her, as enduring as the Earth itself; she does not like surprises in this department. If she loses this "anchor" she may have difficulty bringing her aggressive forces into focus. Where are Mars and Pluto in her horoscope?

75.   Saturn in Gemini (Mutable, yang Air sign, orange color-symbolism.)

Mercury rules: Intellectual, scientific, calculating, critical, restrained verbal expression.

Jupiter in detriment: Sceptical, critical, pessimistic, depressive.

No planet in
exaltation or in fall: Impartial, resourceful, adaptable.

Saturn is a good planet to stabilize Gemini. This person's ego defenses are active, tactical as it were, centered around shifting mental strategems rather than fixed assets or attributes. His intellectual skill and adaptability are his primary means of self-justification. The sign position of Mercury shows the character of his strategems, while its house indicates where his definition (and re-definition) of his ego boundaries is based. His skill may range in depth from dilettante to Renaissance man, as indicated largely by the position and relationships of Jupiter in his horoscope.

76.   Saturn in Cancer (Cardinal, yin Water sign, orange-yellow color-symbolism.)

Moon rules: Tenacious, protective, acquisitive, interested in public welfare.

Jupiter exalted: Lazy, overindulgent, opinionated, lacks buoyancy.

Saturn in detriment: Pessimistic, emotional restraint, needs respect.

Mars in fall: Timid, poorly motivated, uncertain of own capabilities.

In this person's subconscious memory is the parental message "Be careful! You are vulnerable! You are not as capable as you might think." Her parents' efforts to help her actually interfered with her, interrupting her and substituting their obviously more competent skills for hers. Instead of learning the "right way" she learned that hers was the wrong way. She should develop the imagery of her tenth house in the highest and most fulfilling form she can imagine, then "act as if" that is what she already is. How can she link her Jupiter to her Saturn and tenth house? Where is her Mars?

77.   Saturn in Leo (Fixed, yang Fire sign, yellow color-symbolism.)

Sun rules: Authoritative, self-assured, ambitious for recognition, egotistic.

Neptune exalted: Responsible, sensitive to duty, must be honest to thrive.

Saturn in detriment: Authoritarian, controlling, domineering.

Uranus in
detriment: Resentful of limitations, literal-minded, unspontaneous.

Mercury in fall:	Suspicious, negative thinking, difficulty concentrating.

This person justifies himself by the attention, esteem and approval he gets from others. If Neptune is badly placed this may take the form of hypochondria. Where is his Sun? Only when it is clear to him in his heart of hearts what he is here for, will his craving for approval diminish. He needs the detachment and impersonality of Mercury and Uranus to find a career that integrates him with his political and functional context. Where are these planets in his horoscope?

78. Saturn in Virgo (Mutable, yin Earth sign, yellow-green color-symbolism.)

Mercury rules and is exalted:	Methodical, precise, practical.
Jupiter in detriment:	Pedantic, exacting, worrisome, ungenerous.
Neptune in detriment:	Mistrustful, irritable, unempathic.
Venus in fall:	Hypercritical, hard-nosed, ungracious, self-centered.

This person feels surest when carrying out set procedures or following established rules. She justifies herself by her efficiency and accuracy, or by complaining about the inefficiency and inaccuracy of others. Where is her Jupiter? Things beyond her familiar scope will seem inefficient to her, and will be difficult for her to fit into her schedule, but there must be some way to incorporate some of Jupiter's breadth in the structure of her life. Look to her Venus and (circumspectly) her Neptune for ways to stimulate her awareness of her social and psychic contexts.

79. Saturn in Libra (Cardinal, yang Air sign, green color-symbolism.)

Venus rules:	Tactful, particular, creative, kindly, proper.
Saturn exalted:	Impartial, responsible, fair, self-controlled.
Mars in detriment:	Impractical, unmechanical, bloodless.
Sun in fall:	Insincere, austere, lacking ambition, dependent.

This person justifies himself by adapting to others, "adjusting" and getting along. If the Sun and Mars in his horoscope are expressed in extroverted ways, he has the tact and charm of a diplomat or statesman; if inwardly expressed, he involves himself in Virgo-like service and self-sacrifice, but without being so critical. The shape of his career is determined in large measure by the position and relationships of Venus in his horoscope, and what he does with his sensitivity to his social and esthetic environment.

80. Saturn in Scorpio (Fixed, yin Water sign, blue-green color-symbolism.)

Mars rules:	Purposeful, ambitious, passionate about aims, strong sex drive.
Pluto rules:	Strength in reserve, secretive, powerful will, controlling.

Uranus exalted: Abrupt contractual changes, interest in the occult.

Venus in detriment: Cruel, sceptical, selfish, destructive, jealous.

Moon in fall: Secretive, brooding, probing motivated by insecurity.

Saturn in any Water sign indicates a complex personality because the boundaries and defenses of the ego are set deep in the subconscious mind. Where is this person's Mars? Although she looks outward and sees adversaries, they are only projected shadows of inner conflicts. Where is her Pluto? She may seek security and ego strengthening in sex and marriage, but can find only lesser forms of gratification until she is able to disclose her inner fears and vulnerabilities, to herself as well as to her partner. Where is her Uranus? Her insight is partly blindfolded until it has input from her Venus and Moon. Where are these planets, symbolic of the active and passive phases of her subconsciousness? How can she integrate their contents with the outer structure of her ego?

81.   Saturn in Sagittarius (Mutable, yang Fire sign, blue color-symbolism.)

Jupiter rules: Moralizing, ambitious, trustworthy, dignified, frank.

Mercury in detriment: Tactless, insincere, materialistic, indecisive.

No planet in exaltation or in fall: Scattered efforts, afraid of being tied down, indecisive.

This is a good sign for Saturn. With his high self-esteem, this person feels little need to defend himself. He finds his justification in developing his philosophy of life—which he may modestly entitle "The Philosophy of Life." Where is his Mercury? Its position and relationships show how practical he is, and whether it is easy or difficult for him to integrate his ideals with his practice in putting together a career for himself. The position and relationships of his Jupiter may indicate the shape and direction of that career, or in what he invests his ego.

82.   Saturn in Capricorn (Cardinal, yin Earth sign, indigo color-symbolism.)

Saturn rules: Methodical, patient, disciplined, dutiful.

Mars exalted: Hard-working, steady-striving, ambitious, practical.

Moon in detriment: Hard, melancholic, craves reputation and social standing, withdrawn, unfeeling.

Jupiter in fall: Pessimistic, selfish, conservative, materialistic.

Self-esteem for this person depends upon her being a success, and this for her means material achievement, fame and a position of authority. She needs to draw on Jupiter to develop a sense of the many varieties of success available to her in a broad spectrum, beginning with the realm of the mind. Where is her

Moon? She needs to get acquainted with the subconscious images of success that have been programming her goals for her. Only after she has consciously accepted, or amended, these images will her Mars powers be fully available to her. Otherwise, Saturn here is too strong a constraint.

83. Saturn in Aquarius (Fixed, yang Air sign, violet color-symbolism.)

Saturn rules:	Organized, scientific, dogmatic, enduring friendships.
Sun in detriment:	Dutiful, perfunctory, lacks enthusiasm.
Neptune in fall:	Uncompassionate, unempathic, unfeeling, clearheaded.

This person builds his self-esteem on his material and political achievement, but is more sensitive than the person with Saturn in Capricorn to humane issues and the human context. He is an explainer, a justifier needing the esteem and respect of his fellows. If the Sun is well-placed in his horoscope, he will be a benefactor, giving much to society. If the Sun is weak, or if Neptune is stronger or in conflict with the Sun in his horoscope, he will have difficulty individuating, his ego field will be diffuse and permeable, and he will feel that society owes him a living. The relationships of the Sun and Saturn, and their houses, show the focus of these issues of responsibility. How can you help this person take the position of his unique role? How do you enact your own relationship to society?

84. Saturn in Pisces (Mutable, yin Water sign, red-violet color-symbolism.)

Jupiter rules:	Worrisome, retiring, capable of deep understanding.
Neptune rules:	Self-sacrificing, self-pitying, moody, psychic in a practical way, a practical occultist.
Venus exalted:	Loyal, faithful, disciplined imagination.
Mercury in detriment and in fall:	Untidy, depressive thinking.

Deep within her Watery subjectivity, this person wrestles with her own personal negativity, as she defines it. Is Jupiter strong enough in her horoscope to meet her inner hunger for her own approval? The placement of Neptune and Venus will show the particular ways in which she is sensitive to the emotional responses of others. How can she engage her Mercury with those perceptions? She needs objective feedback from other people and from outer events, which can only be provided by her paying deliberate, conscious attention to them. Otherwise, her self-esteem will be too fragile, and will be overset by every unforeseen conflict. She has to get her self-persecution out in the open, to consciously check and verify her self-evaluation, in order to avoid the unconscious projection of paranoia and delusions of persecution. When she clears away the debris, she has gifts to offer beyond anyone's expectations.

Uranus ♅

Uranus has a reputation for being associated with eccentric behavior. Physically, it certainly moves in an odd fashion, rotating backward, rolling around its orbit with one pole perpetually toward the Sun. All its moons move in the reverse direction from other planets' moons.

The root meaning of Uranus in astrology is not change or peculiarity, however, but intuition, the higher octave of Mercurial intellect. Perhaps the poles of the planet, oriented as they are in the same plane as the planet's orbit, symbolize a direct link between the universal mind (the surrounding cosmos) and the inner identity (the Sun).

Intuition, in the sense intended here, is direct perception of truth. It is like looking at a film with meaningless blobs of dark and light on it, then shining a laser beam through it and seeing a three-dimensional image. Intuition is a reorientation of one's perspective, a re-contextualization, in which the significance of what one is experiencing suddenly becomes obvious. It is what Blake means when he says "Truth cannot be told so as to be understood, and not be believed."

Uranus was discovered by accident where no planet was supposed to be. That discovery suddenly recontextualized the solar system and reoriented astronomers so that further discoveries became possible. People are discovering that there are no accidents, and that "coincidence" is merely an as-yet unrecognized manifestation of universal law.

Today's "freaks" may become tomorrow's truth-sayers. Not all freaks are prophets, of course, but somewhere in the wildest of aberrations there is at least a grain of truth, and that truth can be discovered only by intuition. No matter how well-educated you are, no matter how carefully trained your expectations are, the truth is always larger. And thank God for that! If things were otherwise, there would be little fun in life.

Uranus is often said to be in conflict with Saturn. In fact, the faculty of intuition actually widens the scope of our Saturnian understanding of necessity, cause-and-effect and the uses of limitation. Uranus has been associated with anarchy as opposed to Saturnian law and order, but anarchy (from a Greek word meaning "without leaders") ultimately means self-control, control by oneself rather than by some external authority-figure. To assume that simple, essential responsibility, one must know truly what is going on, one cannot rely on the opinions of others.

In many people, however, Uranian energy is poorly integrated and manifests as zany, eccentric or even crazy behavior—or at least so it seems to those who don't share their point of view.

If you wish to develop the following materials into meditation exercises, follow a format like that given at the start of this chapter. No "key phrases" are given; you may want to create some to help crystallize your understanding of Uranus in each of the signs. Review your material on Uranus and on your faculty of intuition. If you were crazy, what would you be like?

Distinctive features: Androgynous (or gynandrous), Airy, pale yellow color-resonance.

85. Uranus in Aries (Cardinal, yang Fire sign, red color-symbolism.)

Mars rules:	Pioneering, inventive, original, fiery, resourceful, healing energies.
Sun exalted:	Independent, courageous, a leader, individualist, self-willed.
Venus in detriment:	Disruptive, selfish, hard to relax, intolerant.
Saturn in fall:	Rebellious, erratic, disruptive, impulsive, hates restraint.

This person experiences intuitive insight in times of crisis and emergency, when something new is emerging and being identified. His intuition will not be deeply engaged in a role of patiently adjusting and improving an existing system, even if other factors, such as planets in Virgo or a good relationship of Venus and Saturn, give the skills for it. If he spends his time tinkering with the status quo, he won't tap into those flashes of insight that make him such an inspiring leader when familiar guidelines can't be trusted. If he gets tension headaches, he can relieve them by stretching and relaxing his neck (ruled by Venus), rotating his head gently, relaxing and expanding his throat and making deep, open sounds.

86. Uranus in Taurus (Fixed, yin Earth sign, red-orange color-symbolism.)

Venus rules:	Charm, magnetism, unique talents, innovative values.
Moon exalted:	Resourceful, seeks independent security, interest in practical occultism.
Mars and Pluto in detriment:	Headstrong, impatient with convention, explosive temper.
Uranus in fall:	Financial reversals, conservatism, powerful subconscious beliefs hamper intuition.

For this person, issues of security and comfort, in physical and financial terms, are the occasion of insight. If Jupiter is well-placed, and there are no great problems in her second house, this person will be free from financial limitations, and even with indicators of want in the horoscope, she will always have a "back door" into security, to which the lock is fear and the key is detached, meditative insight. Her relationship to property is idiosyncratic, and may be iconoclastic. Whether or not she is selfish depends largely upon how she satisfies her security (Moon) and comfort (Venus) needs.

87. Uranus in Gemini (Mutable, yang Air sign, orange color-symbolism.)

Mercury rules:	Nervous, restless, intuitive, inventive, quick to grasp and take up new ideas.
Jupiter in detriment:	Rebels against orthodoxy, unstable judgment, too impatient to integrate insights with actions.

No planet in
exaltation or in fall: Versatile, restless, curious.

Mercurial attention, both outward to the objects of sense and inward to the objects of reason, has as its servant the magical genie, intuition. This genie executes complex chains of logic in a flash, so that conclusions appear to others to be derived out of thin air, by magic. If some task of reasoning proves laborious, this person should realize he must be clinging to some unreasonable belief, some indigestible premise, that not even the universal solvent of intuition can turn to a useful form. He is an intellectual iconoclast who loves new notions that challenge old "common sense." The placement of his Mercury shows where his wit is directed. How can he draw on his Jupiter to broaden and deepen the fundamental beliefs on which that wit flourishes or founders? How can he bring his mind under sufficient Saturnian discipline to focus on one subject in depth rather than scattering itself thinly over all?

88. Uranus in Cancer (Cardinal, yin Water sign, orange-yellow color-symbolism.)

Jupiter exalted: Keen judgment, individualist, unorthodox
                          beliefs.
Saturn in detriment: Rebellious, impulsive, cops out on
                          responsibility.
Mars in fall: Impatient, erratic, disruptive, touchy.

This person is capable of great insight into the nature of human roots, of personal security, of family systems, and so forth. She sees past the outward forms given by tradition and glimpses their root motives—comfort, security, nurturance, growth. The new appliances, home designs and family arrangements which she may try out will unsettle her home life, but they will also energize her household. Where is her Mars? Is she undermining the basis of her standing in the world, to the detriment of her career? She could be a good family therapist.

89. Uranus in Leo (Fixed, yang Fire sign, yellow color-symbolism.)

Sun rules: Strong self-will, spirited, high-minded, proud,
                         eccentric, creative.
Neptune exalted: Intuitive, dramatic, sudden romances,
                         magnetic.
Saturn in detriment: Intolerant, anti-authority, willful.
Uranus in
detriment: Stubborn, intolerant, impulsive, will overrides
                         intuition.
Mercury in fall: Erratic insight, poor grasp of abstract
                         principles.

This person's genius flashes out at any chance for show, to appear as the hero of a sword-and-sorcery fantasy novel, perhaps. He is too enamored of appearances and display for much real insight unless Mercury is well-placed and well-connected with Uranus in the horoscope. He is more swayed by his

Neptunian psychic resonance with others than he is by mental clarity and detachment. If he learns humility—that is, if he has forgotten how to be humiliated—his former egotism may be transmuted to a subtle instrument of service.

90. Uranus in Virgo (Mutable, yin Earth sign, yellow-green color-symbolism.)

Mercury rules and is exalted:	Scientific, technical, or occult work, such as inventor, scientist, medical researcher, nutritionist, mental healer.
Jupiter in detriment:	Opportunities are disruptive or disrupted, myopic judgment, judgment uncoordinated with intuition.
Neptune in detriment:	Insensitive to own impact on others, disruptions with colleagues and employees.
Venus in fall:	Self-centered in love, doctrinaire, imagination can't follow up insights, emotional turmoil.

This person experiences insight in the context of organized work methods. She would do well reforming social service procedures, for example. However, such bureaucratic reforms often illustrate the maxim about good intentions paving the road to hell, due to lack of real direct knowledge (empathy) of the effects on the people served. Where are her Venus and Neptune? To be more than an ersatz "fixit" person in this realm she needs to connect her intuition with her Jupiterian grasp of deeper principles.

91. Uranus in Libra (Cardinal, yang Air sign, green color-symbolism.)

Venus rules:	Unusual tastes, unique talents, unconventional marriage, needs open relationships.
Saturn exalted:	Champion of justice, legal reform (spirit, rather than letter, of the law).
Mars in detriment:	Half-cocked, impulsive in relationships, abrasive.
Sun in fall:	Willful, disruptive, unbalanced, contentious.

This person has the capacity for intuiting what is needed for cooperation and collective effort. If the ego is sound (as shown primarily by the positions and relationships of the Sun and Saturn), he can be a catalyst for social synergy. He can be weak and vacillating, too other-directed, particularly if his Mars is weak, in which case his wishful thinking will anticipate coordination among his fellows where there is not yet a collective spirit, and blame them for not cooperating with him. He may by way of compensation, in such a case, puff up his identity as a lone wolf, or a misunderstood outsider, but clearly his heart is not in it. How can you help him connect his Sun to this façade?

92. Uranus in Scorpio (Fixed, yin Water sign, blue-green color-symbolism.)
     Mars rules: Great will, unusual sex life, healer, rebel.
     Pluto rules: Persistence, perception of underlying causes or
                            motives, sudden revelations and
                            transformations.
     Uranus exalted: Profound intuitive insights, psychic, occultist.
     Venus in detriment: Jealous, envious, sudden vengefulness, passion
                            versus compassion.
     Moon in fall: Possessive, introspective, resentment versus
                            understanding.

The motive for insight here is access to others' resources. This person's intuition is directed by issues of power; she exacts obedience instinctively. If she is cautious, fearful, uncertain or inhibited (Moon or Venus), her circle of followers will be small. If she is comfortable and secure in her Moon and Venus, her magnetism can unify a huge field. Look to the placement of her Sun, and that of her Mars and Pluto, and consider how well she has integrated the whole horoscope, to understand which way her magnetism is polarized.

93. Uranus in Sagittarius (Mutable, yang Fire sign, blue color-symbolism.)
     Jupiter rules: Optimistic, antidogmatic, radical religious
                            views, intuition and judgment integrated,
                            unusual dreams and visions.
     *Mercury in
     detriment:*   Difficulty applying insights, inconsiderate.
     *No planet in
     exaltation or in fall:* Rebellious, extremely independent,
                            freewheeling.

This person is capable of profound insights in the world of ideas, philosophical principles and generalizations. To express this potential, his more mundane powers of observation must be strong and supple to provide their higher octave, Uranus, with clear observations and well-defined facts. Where is his Mercury, and how well does he use it? Is he only a fuzzy cloud-wanderer?

94. Uranus in Capricorn (Cardinal, yin Earth sign, indigo color-symbolism.)
     Saturn rules: Ambitious, political, new methods, conflict of
                            prestige and freedom.
     Mars exalted: Ambitious, great energy, practical inventions.
     Moon in detriment: Impatient with insecurity, unfeeling, resents
                            limits, rebels against the "shoulds" of life.
     Jupiter in fall: Rejects moral doctrines, conflict of judgment
                            and intuition, impatient with generalizations.

This person has glimpses into the roots of necessity. He may generate turmoil in business, commerce and political life by his unconventional *tactics,* but his *aims* are conservative in the deepest sense. Most who style themselves "conservatives" are merely literal-minded fundamentalists, incapable of guessing at the spirit of laws whose letter they so passionately and dogmatically invoke. With such this person has little patience. Where is her Moon? Personal insecurities may inhibit her from carrying out surgery the world sorely needs. She also needs to connect her intuition with the openness and comprehension of Jupiter to ensure the operation is a healing process rather than an execution or an autopsy.

95. Uranus in Aquarius (Fixed, yang Air sign, violet color-symbolism.)

Saturn rules:	Scientific, impersonal, unusual aims, innovative groups, goals abruptly changed, suddenly attained.
Uranus rules:	Inventive, intuitive, independent, works alone.
Mercury exalted:	Scientific, intellectual, impersonal, experimenter.
Sun in detriment:	Willful, disruptive, eccentric, conflict with authority.
Neptune in fall:	Unsympathetic, lacks empathy one-to-one.

The concept of synergy is intuitively obvious to this person. There is no freedom for anyone unless there is for everyone; what cripples anyone cripples me. To act on this insight, to work to raise the level of synergy in the social arrangements of humanity, he must be able really to put his heart into it. Where is his Sun? If it is poorly placed, if his integrity is weak, if he is poorly individuated as a person, he may be a "free rider," turning the proposition of synergy around: "There is no freedom for anyone unless for me; what hinders me hampers you as well, so you owe me a lift." Where is Neptune in his chart? Expect glamour and delusion to play a role in such an outlook.

96. Uranus in Pisces (Mutable, yin Water sign, red-violet color-symbolism.)

Jupiter rules:	Humanitarian, generous impulses, abrupt charity.
Neptune rules:	Very psychic, oversensitive, compassionate, occult interests, freedom through withdrawal.
Venus exalted:	Idiosyncratic tastes, unusual talents, quick devotion, compassionate, easily bored, temperamental.
Mercury in detriment and in fall:	Impractical, indecisive, unreliable, delicate nervous system, oversensitive to drugs and alcohol.

Here the Airy, impersonal intuition of Uranus is directed inward at the Watery, subjective, psychic intuitions of Neptune. Where it leads depends upon the unique subjective psyche of the individual person: Perhaps "art for art's sake," or the inward odyssey of self-discovery and self-development which lies at the roots of the human potential movement. Unless Mercury is well-placed to be a "receiving station" for messages of intuition, or unless this person is a trained, disciplined explorer of inner space by some form of meditation practice, all that precious clarity is lost like a diamond in the depths of the ocean where no Sun's ray ever reaches.

Neptune ♆

Neptune, the eighth planet from the Sun, is the only planet whose discovery resulted from purely theoretical considerations. Two mathematicians independently calculated its position from observed irregularities in the orbit of Uranus, and the German astronomer Galle discovered the planet itself the day after receiving the mathematical prediction in the mail. Neptune has to do with things that are mysterious, hidden, and yet obvious if you look in the right way.

As the god of water and of the sea, Neptune was a masculine ruler of a feminine principle. Robert Graves, poet, scholar and mystic, suggests he was a usurper, taking over the shrines of his feminine predecessor after the worship of the White Goddess was forced underground. The god's feast day was July 23, when the Sun enters the sign Leo, the quintessentially masculine sign where the Sun rules, yet where the yin planet Neptune is exalted. What mystery might lie behind this confusion of genders?

Oceanographers of the psyche have begun to chart its contours and its Gulf Streams, but only the scuba divers of the soul, led by the influence of Neptune, can claim any intimate knowledge of it. Neptune rules the places where your deepest personal need and your social and moral obligations converge and become one and the same. Between that deep level of truth and the surface of social consensus, there are many layers of glamour, wishful thinking and illusion, and these, too, are ruled by Neptune. As the higher octave of the Moon, Neptune governs such diverse matters as hypnosis, hallucinations, astral travel, dreams, religious faith and enthusiasm.

Your age-mates will all have Neptune in the same sign you have (unless you have it near a cusp), yet the connections through the circle of houses and through relationships with other planets will differ from person to person. It is fascinating to explore the differences among your friends and associates, recognizing the common themes that you share as a backdrop. Explore as well the differences between the generations according to the sign Neptune was in for each generation.

If you want to develop meditation exercises based on the following materials, use the example given in the introduction to this chapter as a format. Some of the sign positions for Neptune will not come up among the people you know. Do you know why? Do you know which ones? You may find applications for this information; for example, if a friend has Neptune in the house where you have the sign Aquarius, the section on Neptune in Aquarius might shed some light on your perception of the Neptunian side of his or her personality. Review your material on Neptune and on your powers of empathy, compassion and emotional insight, your capacity for devotion and surrender and your experience of psychism, ESP and so on.

Distinctive features: Yin or receptive, Watery, pale blue color-resonance.

97. Neptune in Aries (Cardinal, yang Fire sign, red color-symbolism.)

Mars rules:	Actions are unobtrusive, covert, occult or spiritualized; magnetic personality.
Sun exalted:	Enthusiastic, idealistic, self-aware, glamorous, mystical.
Venus in detriment:	Dissipation; self-deception in values and in relationships.
Saturn in fall:	Obsessive, confused and restless, subject to psychic interference.

This person's fantasies and personal mythology feature his individualism, pioneering effort, invention, discovery, adventure and so forth; and this generally blocks experience of empathy. He loves to see himself as a person of influence who has decisive impact on events; this would be fine except that he confuses the fulfillment of this image with genuine self-interest. Objective events impress him less than his own aggressive reactions to them. Where is his Venus? He needs to subject his imagination to periodic "reality checks." How can his Saturn help him understand karma (necessity), his dancing partner?

98. Neptune in Taurus (Fixed, yin Earth sign, red-orange color-symbolism.)

Venus rules:	Highly creative imagination, esthetic sensitivity, sexual magnetism, spiritual values.
Moon exalted:	Receptive, dreamy, psychic, responsive, acute senses.
Mars and Pluto in detriment:	Timid, insecure, confused, uncertain, impractical, self-indulgent.
Uranus in fall:	Difficulty interpreting psychic perceptions, spiritual materialist.

This person's empathy is strongly conditioned by the physical, financial and emotional circumstances of her early life. Circumstances of poverty result in subconscious fantasies of want and neglect; but does she develop the fantasy with a desire to escape or with an obligation to ameliorate the need experienced by others? A child who experiences wealth or is otherwise sheltered from emotional or material lack later has subconscious fantasies of universal abundance; but does she carry the fantasy further as a dream of indolence, or as a desire to share the dream with others? The positions and relationships of Venus and the Moon will indicate the symbolism of her personal mythology, but she needs to connect with her Uranian intuition to perceive the inner significance of her symbols, and she needs the force of Mars and Pluto to carry out the obligation implicit in these symbols.

99.   Neptune in Gemini (Mutable, yang Air sign, orange color-symbolism.)

Mercury rules: Mental sensitivity, poetic/inspirational mind, hypnotic, psychic, alert, perceptive, rationalizing, suggestible.

Jupiter in detriment: Exaggeration, poor judgment, unreliable.

No planet in exaltation or in fall: Versatile, restless, desires change.

This person is subtly influenced by fantasies of innovation, change, and novelty in life together with an obligation to appreciate new developments intellectually through study of the world of appearances. He will grasp his observations at a deeper and more satisfying level when he is able to yoke them to lasting philosophical principles, symbolized by Jupiter. He is capable of a vastly tolerant, open-minded creativity welling from deep within his psyche, but this potential may be masked with impatience and irritability, and he may jitter irresponsibly from one project to another, if his intellectual and moral principles are unclear or poorly integrated. (These are the oldest people you are likely to encounter in the flesh, born in the years roughly from 1887 to 1901.)

100.   Neptune in Cancer (Cardinal, yin Water sign, orange-yellow color-symbolism.)

Moon rules: Emotionally sensitive, empathic, psychic, idealizes home, tradition, etc., spiritual emotions.

Jupiter exalted: Idealistic emotions, sincere, compassionate, mystical.

Saturn in detriment: Melancholic, vulnerable, hypersensitive, susceptible to obsession.

Mars in fall: Passive, diffuse will, inconsistent, poorly-directed energies.

The compulsion to recreate her early home environment and to reenact her childhood family patterns is especially strong in this person. Because of the exceptionally powerful influence of the Moon over her higher octave, Neptune, in this sign, it is more than usually important for her to understand the programming in her subconscious mind, and re-condition her emotional habit-patterns. Where is her Jupiter? How can she draw on its exhaustless beneficence to ameliorate her conditioning? If she is dependent, expecting others to mother her and discipline her, how can she contact within herself her own integrity and strength? Where are her Mars and Saturn?

101.   Neptune in Leo (Fixed, yang Fire sign, yellow color-symbolism.)

Sun rules: Glamorous, mysterious, romantic, generous, dignified.

Neptune exalted: Inspired, sympathetic, sensitive, psychic, mysterious.

Saturn in detriment:	Inarticulate insights, dogmatic, passionately certain.
Mercury in fall:	Vague, wishful thinking, self-delusion, unreasoning.

This person can be a great romanticizer for whom all the world's a Gothic novel. The usual Leo preoccupation with (self-) approval and (self-) esteem takes an idealized emotional turn in this person: He craves not approval but *love* for his performances. The position of the Sun indicates his special creative bent, but look to his Moon and Venus to see what constitutes love for him. To realize his full capacities through (self-) compassion he must engage his glamorous, magnamimous personal script with the greater drama of humanity, through the inward-centering discipline of his Saturn, and the outward-clarifying insight of Uranus. However, he may not want to graduate from "As the World Turns" to *War and Peace*.

102. Neptune in Virgo (Mutable, yin Earth sign, yellow-green color-symbolism.)

Mercury rules and is exalted:	Sensitive nervous system, diffuse mental energies, poor concentration, idealizes work.
Jupiter in detriment:	Doubts own judgment, exaggerates, embroiders truth.
Neptune in detriment:	Impressionable, dreamy, neurotic, strange illnesses.
Venus in fall:	Critical, unappreciative, emotions diffuse or confused, must learn to love, hypochondriac.

The psyche of this person was profoundly influenced by the revaluation of work and service that took place during the Depression. Her subconscious fantasy of scarcity and sense of lack may be assuaged by work for its own sake, or at least for the sake of those it serves. Where is her Jupiter, and how can she use it to help focus her attention (Mercury) outward on the working of social, economic and political principles in the world? The key to unlocking her powers lies in the mythological imagery of working people helping one another, so she can't afford to dwell too much on herself.

103. Neptune in Libra (Cardinal, yang Air sign, green color-symbolism.)

Venus rules:	Esthetic inspiration, imaginative, psychic, sexually attractive.
Saturn exalted:	Karmic relationships, obsessed with injustice, public relations skills.
Mars in detriment:	Indecisive, diffuse energies, lacks determination, (self-) deception through anger or passion.
Sun in fall:	Unbalanced, suggestible, distracted from inner purpose.

A fantasy of cooperation and social harmony stirs in the depths of this psyche. His capacity for empathy is strongest with those who seek to align themselves together in a cooperative effort, or with those who most need to unite collectively to ameliorate their social, political and economic circumstances. He may be excessively idealistic, or merely unrealistic, unless Saturn is well-placed in his horoscope. He may feel a subconscious obligation to "volunteer" as a "victim" of injustice, to disclose and demonstrate the imbalance in the tissue of society. Are his Sun and Mars strong enough to carry this role?

104. Neptune in Scorpio (Fixed, yin Water sign, blue-green color-symbolism.)

Mars rules:	Strong physical reactions, confused goals, inconsistent, indecisive, interest in outer space, UFO's, and so forth.
Pluto rules:	Spiritualizes sex, interest in inner space, spiritual disciplines, occultism, life after death, and so forth.
Uranus exalted:	Introspective, meditative, psychic, occultist, mystic.
Venus in detriment:	Self-indulgent, irresponsible, peculiar sex life.
Moon in fall:	Escapist, unstable, misuse of others' resources, unreliable.

Look to the placement of Mars and Pluto to see whether the higher or lower octave of (re)generative power predominates here. This person is fascinated by fantasies about the use and misuse of power. Where these fantasies take her depends in large measure on the subconscious programming of her Moon, and its imaginative elaboration through her Venus. If either of these is in difficulty in the horoscope, or if Neptune is in a difficult house placement or other relationship, she should use great caution exploring the areas indicated above, i.e., psychism, alcohol and drugs, and so forth.

105. Neptune in Sagittarius (Mutable, yang Fire sign, blue color-symbolism.)

Jupiter rules:	Generous, sympathetic, hates injustice, strong intuition, optimistic, high ideals, inspired, prophetic.
Mercury in detriment:	Impractical, poor discrimination, indecisive, unsure, imagination confuses facts, emotion distorts logic.
No planet in exaltation or in fall:	Indecisive, restless, lacks focus.

This person is responsive to the esoteric significance of mythic symbolism in religious traditions, mythologies and prophetic dreams and visions. He wants to explore these realities directly, bodily, in the full spectrum of their manifestation from the physical to the spiritual. To do so, he has to reconcile the mind/body dualism of our cultural myths. To get past the "obvious" (from the Latin *ob-via* "in the way, in the road") he should follow his inner fantasy of adventure and exploration, using his immediate physical perceptions and observations (Mercury) as a "native guide."

106.   **Neptune in Capricorn** (Cardinal, yin Earth sign, indigo color-symbolism.)

Saturn rules:	Patient, educator, enlightened statesman, spiritual guide, practical psychic.
Mars exalted:	Discernment, practical idealism, competent psychism.
Moon in detriment:	Insecure, emotionally unstable, unclear feelings, cloudy aims, feels inferior, doesn't learn from experience.
Jupiter in fall:	Selfish, materialistic, exaggerating, suggestible, misplaced altruism.

A fantasy of worldly success and prestige troubles the waters of the psyche. As always with Capricorn, how well those hard ambitions are achieved depends greatly on the quality of nurturance this person received in childhood, as symbolized by Cancer and the fourth house, and the character of the programming (the Moon) and philosophical attitude (Jupiter) she was given.

107.   **Neptune in Aquarius** (Fixed, yang Air sign, violet color-symbolism.)

Saturn rules:	Philosophical, understanding, retiring, useful dreams.
Uranus rules:	Inventive, spiritual intuition, spiritual/occult service.
Mercury exalted:	Intuitive, prophetic, inspired, poetic, interprets dreams or visions.
Sun in detriment:	Obsessions, ego blocks, confused humanitarianism.
Neptune in fall:	Impractical, dreamer, misleading visions.

In fall here, separated as far as possible from the rulership of the Sun, Neptune more than ever requires a "path with heart." Without that centeredness, this person may easily impose on his friends—and vice-versa. Will this person be a free-loader? Probably not: because he is motivated by true messianic fantasies in which inspired collective actions rather than charismatic individual saviors are the principals. However, Mercury, Saturn and Uranus must be well-placed and in good relationships before immediate, mundane steps can be taken to further his grand aims. Otherwise, his methods may be questionable. "The end justifies the means" is a low-synergy concept, and grotesquely out of place for the generation born with Neptune in Aquarius. Hallelujah! Praise the Lord and pass the inspiration!

108.   **Neptune in Pisces** (Mutable, yin Water sign, red-violet color-symbolism.)

Jupiter rules:	Kindly, courteous, sensitive, intuitive, religious, mystical, inspired.

Neptune rules:	Self-sacrificing, compassionate, psychic, inspired inner life, cosmic insights.
Venus exalted:	Deep love, refined taste, creative inspiration, unassuming, receptive.
Mercury in detriment and in fall:	Confused, imagination vivid but undependable, nervous illnesses like asthma, attention wanders, direction unclear.

It is appropriate that Neptune passes through signs contrary to its basic nature, self-sacrificially through the Moon's detriment (Capricorn) and its own fall (Aquarius), before entering its own rulership in Pisces. We have not yet seen such a back-to-nature movement as this person's generation will bring, acting out their collective fantasy of a contemplative, almost monastic life, bringing about universal harmony. This person can master the art of meditation in action, maintaining her competence in this world through Mercury and Jupiter in her horoscope. She needs the focus of Mercury to use imagination, and not be abused by it. It is very easy for her to disidentify from superficials, barring severe difficulties elsewhere in the horoscope: "I am not what I see—Who is seeing this? I am not what I feel—Who is feeling this? I am not what I think—Who is thinking this? I am not what I imagine—Who is imagining this?" Remember that Neptune is exalted under the rulership of the Sun (in Leo). Throughout this process of disidentification, there remains an inner kernel of perfection, symbolized by the Sun in this gifted server's horoscope. As she seeks to embody that inner identity, it guides her in the process of perfecting both herself and her world.

Pluto ♇

Pluto, the outermost known planet of the solar system, symbolizes power, the power to create and to destroy, the radical power at the root of life where creation and destruction are two faces of the same process, nuclear power, the interconversion of matter and energy. It is no accident that the ninety-fourth element, so important in nuclear fission, is named plutonium.

Many astronomers believe there are planets beyond Pluto. Must we master the power that can destroy our planet in a blast of fission and fusion, or in the slow half-life suicide of radioactive byproducts, before we can discover them and connect with them astrologically?

This power is for life or for death. Atomic energy is not the issue, it merely symbolizes the issue for the human race. Despite the rhetoric of "swords into plowshares" and "the peaceful atom," it turns out that the power of Pluto takes more skill than we have been able thus far to muster; skill of the heart as well as of the brain; the skill to rise above the mere egotism of money and political purchase; the skill to know when and how to ask help from transpersonal parts of ourselves, above our personal egos.

When in Eastern spiritual disciplines they speak of "burning karma" (that is, burning it up, getting rid of it), it is the Fire of Pluto to which they refer. This refiner's Fire brands each age-group of us differently, each generation has a different focus of karma to burn in order to get free. Explore the differences among your age-mates according to the house in which Pluto is placed, and the differences among generations of people according to its sign-placement. The example given at the start of this chapter may be helpful in organizing this information. Review your material on Pluto, on the power in life for death, for change, regeneration and rebirth, and on issues of power in your life. Remember that Pluto is the higher octave of Mars. Because of Pluto's long tenure in each sign (twenty years on the average), the delineations in this section refer to generations, rather than individuals.

Distinctive features: Yang or projective, Fiery, red color-resonance.

109.   Pluto in Aries (Cardinal, yang Fire sign, red color-symbolism.)

Mars rules:	Impulsive, energetic, robust, pioneering, ruthless.
Sun exalted:	Self-assertive, self-reliant, courageous, strong-willed, hungry for power, authority and recognition.
Venus in detriment:	Inconsiderate, cruel, lustful, ruthless, egotistical, lonely because unloving.
Saturn in fall:	Reckless, rebellious, lustful, lust for power, poorly integrated.

Pluto was in Aries for the period of about thirty years culminating in the Gold Rush, a period in U.S. history characterized by political militancy and individualistic pioneering, when sacred cows were fair game and Indians were shot like rabbits for sport. People of this generation were obsessed with personal might and valor, with a compulsion to break free from anything shackling the personal will. This inner fixation pushed them to test themselves beyond the limits of personal exhaustion. Their great lesson was how to prove themselves other than by their impact on others. Their will was constantly thwarted and frustrated, in the nature of the laws of karma, until they could let go of the illusion of separated independence, in exchange for the genuine autonomy that comes with integrated interrelationships. This depends upon their use of Saturn and Venus, the house position of Libra, and their integration of experiences in their connective (Air) houses, especially the seventh.

110.   Pluto in Taurus (Fixed, yin Earth sign, red-orange color-symbolism.)

Venus rules:	Deep love, strong sexuality, procreative, regeneration of values, artistic, magnetic, self-indulgent.
Moon exalted:	Powerful mother figure, sensitive, psychic, emotional extremes, strong sensory reactions.

Mars and Pluto in detriment:	Sensual, antisocial, inhibited feelings that erupt violently, lustful, lacks empathy and compassion.
Uranus in fall:	Inflexible, independent, rebellious, obsessed with material success, power struggles.

The period of American history with Pluto in Taurus, the period of the Reconstruction following the Civil War, was characterized by greed, land speculation and obsession with property both as an index of personal power and as a lasting monument to the personal ego. It was a pragmatic and utilitarian period. People born with Pluto in Taurus tended to invest their powers in material institutions, in a profoundly procreative stance. If Venus is strong in the horoscope they could realize esthetic gifts, particularly for oratory and singing. Their great lesson was to transform the compulsion to possess into dedicated stewardship. For this they needed the depersonalized vision of Uranus to turn the nurturing of the Moon outward from themselves, or else a warm and supportive placement for the Moon and Venus lending itself to emotional generosity and compassion.

111.   Pluto in Gemini (Mutable, yang Air sign, orange color-symbolism.)

Mercury rules:	Original, inventive, self-sufficient, penetrating, mental regeneration, master of the power of suggestion, manipulative.
Jupiter in detriment:	Suspicious, inadequate self-image, sharp but devious, power seeking, strong willed.
No planet in exaltation or in fall:	Very restless, obsessively curious, lacks focus, craves stimulation.

This period (1884-1914) saw a great flourishing of newspapers and periodicals in this country, many dedicated to the special interests of immigrant groups in whose languages they were printed. The First World War, at the end of this period, began with the media hype of a political assassination, and ended with the betrayal of Germany (and of Woodrow Wilson's naively well-intended Fourteen Points) by a public relations man, George Creel, who was born with Pluto in Gemini. Among this generation there is an obsession with mental, verbal power, and a compulsion to vanquish by one's cleverness. The generals behind the lines thought airborn warfare and poison gas were terribly clever. Though communications and media flourished, it was with an incestuous intensity, confined to the range and speed of the horse and buggy, the steam engine and the telegraph. The great inventiveness of this period declined in many cases to novelty-seeking, and to *fin de siecle* boredom and ennui, partly because of the limitations of means. The lesson was to purge the mind of pettiness and acquire more Sagittarian breadth and depth.

112. Pluto in Cancer (Cardinal, yin Water sign, orange-yellow color-symbolism.)

Moon rules:	Emotional extremes, sensitive, psychic, emotional regeneration, powerful mother figure, family transformation.
Jupiter exalted:	Subtle, extrovert, generous, compassionate, cautious optimist, penetrating judgment.
Saturn in detriment:	Strong compensatory egotism, vindictive, jealous, resentful, lust for power, lacks self-mastery and humility.
Mars in fall:	Antisocial, lustful, attracts violence, needs compassion.

During this period (1913-1939), with its political appeals to emotion and sentiment based upon clannishness and the "sanctity of the family," the myth of special privilege flourished. Natives of this time have a compulsion to nurture or to be mothered. Suddenly, during the second half of Pluto's tenure in Cancer, the structures of business and politics could not be relied upon, to the tune of "Buddy, can you spare a dime?" Then government became the great rescuing Mother Hubbard whose children are "all in this together!" These were the parents of those who were to transform marriage (the root of the family) so profoundly when Pluto was in Libra and in Scorpio. They have had to sacrifice their comfortable ideals of family togetherness, forming the anvil for the forging of new social relations. To perform this role in our cultural evolution well, they have needed Capricornian fortitude (Saturn) and vigor (Mars).

113. Pluto in Leo (Fixed, yang Fire sign, yellow color-symbolism.)

Sun rules:	Powerful pride, ruthless, desires power and authority, deeply creative, intense extremes in love and sex.
Neptune exalted:	Dramatic, glamorizes power, transformed by own creations.
Saturn in detriment:	Powerful ego structure, domineering, vindictive, needs humility.
Uranus in detriment:	Rebellious, independent, power struggles.
Mercury in fall:	Intense nervous system, impatient, quick grasp.

The period when Pluto was in Leo (1938-1958) was marked by dictatorial egotism in the rulers of nations, and, among those ruled, a craving for magnificent rulers. F.D.R., an Aquarian, was both kind and father-to-a-nation in his "fireside chats." In their own styles and cultural contexts, Hitler (Taurus),

Mussolini (Leo) and Hirohito (Scorpio) each manifested the same Fixed-sign paternalism. Even the ubiquitous "Kilroy was here" expressed a kind of national ego for GIs. This period was characterized by obsession with government, with "spheres of influence" and megalomaniacal schemes for world government. The people born during this period have a compulsion for personal creativity and some kind of complete personal fulfillment. They need the Aquarian detachment of Saturn, Uranus and Mercury, as their creative gifts must be purged of egotism for their true transpersonal significance to be fulfilled.

114.   Pluto in Virgo (Mutable, yin Earth sign, yellow-green color-symbolism.)

Mercury rules and is exalted:	Analysis in depth, penetrating discrimination, sceptical, manipulative, industrious.
Jupiter in detriment:	Suspicious, devious, conceited, feels inadequate.
Venus in fall:	Unloving, fault-finding, cruel, lustful.

Before Pluto's recent transit through Virgo (1956-1972), nutrition and preventive health care were the obsessions of a kooky fringe, but they have since been transformed into one of the earmarks of a new generation. During this period, the hypocrisies and imperfections of society were challenged by youthful values that were in many ways essentially puritanical. The generation born with Pluto in Virgo must clean up the disarray left by its more flamboyant elders during the sixties.

This period also marks the real onset of the computer revolution, in which those fabulously Virgoan man-made servants have begun a transformation of our commercial world, the repercussions of which will not be fully felt until Pluto is in Capricorn, the next Earth sign.

The practical demonstration, during this time, of alternative forms of healing (natural, mental and metaphysical healing) and their applications has undermined the edifice of the establishment "health care" industry, and will continue to do so.

Natives of this period must take care not to set up a rigid orthodoxy of their own. They must sacrifice their personal notions of what is perfect and what is not, drawing on Venus, Neptune and Jupiter for Piscean universality and tolerance.

115.   Pluto in Libra (Cardinal, yang Air sign, green color-symbolism.)

Venus rules:	Deep love, magnetic, sexy, creative artist, regeneration through relationships.
Saturn exalted:	Diplomatic, idealistic (moralistic), obsessed with justice (judgmental), dedicated to peace.
Mars in detriment:	Antisocial, lustful, troublemaker, attracts violence.

Sun in fall:	Arrogance, inferiority complex, compensatory egotism, cold father figure.

Pluto's orbit passes inside that of Neptune in this sign. Approaching us more closely, Pluto's influence becomes more intense at the same time that its tenure in each sign becomes briefer. During this period (roughly 1971-1984) the formulation of laws and the administration of justice will be profoundly challenged. True world government must begin to emerge during this period, as opposed to the mere outward shows of the past, for there are major planetary imbalances to be rectified. People and organizations must learn to complement what appears foreign and alien, to form a higher-order dynamic unity with each "adversary" in the dance of coevolution. This alchemy of social change rests ultimately upon a change in one-to-one relationships (I-Thou). The love/hate polarity (unity/separateness, merger/individuation) is not an emotion, but a universal principle, the root of *all* emotions. During this period, relationships, notably weddings and marriage vows, are transformed, reflecting this realization. Grand passions and glamorous romance are no longer the prerequisite to wedding bells. Natives of this period (1971-1984) must learn to act decisively, before the wheel of law (karma) turns too far and it is too late. Compulsively impartial, they must learn to transform their obsession with harmony and balance into *necessary action* (karmic intervention).

116.   Pluto in Scorpio (Fixed, yin Water sign, blue-green color-symbolism.)

Mars rules:	Enormous energy, ruthless, courageous, disregards laws and rules.
Pluto rules:	Utter regeneration, penetrating consciousness, drive to purge and reconstruct the ego.
Uranus exalted:	Penetrating insight, clairvoyance, disruptive compassion.
Venus in detriment:	Ruthless, destructive, cruel, lustful, unloving.
Moon in detriment:	A loner, rigid, ingenious but set in ways, emotional crises.

Pluto will reach perihelion, its closest approach to the Sun and its greatest speed, at 17° Scorpio in 1990. During the intense period of its transit through Scorpio (1984-1996) we will feel the psychic consequences of the "I-Thou" social contract being transformed. Ongoing revaluation of "Mine-Thine" boundaries will give the leverage to pry open our subconscious motivations (symbolized by the Moon and Venus). Throughout the vast network of society, wherever separate psyches interface, each person will see as in a mirror his or her own dark side clearly reflected in the other's light. In many, inner barriers will be burnt away and psychic powers will become obvious. From under centuries of cultural sediment, the roots of evil will be exposed, roots that feed those parasitic elements of our collective life which we have refused to integrate with their proper complements. Natives of this period must learn to transform their craving for invulnerability into a thirst for truth. They must link strongly with Uranus,

Aquarian-age messenger of truth, which will be in Sagittarius, Capricorn and Aquarius during this time. (Compare nos. 93-95, above.)

117.   Pluto in Sagittarius (Mutable, yang Fire sign, blue color-symbolism.)

Jupiter rules:	Spiritual regeneration, profound hope, penetrating judgment, prophetic powers.
Mercury in detriment:	Obsessive or fanatical, impractical extremes, must learn to think *thoroughly.*
No planet in exaltation or in fall:	Adventurous, many irons in the fire.

With the turn of the millennium Pluto will approach alignment with the center of our galaxy (at 26° Sagittarius), that higher-order "Sun" about which our solar system slowly orbits. Spiritual energies of a very high order will be focused into our system through Pluto's narrow, intense lens, bringing to many people direct perception of the subtle vibrations of Ether or Akasha. Political and religious distinctions will be burnt to their roots by the heat of realization of the true inner unity of religious ardor and nationalistic faith. Although, like dinosaurs, they may take time to fall, from this time both church and state will be obsolete. Natives of this period, as they come of age in the 21st century, must transform their obsession with freedom into the enormous skill needed to teach mankind to be free together in synergy.

118.   Pluto in Capricorn (Cardinal, yin Earth sign, indigo color-symbolism.)

Saturn rules:	Persistent, patient, moralistic, keen acumen, transformation through career, regenerates commercial values.
Mars exalted:	Ambitious, persistent, courage to discard the outmoded.
Moon in detriment:	Unfeeling, lack of concern for others, lack of public interest.
Jupiter in fall:	Strong will, a loner, power-seeking, feels inadequate, career changes, lost business opportunities.

Like a forest fire that in its ecological role destroys underbrush and smaller trees but leaves the largest and strongest, Pluto's influence during this period will clear away the tangle of conflicting institutions, leaving only the great sequoias of the social order with roots deep in prehistory. Those who could not or would not attune to the "sounding of the trumphet" when Pluto was in Sagittarius will think this a great catastrophe, as the familiar saplings and vines of commerce and politics are turned to ash and swept away by the fiery winds of change. They must make way for the clear expression in society of the psychic and spiritual forces set in vibration in resonance with that call to freedom, arising from the archetypal roots of the social order, roots of those towering sequoias now obscured to our vision, which were seeded in previous ages, when Pluto's power was a part of the constitution of humanity. This generation will be obsessed with "the renewal of all things which are begun afresh in the creation of the world."

119.   Pluto in Aquarius (Fixed, yang Air sign, violet color-symbolism.)

Saturn rules:	Keen judgment, moralistic, perhaps judgmental, good common sense, no excesses, reliable, great stamina when goal is clear.
Uranus rules:	Scientific/metaphysical, inventive, original, intuitive, prophetic, disruptive compassion.
Mercury exalted:	Intuitive, original, disciplined, penetrating mentality, self-sufficient, uses others to advantage.
Sun in detriment:	Detachment from human cares, compensatory strong will covers feelings of inferiority.
Neptune in fall:	Lacks compassion, does not understand devotion.

This will be a time of outward healing, ministering to the wounds in the body politic resulting from the many challenges to humanity for growth. During this period, these very difficult lessons will be interpreted, translated into terms that various beleaguered groups can understand and share. Few will still doubt that they are irrevocable and irreversible, but all must come to understand them as positive growth. The keynote will be discovery, sharing and participation in the benefits of changes that will have occurred. Science, with increased popular support, will greatly expand its exploration of both outer and inner space. The generation born during this period will be obsessed with the experience of synergy. Their personal needs and desires will be transmuted, perhaps unconsciously, into catalysts for harmonious co-evolution.

120.   Pluto in Pisces (Mutable, yin Water sign, red-violet color-symbolism.)

Jupiter rules:	Compassionate, generous, profound understanding, penetrating wisdom, spiritual discipline.
Neptune rules:	Compassionate, unselfish, regeneration through sacrifice of ego, psychic.
Venus exalted:	Compassionate, understands law of love, profoundly creative, regeneration of/through imagination.

*Mercury in detriment
and in fall:* ·   Sensitive nervous system, obsessed by
                                         subjective experiences, destructive
                                         repressions, extremes of sacrifice.

This will be a time of inner healing. During this period, humanity will relinquish its fascination with arcane hardware for exploration and exploitation. Paradoxically, as one branch of science is frustrated in its probing of outer space with machines, which are limited to physical laws and the speed of light, scientists of inner space will discover the freedom to explore those same outer, physical realms psychically. Ways will be discovered to experiment, test and verify results with the inner, nonphysical senses. Science will be freed from the blind alley of extending the physical senses with elaborate hardware, which only shackles the mind. Natives of this period will be obsessed with reconciliation. It will be for them to enact on a planetary scale the fundamental lesson of karma: "When you give it up, you get it back tenfold." What is given up is merely the egocentric demanding which distorts perception and action. Desires, when purged of egotism, are realized as parts of the orderly unfolding of the universe. As such, they are fulfilled literally beyond one's expectations, because egocentric presuppositions would have prevented their fulfillment from being recognized. Only in this spirit may the true power of Pluto as the higher octave of Mars be realized in the excitement of humanity's renewed exploration and discovery of the universe, as Pluto again enters Aries.

As you read the characteristics that astrologers have learned to associate with various planet-sign combinations, ask yourself which distinctive features of the sign they are due to—the element, the mode, the gender, the ruler, detriment, exaltation or fall? What can you discover in the language of astrology?

Some positions of Pluto, Neptune and perhaps Uranus will not occur in the birth charts of people you know. You may use the corresponding descriptive paragraphs for historical study. There are also ways to use this information with living acquaintances. You and your friend may both have Pluto in Virgo, but suppose you have Aries rising and she has Virgo rising, with Pluto on her Ascendant: In some respects your relationship would be like your having Pluto in Aries.

This chapter provides a framework for synthesizing and applying all the material of the first four chapters of this book. So far, this has been a static view of the horoscope as a kind of fixed "snapshot" of your energy pattern at the moment of birth, frozen in memory. It is limited to the three dimensions of space. Chapter 6 develops the fourth dimension, time, the axis of dynamic change and flow.

Implicit in all of this is another and more mysterious fifth dimension, the axis of evolution. You may think of it as the dimension of perfection, or of degrees of realization. The ultimate point of this book is your own self-unfoldment on this fifth dimension.

6

Cycles and Harmonics in Your Life

So far in this book, we have looked at your horoscope as a "snapshot" of the energies present at your birth. We have ignored the fourth dimension, time. In this chapter, we will explore the time dimension of your horoscope. You will learn how astrological cycles affect you and influence your experiences in your circle of houses. You will learn how the energies of the planets and the rhythms of their individual cycles overlap and harmonize with one another, just as sound vibrations are combined in music.

Through our exploration of cycles and their harmonics, we will come to a proper understanding of aspects, the angular relationships in your "snapshot" horoscope. This is an area of astrology that is subject to confusion and mystification in much of the astrological literature.

A cycle is a process that repeats itself rhythmically, over and over. Every day, the Sun, the Moon, each of the planets and each of the signs of the the zodiac in turn rises over the eastern horizon, passes through the sky, sets in the west and returns on the other side of the Earth from you. This diurnal (daily) cycle is based on the Earth's rotation on its axis. Every month, the Moon cycles through the zodiac as it orbits around the Earth. Every year the Sun does so, due to the Earth's orbital motion. Each of the planets moves through the zodiac at its own pace, determined by the planet's orbit around the Sun, combined with the Earth's changing orbital position through the year.

The point of studying these cycles is to increase your freedom of choice. As you increase your awareness of how they manifest as changing energies and potentials in your life, you also increase your ability to choose how they will manifest in your behavior and your experiences. You can learn to emphasize those characteristics of a given cycle that are desirable to you, and to transmute those that seem less desirable. The same universal rhythms will still reverberate through your personal powers and faculties, but you will be more able to choose how your personality will experience them and express them.

The Cycle through the Houses

We will look at the cycles of planets through the houses of your natal horoscope first, because you are familiar with looking at planets in various houses. We have been referring to the circle of houses as "the cycle of experience" from the beginning of this book. Now you will see why.

As the planets transit (pass through) the zodiac, eventually they get to the point that was on the eastern horizon when you were born. When a planet crosses your natal Ascendant, it begins a cycle through your circle of houses. As it passes through each house in turn, you tend to apply its energies, and the corresponding faculty of your personality, primarily to the area of experience represented by that house. The cycle through the houses, therefore, has to do with your application of available planetary energies, whereas the return cycle, which we will consider in the next section, refers to your access to those energies, and to changes in their strength and quality.

To illustrate the cycle through the houses, suppose you had 15° Sagittarius rising. Every winter around the sixth of December you would experience the beginning of your subjective spring season, as the Sun crossed your natal Ascendant. For about three months, the Sun would be in the first quadrant of your circle of houses. During that time, your awareness of your inner life-purpose (the Sun) and your efforts to find appropriate means for expressing it would be focused on yourself as a person: on your self-image, your style, your personal values and other matters associated with the first three houses.

In late February or early March, when the Sun crossed into your fourth house (still assuming that you have Sagittarius rising), your new ways of expressing yourself would come into increasing conflict with the image of you that is familiar to your family. There is a tendency during this time to "regress" to the more comfortable ways of being that preceded the new developments in this current cycle. Old images of you in the eyes of others, like ghosts, come back to haunt you. Both the old and the new selves may seem equally unfamiliar by turns. There is a need to integrate the old with the new; not only to create a new way of being that is more true to your inner self than your old way, but to retain and renew what is valid from prior cycles.

About the ninth of June, as the Sun crossed your Descendant and entered your natal seventh house, one-to-one relationships would become more vital and more important to you. Your newly-integrated self-image emerges fully into your interactions with others, having been given a "test run" three months earlier when the Sun was in your fourth house. If you avoided the task of integration then, you will experience difficulties in your relationships at this time.

In late August or early September (if you had Sagittarius rising), the Sun would cross your Midheaven and enter the fourth quadrant of your cycle of houses. At this time you would express your inner purpose primarily in connection with your status and reputation in the eyes of others. If your position in society is based upon an image of yourself that no longer fits you, and if you were unsuccessful in integrating your new growth in this cycle with the results of earlier cycles, this can be a distressing period. It is difficult to accept the gratification and rewards of a person you used to be but no longer are. On the other hand, if you were successful in integrating your new growth into your established ways of living and being, this is a time to enjoy the fruits of your efforts to rediscover and express your inner life-purpose.

Toward the end of the fourth quadrant, as the Sun passes through your twelfth house, there comes a time when your image of yourself fades and your sense of inner purpose seems more and more unreal. It is a time when you are more suggestible than usual, and perhaps more impatient to find the real meaning of your life. This is the end of your subjective winter season, with spring coming on; you need to take care which seeds are planted in your consciousness at this time. Look within yourself for the first glimmerings of direction for your life. Set aside time for meditation on the meaning of your Sun sign during the week or so when the Sun is crossing your Ascendant.

The same principles apply to all the planets as they transit your circle of houses. To determine the timing of these transits you will need an ephemeris. I recommend *The American Ephemeris*, by Neil Michelson (Astro Computing Service, distributed by Para Research). A sample page from this ephemeris is given in Appendix 3, together with an explanation of its use.

I can also highly recommend Rob Hand's *Planets in Transit* for suggested interpretations of planetary transits (see the Bibliography).

Exercise 1: Review the symbolism of the cycle of houses in Chapter 1 and in your notebook.

In the Sun section of your notebook, list the twelve house cusps of your horoscope; next to each, write the date that the Sun transits that point in the course of the year. Underline the angular cusps, the cusps of the first, fourth, seventh and tenth houses. Using the dated entries in your notebook, review the events of the past year in terms of your solar cycle. Don't try to attribute every event and change of attitude to the solar transits—there are after all nine other planets, and at least one other major type of cycle to consider—but notice when the major shifts of emphasis occured, when the Sun crossed one of the angles into a new quadrant, and meditate on events at that time.

When did the current cycle of the Sun through your houses begin? Where are you in that cycle now? Look for signs of the current phase of this cycle in your daily experiences. What is coming up in the near future? What house is the Sun currently transiting? Is this an area of experience with increased vitality and interest for you at this time?

Suggestions for further meditation: In your ephemeris, determine the position of Saturn at the present time. What sign is it in? What degree of that sign? What house of your horoscope does this degree fall in? Where is the cusp of this house? When did Saturn enter this house? Meditate on the part of your life that this house symbolizes. Is this an area where you are experiencing increased responsibility at this time? Determine the date when Saturn will enter the next house. Review your meditation notes for the period that it has been in this house. Reconstruct what has been going on for you during this period.

Which quadrant of your horoscope is this house in? From the ephemeris, determine the date of Saturn's entry into this quadrant (the date when it last crossed an angular cusp). Were there important changes of direction in your life at this time?

Determine the date when Saturn crossed your Ascendant last, beginning the current cycle through the houses, and the dates of its entry into each new quadrant since then. When will Saturn cross your Midheaven and enter your tenth house, so that you experience the fruits of this cycle? Meditate on your career development in terms of the Saturn cycle.

Saturn is treated first because its cycle is generally more obvious in people's lives, providing the basic framework and context for developing one's social role.

Where is Jupiter now in your cycle of houses? Does this house represent an area of your life in which you are particularly aware of opportunities for growth and expansion? When did Jupiter enter this house, and when will it leave? What can you find relating to Jupiter in your meditation notes for this period? When did Jupiter enter this quadrant? Was this a significant period of openness and ease in your life? When did Jupiter cross your Ascendant, beginning this cycle through your houses, and when did/will it cross an angular cusp into each of the four quadrants? What can this pattern teach you, in meditation, about your cycles of growth and learning?

Where is Mars now in your cycle of houses? Does this house represent an area of your life in which you are particularly able to take care of your needs with aggressive energy; or does it represent issues about which you are currently particularly prone to show impatience? Review the dates of Mars moving through your quadrants and houses. How have your applications of your Mars energy acted as triggers or focal points for the release of energies from the slower planetary cycles?

Consider one of the experiences that you have linked with the positions of the planets, above. Where in your cycle of houses were the Sun, Mercury and Venus at that time? Do they tell you anything about your motivation, interest and assignment of personal value to that experience?

The transpersonal planets Uranus, Neptune and Pluto move too slowly to be considered in terms of the whole cycle through the houses. Their influence is felt more through other cycles, to be considered below. Nevertheless, you may fruitfully ask similar questions about their transits through your cycle of houses. What houses are they in now? When did they enter those houses, and when will they move to the next? In the house Uranus is transiting, what unexpected, startling changes are going on? Do unexpected events here challenge you to shift your perceptions to a different perspective on a higher level? In the house Neptune is transiting, how is your self-worth being questioned, along what paths does your wishful thinking wander, and how does your egotism lead you into confusion? In the house Pluto is transiting, what radical experiences of death and rebirth, destruction and reconstruction, purging and renewal, are you undergoing? Review events of the preceding phases, when these planets were in the next prior houses. Does this review give you more ideas of the kinds of experience to look for now?

If you wish, meditate on the house positions of Neptune and Pluto prior to your birth as indicators of past-life patterns. Where are Neptune and Pluto likely to be at the end of your current lifetime?

Planetary Return Cycles

The second major type of astrological cycle that we will look at is defined by the location of a planet at the time you were born. When the planet returns to its natal position, one return cycle is completed and another begins. Whereas the cycle through the houses indicates how and where you apply the energies symbolized by the planet, the return cycle indicates the waxing and waning of the energies themselves, or, rather, the changing quantity and quality of your access to planetary energies through your horoscope.

Let me make an analogy. When you are driving your car and listening to the radio, the reception will vary, depending upon your location. It is the same with your horoscope. Your strongest "reception" of a planet's energies is when it returns to its natal position, with lesser peaks elsewhere in the cycle, to be discussed presently. (For now, ignore the planet's cycle through the zodiac, according to where it is exalted, which sign it rules and so on, which provides a kind of background variability, like the strengthening and weakening of signals on your radio at home.)

The position or phase of a planet in its return cycle tells you what energies are available to you, and its position within the cycle of houses tells you what you are doing with those energies. The planetary return cycles are keyed to the zodiac, so they operate on a higher level or deeper level than the cycle through the houses.

Near your birthday, the Sun transits (passes over) the place where it was when you were born. This event is called your solar return. If you are attuned to what you really want in life, this is a time for celebration and personal renewal. The form of the celebration and renewal is indicated by the house the Sun is in, and the nature of the inspiration, which is really a renewal of your inner life-purpose, as indicated by the sign.

However, if you are not following your deepest (solar) motivation and are not on "a path with heart," the intensification of your inner life-purpose at this time may manifest in unhappinesss or depression. You might avoid anything connected with the house the Sun is in because you would find it "too depressing," especially on your birthday! Ironically, you would be avoiding exactly the issues with which you most need to get in touch.

Each of your planetary powers and faculties has a "birthday" when the corresponding planet returns to its natal position. This is a time for refocusing that part of yourself and recharging its batteries, a time for renewing and reaffirming the role played by that faculty in the life-pattern that you assumed when you were born.

Every cycle has phases. We will look at planetary return cycles in terms of two phases, waxing and waning; four phases, like the four quarters of the Moon; and twelve phases, like the cycle of the houses or of the zodiac.

The easiest way to represent these phases would be to divide the circle first into halves, then into quadrants, and finally into twelve phases, as we did in Chapter 1. We already have the circle of houses laid over the circle of the zodiac, each divided in a different way into twelve phases. To try to add to this composite map called a horoscope another twelve phases, or even just four quadrants, for each planet's return cycle, would be impossibly confusing.

Instead, let us look at another way of representing astrological cycles. In figure 102, the horizontal line represents the dimension of time from left to right. The sine wave curving across the center line represents the waxing and waning phases of a cycle, and shows the changing intensity or quality of the planet's energies in some way as yet to be defined.

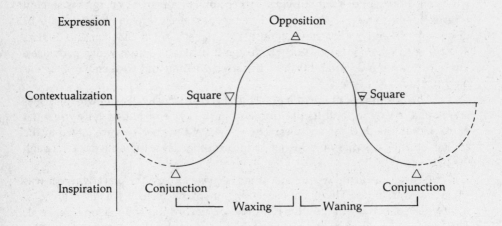

Figure 102. Graph of a planetary return cycle

The alchemical elements archetypally represent four phases of every creative process (see the introduction to Chapter 5). Their symbols are drawn at four critical points in figure 102. The waxing phase begins at the lowest point of the curve with an intention or an initiating impulse (Fire). It proceeds into manifestation by interaction with pre-existing patterns (Water). The challenge of the status quo is greatest at the point where the curve crosses the center line. Because it is 90° from the starting point, this phase is called a square, or, more precisely, the waxing square in the cycle.

At the peak of the cycle, after it has been modified to "make sense" in pre-established terms (Water), the original Fiery impulse must mesh with all the other cycles and processes (Air) that are implicated by your activities giving expression to it. This "full-Moon" phase is called opposition.

Finally, at the waning square or "third-quarter" phase, a new "status quo" is established embodying the results of the cycle (Earth).

Let's look at an example. Suppose you were born with the Sun at 12° Taurus. The starting point of your solar cycle (called conjunction) would occur about the third of May, when the Sun transited conjunct its natal position. You would experience a revitalization of your inner motivation as a Taurus, in the particular manner indicated by the Sun's house position in your horoscope. This would involve the stewardship of material possessions, practical values and kindred Taurean issues.

During the next three months, as you sought ways to express your inner motivation, you would increasingly have to grapple with established standards of artistry, pre-existing conventions regarding what constitutes effective self-expression. This would come to a peak around the third of August, when the Sun transited the waxing square of the cycle, at 12° Leo. Your own performance in prior cycles might come back to haunt you, so to speak, bidding comparison either to tell you that the new inspiration of the cycle does not measure up to your past achievements, or that you could not measure up to established standards of excellence in prior cycles, so why try now? The pressure for conformity peaks at just the point when the original inspiration seems weakest (where the curve crosses the center line in figure 102).

At the waxing square, you are deeply involved in creating structures to express your new realization of your inner identity and purpose; so deeply involved that you are more clearly aware of the mechanics of expression than you are of the original inspiration that you set out to express. For this reason, circumstances test the validity of the aims that you undertook three months earlier, at the conjunction.

During the next three months, as the Sun transits Leo, Virgo, Libra and the first part of Scorpio, the pressure for conformity would lessen and you would once again feel your individuality more strongly. Your sense of inner purpose would re-assert itself in forms that are easier to exteriorize and examine objectively than they were six months earlier, at the conjunction, often being reflected back to you from other people through your relationships and interactions with them. Taurean issues of stewardship versus ownership are even more intensely expressed in Scorpio, and they would come to a head around the third of November when the Sun transited the opposition phase of your solar return cycle. You would be forced to put your principles into practice. Whatever structures you had built in the waxing half of the cycle to express your unique approach to these issues might or might not serve you well at this point, depending upon how well you had integrated the new with the old at the time of the waxing square, when the Sun was in Leo.

The first half of the waning phase of the cycle involves you increasingly with the establishment of a new "status quo." Like the waxing square, the waning square marks the peak of a period of regression or conservatism. This is a rather matter-of-fact time of assessment and summing-up, cutting one's losses if the earlier crisis-points were not successfully negotiated, capitalizing on your enhanced position and reputation in the world if you did well with the earlier transitions. If you have compromised too much, the rewards of your position may seem empty to you. Your identity in the eyes of society may be a source of pain or inner conflict for you. On the other hand, if you failed to integrate your sense of individuality with the available means for expressing it, your experience at this time might range from aggravated frustration at being "misunderstood" and unappreciated, with a reintensified desire to discover and express your unique contribution to the world, to discouragement and despair because your life was not working.

In the last three months of your solar return cycle, there is increased detachment as you disengage the energies which you had invested in various structures and activities. This is a process of freeing yourself and your solar energies for a new cycle, which intensifies as the conjunction of the solar return cycle approaches.

All the imagery which applies to the cycle of houses or the zodiac also applies to planetary return cycles. The energies of the planet sprout from a seed-point at the conjunction, with branch, leaf and root (waxing square), then flower (opposition) and fruit (waning square) bearing within it a new seed. The cycles can be broken down into twelve phases or more, as you will see in the discussion of the aspect cycle later in this chapter.

A tremendous amount can be learned about cycles from the symbolism and imagery associated with the signs and houses. For example, let's look at the mode, element and gender of signs at the four "crisis points" of the planetary return cycle. All four signs must share the same mode, since they are 90° apart. In the example, Taurus, Leo, Scorpio and Aquarius are all fixed signs. The two squares are in signs with the opposite gender from the conjunction or starting point, while the opposition or midpoint has the same gender. At the first square, ghosts of past achievements come back to "haunt" you, in a sign with the same gender as the waning square in the previous cycle. At the opposition, when the life-structures you built in the waxing half-cycle are publicly "unveiled" as it were, your original motivation is echoed in a sign of the same gender, parallel yet with a subtle reversal, as in a mirror. It is somewhat like watching someone put on a garment you had made for yourself, or seeing someone else drive off in your car. It is an ideal time for getting feedback from others, directly or indirectly, about the meaning of this planet in your horoscope and in your life.

At the waning square, an element of opposite gender again appears. The conflict of genders, yin and yang, like the symbolism of Sun and Moon, is the essential tension that makes the creative process possible. Each gender conditions the other and is conditioned by it. The contradictory gender of the signs at the waxing and waning squares represents the circumstances and limitations of the world with which the individual must interact. At the waxing square, it represents a subjective aspect of the world, as suggested by the symbolism of Cancer and the fourth house; at the waning square, it represents the objective world of social institutions, congruent with the symbolism of Capricorn and the tenth house.

In terms of your access to the energies of the planet, there is a peak at conjunction and opposition, and a low point at each of the two squares. At the low points, the squares, you are subject to being "haunted" by ghosts of other cycles. At the waxing square, previous successes (or failures) distract you; at the waning square, you may have premonitions of the cycle to come. The long-range challenge is for you to develop continuity among all the repetitions of a given planetary return cycle, so that they build on one another, rather than conflicting, and the challenges become more productive and less disruptive.

Planetary cycles differ in length. The Moon takes about twenty-eight days, just short of a month, to cycle through the zodiac. The Sun, Mercury and Venus all have return cycles about a year in length. Mars takes about two years, Jupiter almost twelve, Saturn about twenty-nine and Uranus about eighty-four. Neptune and Pluto have return cycles of one hundred sixty-five and two hundred forty-eight years, respectively, longer than the usual human life-expectancy.

These cycles overlap in very revealing ways. Figure 103 shows the return cycles of all the planets except the Sun, Moon, Mercury and Venus; if they were included, you would see nothing but dense black lines, almost solid ink, because they are too fast for a graph on this scale. Only part of the cycles of Neptune and Pluto are shown, because they are so long. Pluto is shown together with Neptune, and again, parenthetically, with a much longer dotted curve, because its cycle is so irregular. At present, Pluto's cycle corresponds rather closely to that of Neptune.

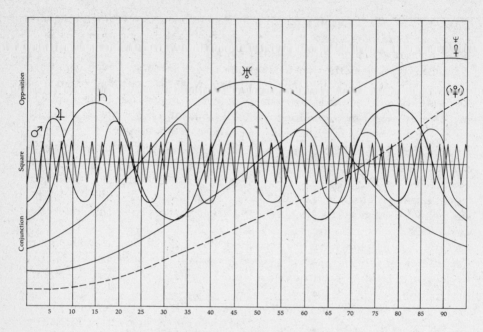

Figure 103. A lifespan of planetary cycles

Each planetary cycle is represented by a sine wave; conjunctions with the natal position are at the troughs of waves, and oppositions at the peaks; the waxing phase rises from trough to peak, and the waning phase falls from peak to trough; the squares occur where the sine wave crosses the center line.

Any of these four points in a cycle may mark times of high energy and/or transition for a person, especially where more than one coincide. Look at figure 103. Do you see where times of transition or challenge might occur? There are many books and articles available now on predictable crises in adult life, such as Gail Sheehy's best-seller *Passages.* Lois Rodden has written a fine article in the *Journal of Geocosmic Research* correlating such research with astrological cycles (see the Bibliography).

To become more intimately acquainted with these patterns, draw your own version of the life-span graph in figure 103. In an ephemeris, look up the times when the planets actually form squares, oppositions and conjunctions to their natal positions in your own horoscope. These will not always be the times indicated in figure 103, because the speed of planetary cycles is not constant. For a person born around 1900, the midpoint of the Uranus cycle came at around age forty-six, but for a person born in 1950 it will come at age forty. A person born in 1900 experienced the waxing square of Pluto around age sixty-five, but a person born in 1950 will experience it at about age thirty-nine! (Pluto has the most irregular orbit of all the planets, and is currently moving at its greatest speed, inside the orbit of Neptune.)

Exercise 2:   See Appendix 3 for instructions on the use of an ephemeris. Using your ephemeris, determine the date when Jupiter last returned to its natal position in your horoscope. What was happening in your life at that time? Was this a period of special opportunity to broaden and deepen your experience? Did you experience renewed interest in education or travel, or in expanding your business? Review your material on Jupiter and on the sign and house it is located in for other ideas about this time.

Determine when Jupiter transited the waxing square, the "first-quarter" phase, about three years later. Was your optimism and ambition challenged by circumstances? Had you taken on too many ambitious projects in the interim, in addition to the ones you were inspired to begin at the time of your Jupiter return? If there were difficulties and challenges, how did you cope with them? Review your material on the sign and house Jupiter was transiting at the time for other ideas about this period.

Determine the date when Jupiter last reached opposition to its natal position. Were your projects again demanding extra attention, time and energy, perhaps beyond your capacity? Did you feel obligated to prove or demonstrate your capacities to others? Did someone feel threatened by your ambitiousness, or did someone challenge your optimism? Review your material on the sign and house opposite Jupiter's natal placement for other ideas about this period.

Determine the date when Jupiter last reached the waning square in its return cycle, the "third-quarter" phase. Refer back to your reconstruction of the preceding conjunction, the beginning of that cycle; how much of your original inspiration survived for you to enjoy? How well had you balanced optimism and practicality? Was this a retrospective time? Did you feel appreciation of your growth and development over the preceding nine years, or did you feel regret at opportunities missed and energies squandered? Review your material on the sign and house Jupiter was transiting at this time for other ideas about this period. (You may have to reconstruct the Jupiter cycle before the one you are currently in to complete this exercise.)

Suggestions for further meditation: To explore this cycle in greater depth, divide it into twelve phases, as though the conjunction at Jupiter's natal position were the start of Jupiter's own "zodiac." Use the familiar symbolism of the houses and signs to help you understand the intermediate phases of Jupiter's return cycle, between the four "quarter-phases" with which you have already worked. Review your astrological journal and your memories of events at the indicated times.

Exercise 3:   Determine the date when Saturn last returned to its natal position in your horoscope. Was this a time when you experienced an especially strong sense of responsibility for the purpose and direction of your life? Did you feel that events were "fated" in some way? Did you feel that the choices you made at this time were especially decisive, directing your life-span for many years to come; or do you feel that now, looking back?

Consider the time of the waxing square, about seven years later. Was this a time of questioning and self-doubt? Did you wonder whether or not the choices you had made in the previous seven years were good for you in the long run? Were you particularly vulnerable to challenge and criticism from competitors or superiors? How did you handle career issues in your life at that time?

Determine the time of Saturn's last opposition to its natal position, about fourteen years after the start of the cycle. Did you experience more responsibilities than usual in your life at that time? Was the work and responsibility rewarding or onerous? Can you relate your answers to these questions to the testing you experienced at the time of the waxing square about seven years earlier? If you experienced especially heavy burdens then, without a sense of fulfillment, did that feeling stem from conflicts that you were unable to resolve adequately? What had you made of yourself during the first fourteen years of this Saturn cycle, and what messages had you communicated about yourself as a consequence in your interactions with other people?

When did Saturn last transit the waning square (third-quarter phase) of its return cycle? At that time, how did you experience the meaning and value of your development over the previous twenty-one years? How did you feel about the feedback you got about yourself from the world at this time? What had you made of yourself, and what did you wish you had made of yourself? Did your responsibilities take the form of harvesting and distributing the benefits of your success, or were you concerned rather with clearing away fragments of failures and partial successes? Was this an "up" time or a "down" time for you?

Exercise 4:   The waxing square or "first-quarter" phase of the Uranus cycle occurred about the time of the waning square in your Saturn cycle, in your early twenties. Was this a time of radical reorientation for you, a time when you felt a need to question what others took for granted? Or was this a time when you felt a need to reaffirm traditional values or to conform to the social consensus because the undercurrent of change was threatening to you? Your choice of how to experience this transit may have been conditioned in part by the relative timing of the Jupiter and Saturn transits just mentioned.

The opposition phase comes around age forty, just before the second opposition in the Saturn cycle. This is the middle of what Gail Sheehy calls the "deadline decade." If you have experienced this transit, use your astrological journal to help you reconstruct events at that time. Was this a time of contentment with your achievements? Were you happy to bring your outward exploration and rebellion to a close and turn to inner exploration and the spiritual meaning of your life? Or was it a time of urgent attempts at rejuvenation, your last chance, before your time is up, to realize opportunities you were afraid you had wasted?

Uranus represents the eternal youth in us, pictured in Tarot as The Fool. Have you experienced the freedom of the untrammelled spirit in your life, or have you become stuck in some imagined model of adulthood, on a path without heart for you?

The waning square of the Uranus cycle comes in your early sixties, the time marked as a typical retirement age in our culture. The question here is: are you dependent upon your socio-economic role for the meaning of your existence? Or were you successful at earlier phases of this cycle in rebelling against your cultural conditioning and turning inward for the spiritual meaning of your life?

Learn what you can from the experiences of other people at these later stages of their life cycles, if they are still in the future for you.

The Uranus return occurs at about age eighty-four. At this point, people feel less inhibited and more free to "speak their mind." Generally, purely mundane issues of sustenance and social role are of much less concern than they are for younger people, and a higher perspective opens on life. Life is viewed in a more spiritual context, and consequently is much more enjoyable. The "wisdom of age" includes sharpened intuitive perception. As other faculties dim, making it less and less easy to "do something" about things, intuition discloses the underlying ecological unity of events so that there is less felt need to change anything.

Exercise 5:   The waxing square of Neptune's return cycle comes at about age forty-two, in the middle of the "deadline decade." Jupiter, Saturn and Uranus all reach opposition in their respective cycles at about this same time. What unfulfilled dreams come back to haunt you, glamorous visions of your unrealized potential? What happens to your ability to discriminate clearly between reality and illusion?

Neptune comes to the opposition phase of its return cycle in your mid-eighties, at about the same time as your Uranus return. How do people deal with the "transvaluation of values," and its attendant confusion, that occurs at this time? Do they enjoy the perception of new ranges of meaning? Do they find themselves more empathic with people and situations? If they choose to retire from active life, is it because they desire rest and peace at the close of life, or because they are fearful when their old familiar values and concepts no longer "hold water"?

Because of the great eccentricity of Pluto's orbit, it reaches the waxing square of its cycle at very different ages for different people. The following table shows the age at which the waxing square occurs for people born in different decades in this century:

Birth Year	Age at which waxing square occurs
1900	64
1910	60
1920	55
1930	50
1940	45
1950	40
1960	38
1970	37
1980	39
1990	44
2000	53

This table shows how Pluto is moving faster as it approaches perihelion (when it is closest to the Sun and moving its fastest). Pluto's perihelion is at 13° Scorpio, where it will be in 1989.

Exercise 6:   When does Pluto reach the waxing square of its return cycle in your horoscope? What can you learn from the myth of the phoenix at this time? What unconscious parts of yourself might surface to be dealt with? What things in your life might be destroyed or blasted away? Can you see the unconscious roots of these issues and of their destruction (or radical regeneration) in your past actions and failures to act? How might sprouts of new life break apart the shells of the old forms?

Exercise 7:   Using your ephemeris, correlate the cycles of the faster-moving planets with those of the outer planets. Reconsider the major events and transitions that you have explored in earlier exercises in this chapter: When during those periods did major phases of the return cycles of Mars, Venus and Mercury occur? Did the energy of Mars trigger or release changes symbolized by phases of one of the slower cycles? Did the cycles of Venus relate to your personal response and evaluation of those experiences? Did the phase of your Mercury return cycle mark times when your perceptions and mental acuity were especially clear, or when you were not sure of your objectivity?

Exercise 8:   Obtain a horoscope for the precise time of your next solar return (your astrological birthday). Consider its symbolism as a forecast for the subsequent year of your life. What house is each planet in? At what phases are they in their respective return cycles? What relationships can you find between the planets at your solar return and in your natal horoscope, based upon rulerships, exaltations and other distinctive features of the planets, signs and houses?

Complex Cycles

Planetary cycles may be defined with various starting points other than the natal position and the Ascendant. The natal positions of other planets may be taken as starting points. Interpretations for transits of planets relative to the natal positions of other planets are given in Rob Hand's *Planets in Transit,* along with interpretations for twelve phases of each of the planets' return cycles.

Planets may also have cycles relative to other transiting planets. Most important among these is the relationship of the Sun and Moon. The location of the new Moon each month in your circle of houses is said to indicate an emphasis for the ensuing twenty-eight-day soli-lunar cycle; a horoscope cast for the exact time of the new Moon may be examined for its relationships with your natal horoscope to forecast the month in greater depth.

The soli-lunar return occurs when the Moon and Sun return to the exact angle that was between them when you were born, regardless of what sign or house they are in. In other words, if you were born at the first quarter of the Moon, the waxing square of the soli-lunar cycle, then the first quarter of the Moon is especially significant for you each month. The soli-lunar return has been linked with fertility in some research, and is an important factor in astrological birth control.

Retrograde Cycles

Periodically, each of the planets spends a period of time moving backward through the zodiac. This is called *retrograde* motion. It is an illusion, due to the relative speeds of the Earth and the other planets.

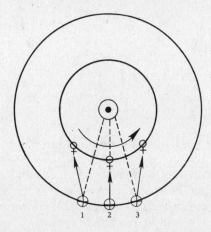

Figure 104. Retrograde motion of an inner planet

Mercury and Venus both move faster than the Earth. Figure 104 shows the positions of Earth and Venus at three separate times in their orbits around the Sun. At time 1, for an observer on the Earth, Venus appears to be in Capricorn while the Sun appears to be "behind" Venus at the cusp of Capricorn. At time 2, both Venus and the Sun are at the cusp of Capricorn together. At time 3, the Sun appears to have moved steadily onward into Capricorn, but Venus appears to have moved backward (retrograde), returning to Sagittarius. This is actually because Venus is moving faster than the Earth.

Have you ever been in your car, stopped at a light, when a bus next to you began to move forward and you thought your car was rolling backward? This is what retrograde motion is all about.

Figure 105 shows a slower planet in retrograde motion. This could be any of the planets outside Earth's orbit, from Mars to Pluto, because they move more slowly than the Earth. When the Earth is between the Sun and one of these planets, it bypasses the planet, so that the planet appears to be moving backward or retrograde for an observer on the Earth. In figure 105, at time 1, Jupiter appears to be in Cancer for an observer on the Earth, but at time 2 it appears to have moved retrograde into Gemini. In this case, it is because the Earth is moving faster.

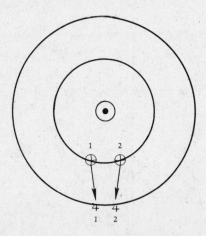

Figure 105. Retrograde motion of an outer planet

Retrograde motion occurs whenever the Earth and another planet are on the same side of the Sun. Therefore, when a planet is moving retrograde, it is at its closest approach to the Earth. This suggests that the influence of a planet may be more powerful when it is in its retrograde cycle.

Retrograde cycles have three phases, as shown in figure 106. Phase one is normal, direct motion through the zodiac. During this phase, that part of your personality that corresponds to the planet is pressing forward into new areas of experience. Gradually, its speed diminishes, and it comes to a halt (from the point of view of an Earth observer).

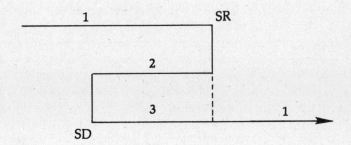

Figure 106. Three phases of the retrograde cycle

This halt is called "stationary retrograde," abbreviated "SR" in your horoscope and marked with an "R" in your ephemeris. (Note that the "R" also appears at the beginning of a month if the retrograde phase, phase two, is carried over from the previous month.) Planetary "stations" are considered to be times of especially powerful influence, perhaps because the planet stays in one location long enough for greater intensity to build up.

This station marks the beginning of phase two, wherein the planet moves backward over a portion of the zodiac that it had just transited in direct motion. It picks up speed, albeit only a fraction of its direct-motion speed, then slows to a halt again.

The second halt is called "stationary direct," abbreviated "SD" in your horoscope and marked with a "D" in your ephemeris. This station is also considered to be an especially powerful state for a planet.

It marks the beginning of phase three, the first part of the planet's renewed direct motion. During phase three, the planet advances through a part of your horoscope that it has already transited twice, once direct and once retrograde. This phase ends when the planet reaches the point at which it last turned retrograde.

Phase one is like the cardinal mode of the signs, introducing new energies and new impulses. Phase two is like the fixed mode, turning back in the contrary direction, as if to say "Wait a minute, not so fast—how did that go again?" It is a time of inward assimilation, with fewer outward challenges; it is a retrospective period, as if asking "Just how did I get here, and what was I doing anyway?," checking step by step, slowly, in reverse order. Phase three has the feeling of "Now I've got it!" or "This is a snap!" It is the shortest of the three phases of the retrograde cycle.

Think of the phases children go through. During "difficult" periods, they are testing boundaries, stretching, breaking into new territory. Then they quiet down and regress to an earlier, less challenging stage of development, while inwardly their subconscious minds are assimilating what they have learned. In this "phase two," they are usually considered "good kids" who are "well-behaved." In phase three, they suddenly seem magically to have acquired the skills that were so distressing and new in phase one. Often, the relationship between their new skills (a source of parental pride) and their earlier "misbehavior" in phase one (cause for distress or even shame) is not obvious.

The retrograde cycle may occur at any point in a planet's return cycle or its cycle through your houses. The relationship between Mars' return cycle and its retrograde cycles could account for many "problem children." Little or no research has been done in this area, however. If you were interested, you could easily put together a very interesting article for an astrological journal, correlating cycles of "behavior problems" with the interaction of these two cycles of Mars.

Retrograde planets have been a murky area for astrologers. In my own horoscope, the five outer planets (Jupiter through Pluto) are all retrograde. For me, this correlates with a tendency to "preview" areas of experience and growth before they happen. For example, during the year or so preceding my Saturn return, I made some new friends (Saturn is in my eleventh house) through whom I was exposed to Tarot and astrology in a superficial way, and I bought several books on these subjects. When I realized that to learn these things adequately required more time and energy than I was prepared at that time to invest, I sold the books back to a used bookstore; but not until I had had a preview of an area of learning and experience which in fact became very important to me in the years following my Saturn return.

Another example concerns a project I am actively engaged in with a computer programmer, developing programs that will enable computers to use English in a normal, natural way in their interactions with people. This is based upon proposals I made in my Master's thesis in linguistics at the University of Pennsylvania in 1970. At that time computers were not capable of what I wanted to do; nor was I capable of coping with the psychological, social and political stresses of the research and development period that must come first. Experiences in the ensuing ten years have opened the way, and have taught me many things, such as patience. I feel like I am returning from exile.

But is it not rather that my characteristic approach to life involves the three stages of the retrograde cycle? After an advance into new territory, providing a glimpse of vistas to come, I characteristically turn to an incubation period during which the necessary groundwork is done, through experiences which often seem unrelated to the achievement I had "previewed." When the time comes at last, the way opens, the strengths and means are at hand, I re-cross the old ground with accelerating speed (whereas the first time I had been slowing down, finding increasing resistance), and move on into new territory with assurance, with a running start, as it were.

Exercise 9:   With your ephemeris, determine where each of your planets is in the retrograde cycle. Is it approaching stationary retrograde (SR), slowing down as it passes through a part of the zodiac which it will shortly be traversing in retrograde motion? To find out, look ahead in the ephemeris, past the date when the planet turns stationary retrograde, through the period of retrograde motion, and locate the date when it is stationary direct. If this SD point is earlier in the zodiac than the planet was when you were born, then your planet is in phase one; if the planet had not yet reached its future SD point when you were born, then it is still in phase three in your horoscope. If you have a planet in retrograde motion or stationary retrograde, then it is of course in phase two. Stationary direct is the beginning of phase three (see figure 106).

When you have determined where each planet is in its retrograde cycle, review your notes on each planet in turn, and see how the symbolism of the retrograde cycle fits with your experience of the corresponding faculty in the personality and in your affairs. Remember that retrograde planets are always closer to the Earth than otherwise (figures 104 and 105): are these planets stronger influences in your life? Tradition states that retrograde planets are less directly or observably expressed. Is this so? If you have "preview" or *deja vu* experiences, which planets are most involved in them, and where are they in their retrograde cycles?

For further investigations, you may want to study transits from the point of view of the retrograde cycle. This may have bearing on mass astrology (the astrology of humanity as a whole, or of masses of people). Everyone experiences retrogradation of the transiting planets at the same times each year. Retrogradation of the outer planets begins when the Sun is two-thirds through the waxing phase of its cycle relative to the planet (more exactly, when it is roughly 100° to 110° later in the zodiac). Retrograde motion is fastest when the Sun is opposite the planet. The retrograde phase ends when the Sun is two-thirds through the waning phase of its cycle relative to the planet (roughly 100° to 110° earlier in the zodiac).

Retrogradation is thus a seasonal phenomenon. Presently, the outer planets are all in autumnal signs (Libra, Scorpio and Sagittarius). As they move, the relative timing of their retrograde cycles shifts. Can you feel a release of everyone's energies as Saturn goes direct in May? This is well after the end of winter and the onset of spring. Can older relatives and friends tell you what they experienced during the years when Saturn went direct around the time of the winter solstice? Saturn's direct station in 1907 occurred in November; in 1908 and 1909 it was in December; in 1911 it was in January. Are people with Saturn retrograde in their horoscopes more susceptible to this sort of influence? These are questions to which no one has found the answers. Will you be the one to discover some new laws of nature here?

Harmonics

The pioneering astrological researcher, John Addey, has made the topic of harmonics in astrology perhaps the single most exciting and fruitful concept in the field (see the Bibliography for references). This simple concept, borrowed from the physics of music and acoustics, promises to be the cornerstone of astrological theory and research for many years.

We have dealt much with concepts of vibration and resonance in this book, even going so far as to correlate the vibrations of sound, light, and astrological entities (signs and planets). Addey's research puts all of this on a solid scientific basis.

Vibrations are graphically represented by sine waves, such as those we have seen already in this chapter. Figure 107 shows a vibration with two complete cycles in a given period of time. Directly under it, on a second line, is a vibration with four complete cycles in the same period of time. This second vibration is twice as fast as the first.

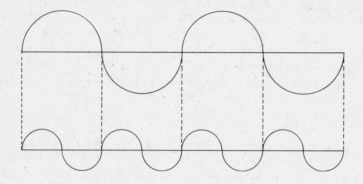

Figure 107. Two vibrations that harmonize

The lower-frequency vibration (two cycles for the given unit of time) is called the fundamental frequency or the first harmonic. The higher-frequency vibration in figure 107 is called the second harmonic relative to the first one, because it is twice as fast.

The important thing is that harmonics combine well together; they "harmonize." This is because their peaks and troughs coincide and reinforce one another.

In figure 108, notice how the crests of the second and fourth harmonics reinforce one another to produce an extra-high crest in the combined wave-form (the dotted line), followed by a slight dip. Even though the wave-pattern is no longer a simple, regular sine wave, it is still perfectly regular; it is repeated in exactly the same double-humped form, above and below the center line, for every cycle of the vibration.

Harmonics are always multiples of the fundamental frequency or first harmonic; more precisely, they are integral multiples, multiplied by one of the integers one, two, three and so on. In the fourth harmonic, which is twice as fast as the second, every other wave-crest coincides with a wave-crest of the second

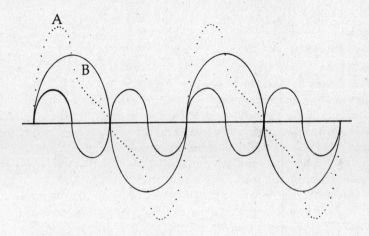

Figure 108. Second and fourth harmonics combined

harmonic, and every other trough coincides with a trough of the second harmonic. In figure 108, the hump (A) in the combined wave is the result of the two wave-crests reinforcing one another, and the dip (B) that follows it results from the trough of the fourth harmonic interfering with the crest of the second harmonic. This pattern of reinforcement and interference is perfectly regular and stays the same no matter how long the vibrations continue together.

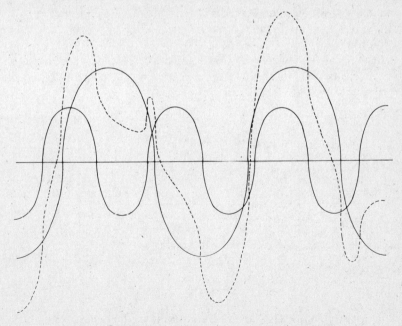

Figure 109. Two vibrations that do not harmonize

If the higher-frequency vibration were not an integral multiple of the fundamental frequency, the wave resulting from combining the two vibrations would not be a regular wave-form; the two wave-forms would not "harmonize" (figure 109).

Notice how the two vibrations in figure 109 move in and out of phase with each other in an irregular manner. The reinforcement by the higher-frequency vibration comes first at the beginning, then at either end, then in the middle of the crests of the lower-frequency vibration. The combined wave-form represents a vibration that waxes and wanes in an irregular way. In terms of sound vibration, this is like the "fluttering" quality of a dissonance, for example when you play two adjacent notes on the piano at the same time.

It is possible to look at a complex wave-form, like that in figure 108, and analyze it into its constituent harmonics. Indeed, very complex wave-forms can be analyzed into the simple sine-waves that compose them. A moog synthesizer works on this basis, since it is the relative strengths of various harmonics that give the characteristic quality or "timbre" of different musical instruments.

How does this connect with astrology? This is where the genius of John Addey comes in. Looking at graphs that showed the statistical distribution of certain planets in the circle of houses for large numbers of horoscopes (the work of the French researchers, Michel and Françoise Gauquelin), he discovered that they formed complex wave-forms that could be analyzed into simple sine-waves of varying strengths and orientations.

We will not go into Addey's findings here, they have been very well covered in his own books, and there is a fairly full discussion in *Recent Advances in Natal Astrology* and the *Larousse Encyclopedia of Astrology* (see the Bibliography).

Instead of reviewing the hard scientific evidence for harmonics in astrology, let's take a look at how the theory affects the picture of astrological cycles that we have been developing in this chapter.

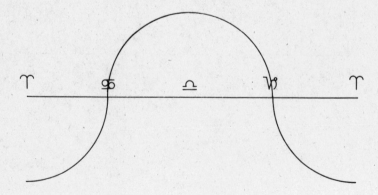

Figure 110. The first harmonic in the zodiac

Let's assume that the zodiac, an energy field around the Earth established by the Earth's relationship to the Sun, varies in intensity in a regular way. Since the zodiac begins in Aries, we can imagine a sine-wave beginning at 0° Aries, waxing through the summer signs to a peak at 0° Libra, then waning through the winter signs until it returns to 0° Aries again. This is the first harmonic in the zodiac (figure 110).

The second harmonic, beginning at 0° Aries again, waxes to a crest at 0° Cancer, wanes to a trough at 0° Libra, waxes again to a second crest at 0° Capricorn, and returns to 0° Aries (figure 111).

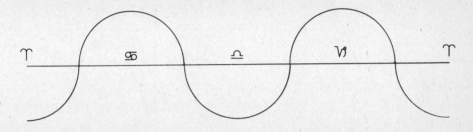

Figure 111. The second harmonic in the zodiac

The third harmonic has crests at the Air signs Gemini, Libra and Aquarius, and troughs at the Fire signs Aries, Leo and Sagittarius. (Remember to judge a thing by the direction it is moving, rather than by where it happens to be: the energy of the Fire signs is waxing, even though they are located in troughs of the wave; the diffusive quality of the Air signs is waning, even though they are located at the crests of waves. See figure 112.)

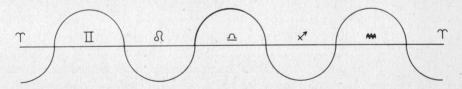

Figure 112. The third harmonic in the zodiac

Rather than show a graph for the fourth harmonic now, I will leave that for you to do. Assuming that the first waxing phase starts at 0° Aries, as with all the other harmonics, where would the first complete cycle end, and the next waxing phase begin? Divide twelve, the number of signs, by four, the number of complete cycles that the fourth harmonic will make in the zodiac.

Figure 113 shows the first four harmonics plus the sixth in one graph. The fifth harmonic is omitted because its crests and troughs do not come out evenly in the zodiac; five does not divide evenly into twelve, but one, two, three, four and six do.

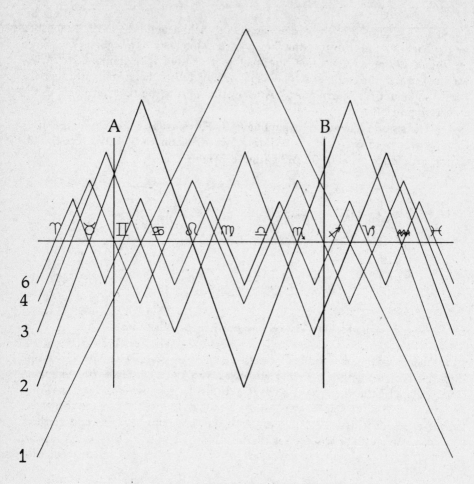

Figure 113. Five of the first six harmonics

It would be possible to make a graph showing the combined wave-form for all of these harmonics together, but it would be relatively meaningless, because we do not know the relative strengths of the harmonics. We cannot add the waves together if we do not know how strong they are.

Indeed, there is evidence that the relative strength (or "amplitude") of the harmonics depends on how we measure them. We cannot see them directly by looking up at the zodiac in the sky. If we look at the statistics of career choices, however, and use that sort of graph as our measuring device, the fourth harmonic appears to be strongest. The fourth harmonic has to do with challenge, difficulty, effort and achievement. As we look at vocations that are more creative or artistic, the third harmonic increases in importance. The third harmonic has to do with play, harmony, and an easy, intuitive flow of energy. (See John Addey's work, cited above, for more detail on this.)

Resonance among the Planets

Now, imagine planets at two positions in the zodiac; one at the cusp of Cancer and the other at the cusp of Capricorn. In figure 113, you can see that both planets would be located at a crest of the second-harmonic wave. Since they are at the same relative position on two waves of the same harmonic, they are *in resonance* with one another on the second harmonic.

Similarly, imagine a planet in Gemini at the point marked by the vertical line A in figure 113, and a second planet in Sagittarius at point B. Both planets are three-quarters through the waxing phase of a second-harmonic wave. Again, since they are at the same relative position on two waves of the second harmonic, they are in resonance with one another on the second harmonic.

Look at the cusps of Cancer and Capricorn again. Notice that troughs of the fourth harmonic are located at both these sign cusps, and that crests of the sixth harmonic are located there also. When the two planets are at the cusps of Cancer and Capricorn, respectively, they are in resonance on the fourth and sixth harmonics as well as on the second harmonic. To verify this, observe where the vertical lines A and B fall on the fourth and sixth harmonic waves; since they are in corresponding positions on both marked waves of those harmonics, they are in resonance in those positions as well.

This is because four and six are multiples of two. Two planets in resonance on the second harmonic will also be in resonance on all multiples of the second harmonic. Thus, you know that they will be in resonance on the eighth, tenth and twelfth harmonics, for example, even though these harmonics are not shown in figure 113.

Observe where positions A and B fall on the third-harmonic wave, however. A is just past the first crest of the third harmonic, and B is just past the second trough. Planets at these two points are not in resonance on the third harmonic; and three, of course, is not a multiple of two.

The relative positions where planets come into resonance with one another are called *aspects*. Aspects are usually measured in terms of angular distance, the number of signs and degrees apart the two planets are. For example the second-harmonic aspect, called the opposition, occurs when two planets are six signs or 180° apart (360° divided by 2); the third-harmonic aspect, called the trine, occurs when two planets are separated by four signs or 120° (360° divided by three) or eight signs or 240° (two-thirds of 360°).

The relative strengths of different harmonics in your horoscope help to determine your personal qualities and your character, just as the relative strengths of different harmonics in a musical sound determine the qualities or timbre of a musical instrument. That is the personal relevance of harmonics in astrology.

The Cycle of Aspects

We have looked at cycles of planets relative to the Ascendant and relative to their natal positions. In both the planetary return cycle and the cycle through the houses, the beginning/ending point is a fixed location in the zodiac.

In the cycle of aspects, the beginning/ending point of the cycle is the slower-moving of two planets. An example is the lunation cycle (or soli-lunar cycle), which ends and begins anew at the new Moon, when the Moon catches up to the Sun. The phases of the cycle of aspects (as exemplified by the phases of the Moon) are the aspects, the angles that result from dividing the 360° of the zodiac by the integers, one, two, three, four and so forth.

The traditional term "aspect" preserves the archaic meaning of "look, glance or gaze," since aspects were thought of as indicating how the planets "looked at" each other, whether they were friendly or unfriendly to each other, and so forth.

When two planets come together at the same degree of the zodiac, as the Sun and Moon do at the new Moon, they form the aspect called conjunction, resonating on the first harmonic.

The qualities of the first harmonic all stem from the root idea of union or unity. Planets in conjunction interchange and blend their energies. The slower-moving planet may be thought of as the initiator of the cycle, extracting the essence of the cycle just ended and imparting fresh inspiration to the faster-moving planet. At the new Moon, for example, the Sun is the source of inspiration and life for the ensuing lunar month, to be carried out into successive phases of manifestation by the faster-moving Moon.

As the planets move apart from conjunction, they move progressively through the cycle of aspects. The aspects are listed below in the order of the harmonics from the first to the twelfth harmonic.

First harmonic
☌ Conjunction = within about 12° of the same space.
Orange color-symbolism. Blending, uniting, enriching, inspiring. (This aspect is generated by every harmonic.)

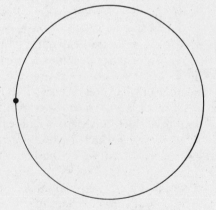

Figure 114. First harmonic

Second harmonic
♂ = 0° (see 1st harmonic)
♂ Opposition = 180° within about 6°
Orange color-symbolism. Tension, polarity,
complementarity.

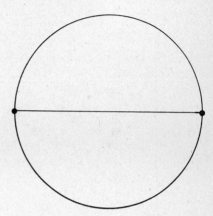

Figure 115. Second harmonic

Third harmonic
♂ = 0° (see 1st harmonic)
△Trine = 120° within about 4°
Blue color-symbolism. Ease, flow, play,
harmony.

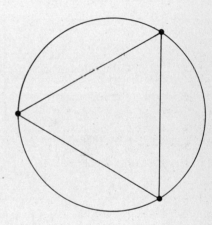

Figure 116. Third harmonic

Fourth harmonic
♂ = 0° (see 1st harmonic)
♂ = 180° (see 2nd harmonic)
☐ Square = 90° witin about 3°
Red color-symbolism. Challenge, difficulty,
effort, achievement.

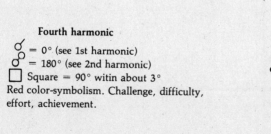

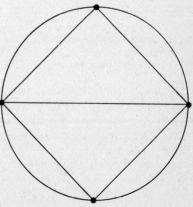

Figure 117. Fourth harmonic

Fifth harmonic

♂ = 0° (see 1st harmonic)

☆ Quintile = 72° within about 2° 24'

2 ☆ Biquintile = 72° within about 2° 24'

Yellow color-symbolism. Art, mind, discrimination, craft. (Applies to both ☆ and 2 ☆ .)

Figure 118. Fifth harmonic

Sixth harmonic

♂ = 0° (see 1st harmonic)

✶ Sextile = 60° within about 2°

Green color-symbolism. Cooperation, coordination, application, activity.

△ = 120° (see 3rd harmonic)

☊ = 180° (see 2nd harmonic)

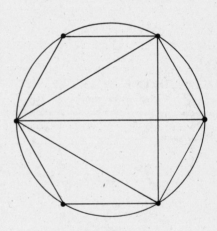

Figure 119. Sixth harmonic

Seventh harmonic

♂ = 0° (see 1st harmonic)

✹ Septile = 51° 25' within about 1° 43'

2 ✹ Biseptile = 102° 50' within about 1° 43'

3 ✹ Triseptile = 154° 15' within about 1° 43'

Violet color-symbolism. Creativity, inspiration, spiritual guidance, the sacred, fulfillment. (Applies to both ✹ , 2 ✹ , and 3 ✹ .)

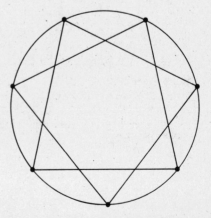

Figure 120. Seventh harmonic

Eighth harmonic

☌ = 0° (see 1st harmonic)
∠ or ⌐ Semisquare = 45° within about 1° 30'
□ = 90° (see 4th harmonic)
⊡ = Sesquiquadrate = 135° within about 1° 30'
☍ = 180° (see 2nd harmonic)
Pink color-symbolism. Challenge, stimulus, circumstance, stress, feedback. (Applies to both ∠ and ⊡.)

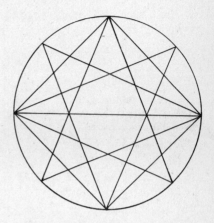

Figure 121. Eighth harmonic

Ninth harmonic

☌ = 0° (see 1st harmonic)
∇ Novile = 40° within about 1° 20'
2∇ Binovile = 80° within about 1° 20'
△ = 120° (see 3rd harmonic)
4∇ Quadrinovile = 160° within about 1° 20'
Red-violet color-symbolism. Potential, ideal, goal, completion. (Applies to ∇, 2∇, and 4∇.)

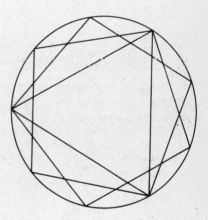

Figure 122. Ninth harmonic

Tenth harmonic

☌ = 0° (see 1st harmonic)
D Decile = 36° within about 1° 12'
☆ = 72° (see 5th harmonic)
3D Tredecile = 108° within about 1° 12'
2☆ = 144° (see 5th harmonic)
☍ = 180° (see 2nd harmonic)
Yellow color-symbolism. These aspects were introduced by Kepler, but are little used today.

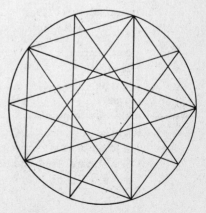

Figure 123. Tenth harmonic

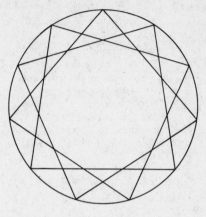

Eleventh harmonic
♂ = 0° (see 1st harmonic)
No other named aspects.

Figure 124. Eleventh harmonic

Twelfth harmonic
♂   = 0° (see 1st harmonic)
⊻ Semisextile = 30° within about 1°
⚹   = 60° (see 6th harmonic)
☐   = 90° (see 4th harmonic)
△   = 120° (see 3rd harmonic)
⊼ Quincunx (or Inconjunct) = 150° within about 1°.
♂°= 180° (see 2nd harmonic)
Yellow-orange color-symbolism. Contrast, alternation, phasing, diversity.

Figure 125. Twelfth harmonic

Exercise 10: Set aside a section in your notebook for each of the traditionally most important aspects:

conjunction	(first harmonic)
opposition	(second harmonic)
trine	(third harmonic)
square	(fourth harmonic)
quintile, biquintile	(fifth harmonic)
sextile	(sixth harmonic)
septile, biseptile, triseptile	(seventh harmonic)
semisquare, sesquiquadrate	(eighth harmonic)
semisextile, quincunx (or inconjunct)	(twelfth harmonic)

Why do you think the ninth, tenth and eleventh harmonics are omitted? The fifth- and eighth-harmonic aspects are often omitted also. Look again at the way harmonics reinforce one another if they may be divided by the same number, that is, if they are multiples of the same fundamental vibration.

Meditate on the nature of conjunction. Draw the geometrical image given in figure 114, a spot at the beginning/ending point of the cycle. Draw the symbol for conjunction, ♂ . Meditate on these images. Meditate on the number one, and on ideas like unity, unison, union, reunion, merger, blending and so forth. Meditate on the nature of the ending/beginning point of all the cycles you have studied. Meditate on the nature of initiation. Record your observations in the conjunction section of your notebook.

Suggestions for further meditation: In the opposition section of your notebook, draw the geometrical image given in figure 115, a circle with a horizontal line across its diameter, connecting the beginning of the cycle with its midpoint. Draw the symbol for opposition, ♂° . Meditate on these two images. Review your material relating to your experiences in opposite houses, and reflect on the nature of conflict and other one-to-one relationships with others. Meditate on the number two. Meditate on ideas like duality, duplication, reflection, memory, receptivity, dependence, alternation, antagonism. Meditate on the nature of the midpoints of the cycles you have studied. Record your observations in the opposition section of your notebook.

In the trine section of your notebook, draw the geometrical image given in figure 116, a circle with an equilateral triangle inscribed in it, connecting the beginning of the cycle with the other two nodes of the third harmonic. Draw the symbol for trine, △ . Meditate on these two images. Review your material relating to signs and houses with a common element (Fire, Water, Air and Earth). Meditate on the number three, and on ideas like multiplication, development, growth, unfoldment, expression, creativity, play, imagination.

In the square section of your notebook, draw the geometrical image given in figure 117, a circle with a square in it, connecting the beginning/ending point of the cycle with the other three "quarters" of the fourth harmonic. Draw the symbol for the square aspect, ☐ . Meditate on these two images. Why is the horizontal line of the second harmonic present in the first image? Review your material on houses and signs that share the same mode (cardinal, fixed or mutable signs; angular, succedent or cadent houses), and on the quarter-phases of the planetary return cycles which you studied previously. Meditate on the number four, and on ideas like challenge, difficulty, stress, endeavor, construction, constitution, order, measurement, classification, dispensation.

Construct other suggestions for meditation for the fifth, sixth, seventh, eighth and twelfth harmonics, on the model of the suggestions given here. Do the same with the omitted harmonics, the ninth, tenth and eleventh harmonics, if you wish.

Orbs of Aspects

Aspects do not suddenly blink into effect when planets reach the precise angle required, then blink off again when the planets move on. They become stronger as the two plants approach *partile* (exact aspect), and then taper off again gradually as the planets continue through the zodiac. There is considerable disagreement among astrologers about how far planets can be from an exact or partile aspect before its influence is felt. In the broadest terms, this distance, called the *orb* of the aspect, is always less than half a sign (15°), much less for the higher harmonics.

The reason for this becomes apparent when we look at the way higher harmonics reinforce lower ones. The most intense part of the first harmonic is, let us say, within 12° of partile (exact aspect), or one-thirtieth of the 360° of the zodiac. The wave-length of the first harmonic is the whole 360° circle, so the orb for conjunction is one-thirtieth of the wavelength of its harmonic, the first harmonic.

As two planets approach conjunction, when does the second harmonic come into effect, reinforcing the first harmonic? The wavelength of the second harmonic is half that of the first harmonic; there are two complete cycles of the second harmonic in the zodiac, as against the one complete cycle of the first harmonic. Therefore the orb for the second harmonic is half that of the first harmonic, or 6°.

It may help to visualize the tip of the wave-crest as being the most intense part; since the tip of the second-harmonic wave is smaller, the area where it is most intensely felt is also smaller.

So the conjunction begins to be felt as the two planets resonate on the first harmonic, around 12° from each other, and its influence becomes stronger as the two planets resonate on the second harmonic, when they are around 6° apart. When would the third harmonic come into effect? Divide twelve by three, and the answer is a 4° orb for the third harmonic. The fourth harmonic is felt at about 3° and so on.

These orbs are included in the descriptions, above, of the aspects associated with each harmonic. They were originally suggested by John Addey. Most astrologers follow the textbooks and assign certain fixed orbs to the "major aspects" (the first four harmonics, and sometimes also the sextile), usually 10° or 8° for all of them, and smaller orbs to the "minor aspects."

The purpose of these orbs is to determine when an aspect should be included in the delineation of a horoscope, and when not. In practice, they devolve to a kind of rule of thumb for new astrologers. If the Sun or Moon is involved, a larger orb is allowed; likewise, if more than two planets are linked by aspects, forming an aspect pattern. (Aspect patterns will be discussed further on in this chapter.)

Figure 126 shows how harmonics reinforce one another in the most commonly-used aspects, the conjunction, opposition, square, trine, sextile, semisextile and quincunx (also called the inconjunct).

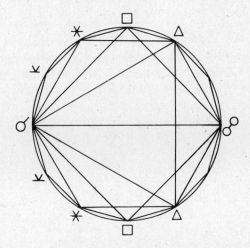

Figure 126. Mutual reinforcement of harmonics

Exercise 11:   Draw a larger version of figure 126 on a sheet of paper. Which harmonics are involved here? Which harmonics reinforce the conjunction? Which harmonics reinforce the second harmonic in the opposition? Which harmonics reinforce the third harmonic in the two trines? Which harmonics reinforce the fourth harmonic in the two squares? Which harmonics reinforce the sixth harmonic in the two sextiles? Which harmonics and aspects are reinforced by the twelfth harmonic? How does this account for six of the first twelve harmonics being omitted from figure 126? Or, to turn that question inside out, which of the harmonics in figure 126 would be reinforced by the fifth, seventh, eighth, ninth, tenth or eleventh harmonics? How does this account for the importance of the number twelve in astrology? Meditate on the number twelve and all the associations to it that you can discover. Meditate on the numbers two and one, and consider the number twelve as the expression of the number two through the agency of the number one.

Higher Harmonics

Any fraction of the zodiac is an aspect, and the harmonic involved is named by the denominator of the fraction. For example, planets separated by one-fourth or three-fourths of the zodiac are square one another, and resonating on the fourth harmonic. In the same way, planets separated by 12° are in aspect on the thirtieth harmonic (360° divided by 12° yields thirty); planets just slightly closer together are in aspect on the one-hundred-twenty-seventh harmonic (4/127 of 360° is 11°31′ 12″).

This means that there is really an infinite number of aspects. Although the most important aspects in the practice of clinical astrology are still those of the twelfth harmonic and lower harmonics, as shown in figure 126, the higher harmonics are becoming increasingly important in astrological research.

Figure 127 shows how the higher harmonics reinforce the lower ones. The 360° of a circle have been rolled out into a straight line to make the graph easier to draw and to read. The starting point of the cycle of aspects, the conjunction or 0°, is in the center of the line; the waxing square or 90° is half-way to the right end; the opposition or 180° is located at the right end of the graph, and again at the left end, so that if you were to cut out the graph and form it into a circle, the two ends would meet at one point opposite the conjunction; the waning square or 270° is at the half-way point in the left side of the graph.

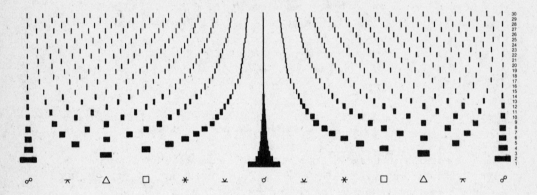

Figure 127. Resonance points of the first thirty harmonics

Only the first thirty harmonics are shown, because the thirtieth harmonic has a wavelength of 12°, as noted above. In other words, the first resonance point for the thirtieth harmonic comes in at 12°, just where the orb assigned to the conjunction ends. The resonance points of the thirtieth harmonic—all thirty of them—are shown on the topmost horizontal line of the graph, numbered "30." Immediately after that, the first resonance point for the twenty-ninth harmonic comes in (on the twenty-ninth line of the graph), followed by the twenty-eighth and so on. The sequence of resonance points for harmonics descends in a gradually opening curve down toward the opposition.

When the resonance of the fifteenth harmonic is reached, it is reinforced by the thirtieth harmonic, directly above it on the graph. This is the starting point of a second curving line of resonance points an octave above the first. (An octave is a relationship between harmonics where one is twice as high in frequency as the other.) The twenty-ninth harmonic comes next, followed by the twenty-eighth, and so on. The twenty-eighth harmonic reinforces its lower octave, the fourteenth, but there is no lower octave for the twenty-ninth harmonic to reinforce (since twenty-nine cannot be divided evenly by two).

Above the tenth-harmonic resonance point a third curving line of reinforcing harmonics begins, three times the frequency of those on the first curving line. A fourth curving line begins two octaves above the seventh-harmonic resonance point, a fifth above the sixth-harmonic resonance point and so on. How many can you find in figure 127?

Now, imagine a pair of planets moving through the aspect cycle. The slower-moving one is represented by the symbol for conjunction at the center of the graph in figure 127. At the conjunction, the two planets are in resonance on all harmonics, in unison, so to speak. As the two planets separate, they go out of resonance, first on the highest harmonics, then on progressively lower harmonics. At 3° separation, the limit of the orb assigned to the fourth harmonic, only the first three harmonics are strong enough to be considered. (We are not including harmonics that are off the top edge of the graph in figure 127, such as the 120th, which has a resonance point at 3°.) The third harmonic fades out at 4° and the second harmonic at 6°, leaving only the resonance on the first harmonic between 6° and 12°.

At 12°, the descending curve of resonance points comes into range of our graph at the thirtieth harmonic. At 24°, the fifteenth harmonic is felt, reinforced by a second resonance point on the thirtieth harmonic. At 30° separation, the first named aspect comes into resonance, the semisextile.

The twelfth harmonic is more significant in astrology than the eleventh or the thirteenth, for example, because it resonates with harmonics one, two, three, four and six. These six harmonics form a synergetic unity (see the discussion of synergy in connection with the eleventh house and with Aquarius). That is why the conjunction, opposition, trine, square, sextile, semisextile and quincunx (or inconjunct) are more prominent aspects than, for example, the novile (ninth harmonic) or the endecile (eleventh harmonic).

The pattern of reinforcement shown in figure 127 also gives a means for interpreting the orbs of aspects, and shows how they have no absolute cut-off point. The conjunction's first-harmonic resonance is rather weak at 10° separation, but perhaps not as weak as the thirty-sixth harmonic which comes into resonance at that point to compete with it. If the thirty-sixth harmonic figures strongly elsewhere in the horoscope, indicating a thirty-sixth-harmonic resonance for the personality as a whole, then perhaps an aspect of 1/36 would take precedence over a weak conjunction with a 10° orb. In any case, a conjunction with a 10° orb would have overtones of the thirty-sixth harmonic, and this could be used to help interpret the differences between aspects with different orbs.

This is a topic worth a book in itself. If you want to pursue this approach to interpreting the orbs of aspects, you will need the *Astrologers Guide to the Harmonics* by James S. and Ruth E. Williamsen (Cambridge Circle, 1977, distributed by Para Research). The following table gives the lowest harmonic in resonance for 1°, 2°, 3°, etc. orbs for all the major aspects (conjunction, sextile, square, trine and opposition).

Orb	Harmonic	Exceptions
1°	360th	
2°	180th	45th for approaching, waxing square (88°) and for departing, waning square (272°)

Orb	Harmonic	Exceptions
3°	120th	40th for approaching, waxing trine (117°) and for departing, waning trine (303°)
4°	90th	90th for conjunction and for waxing trine
	45th	45th for opposition and for waning trine
5°	72nd	
6°	60th	
7°±	46th	46th harmonic resonates at 7°0'47" and the 52nd at
	52nd	353°00'35", not at 7° exactly
8°	45th	
9°	40th	
10°	36th	
11°±	98th	98th harmonic resonates at 11°1'13" and at 348°58' 47", not at 11° exactly
12°	30th	

If this table doesn't make sense to you at this point, just pass over it. It is intended for more advanced students who wish to do research in this relatively new and unexplored area.

Exercise 12: Meditate on the pattern of harmonic resonances shown in figure 127. See how in the waxing half of the aspect cycle two planets move apart step by ever wider step out through the opening spirals of harmonics, until they reach opposition. The number of descending curves in the diagram increases to a maximum at that point, where the two planets resonate on every even-numbered harmonic.

Then in the waning half of the cycle (the left half of the graph), as the planets move progressively closer again, see how the harmonics become progressively more subtle, higher and in closer and faster steps, through the third harmonic (the waning trine), the fourth (the waning square), the fifth (quintile) and so on until they reach conjunction. As they approach conjunction, the rising curve of harmonics becomes very steep. What does this suggest to you about the subjective knowledge of unity experienced by mystics?

Meditate on the cycle of aspects opening and closing like a flower; or like the inflowing and outflowing of breath.

Suggestions for further meditation: Apply this picture of the cycle of aspects to the other cycles you have studied. Review your material on planetary return cycles and cycles of planets through the houses. How many phases there are in a cycle depends upon which harmonic you are focusing on.

Finding Aspects in Your Horoscope

The preceding section on harmonics is the most difficult in this book. To future generations of astrologers, it will appear simple and obvious; however, that will be because people learning astrology now will have an understanding of harmonics before their heads are cluttered with the traditional rules of thumb and heuristic procedures by which most astrologers today have learned to use aspects.

With some understanding of harmonics, however, the practical techniques for recognizing and interpreting aspects are much easier to learn.

Figure 128 shows a horoscope with planets in the following positions:

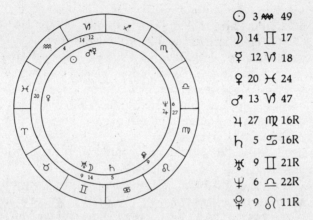

Figure 128. A horoscope (no house cusps)

No house cusps are shown in figure 128 because they are not relevant to the purely planetary aspects we are about to look at. The positions of planets are rounded off to the nearest whole degree, indicated by the numbers in the circle between the symbols for the signs and those for the planets. (You last saw this horoscope in Chapter 4.)

The conjunction and the opposition are the most obvious aspects in any horoscope. By simple inspection, you can find planets that are within 12° of one another, or within 6° of exact opposition. When two planets are in adjacent signs, you have to do some mental subtraction and addition, but this is not difficult. For example, how far apart are Jupiter and Neptune in this horoscope? Neptune is 6° from the cusp of Libra, and Jupiter is 3° from the cusp of Libra (30° minus 27°), so the two planets are a total of 9° apart. There are three conjunctions in this horoscope; can you find the other two?

There are four candidates for oppositions in this horoscope, four pairs of planets in opposite signs. Which of them come within the 6° orb assigned to the opposition? (Answers will be given below.) Notice that opposite signs have the same mode; thus, one may speak of cardinal, fixed and mutable oppositions in a horoscope. If planets are located near sign cusps, you may find an opposition with mixed modes (cardinal-fixed, fixed-mutable or mutable-cardinal).

The fixed opposition in this horoscope has an orb of 5°. The other three candidates have 7° and 9° orbs. We will find later, in the section on aspect patterns, that we might want to include one of these despite its wide orb, because it is supported by other aspects in the horoscope.

Next, let's look for third-harmonic aspects, the trines. These are usually in signs with the same element, except for pairs of planets near sign cusps. Thus, we may speak of Fire, Water, Air and Earth trines. First, find possible candidates, then check to determine if they come within the recommended 4° orb for a trine.

There are four candidates for trines in this horoscope, one of them crossing sign cusps from Earth to Air. They have orbs of 2°, 3°, 4°, and 7°. Can you find them all? (Again, answers will be provided below.)

Squares usually involve signs with the same mode, as the oppositions do, except of course that they are 90° apart rather than 180° apart. Also, squares always involve signs of opposite gender. Thus, where one might speak of yin or yang oppositions, as well as cardinal, fixed or mutable, one may only speak of cardinal, fixed or mutable squares, unless the planets are near sign cusps, resulting in a mixed-mode square.

There are three candidates for squares in this horoscope, with orbs of 1°, 6°, and 6°, respectively. Can you find them?

Sextiles skip a sign, linking signs of the same gender (except for planets on the cusps). Since the sextile allows only a 2° orb, candidates are somewhat harder to find. Venus has moved 6° past a sextile with Mars, and the Moon has another 6° to go to make a sextile with Venus. There is, however, one exact sextile in the chart, and another candidate with a 3° orb which will later be included because it is supported by other aspects.

We skipped quintiles because they are a bit more complicated to find. In fact, all the other aspects, except the twelfth-harmonic semisextile and quincunx, involve some mental math to find. For beginning work, you may wish to ignore them.

The quintile is a sextile plus 12°. Measuring in zodiacal sequence (counter-clockwise), add 12° to the position of a planet and look two signs further on at the resulting degree for a second planet. For example, adding 12° to the position of Mercury gives 24°, and two signs further on from Capricorn would be 24° Pisces. Venus is at 20° Pisces and the quintile allows less than 3° orb, so there is no quintile there unless it is part of a strong aspect pattern such as we will discuss later in this chapter. A quintile from Mars would be 2° further on, at 26° Pisces. Where would a quintile from the Sun fall? Add 12° to 4°, and carry the result two signs ahead into Aries. Continue around the horoscope until you have checked each planet in sequence.

The biquintile is a quincunx (150°) minus 6°. Subtract 6° from each planet's position and look five signs ahead for another planet. (Five signs is one sign less than an opposition.)

Rules of thumb can be devised for all the other aspects. How many degrees and signs would you add to find a semisquare? (Answer: 15° plus one sign, to total 45°.) The sesquiquadrate is always 180° from the semisquare.

The "major" aspects in the example horoscope of figure 128 are as follows (see figure 129). A raised "w" (for "wide") indicates that the aspect exceeds the suggested orb, but may be close enough to be considered if there are supporting factors in the horoscope.

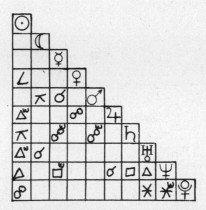

Figure 129. Table of aspects in the horoscope of figure 128

In this matrix, aspects are written where the vertical column associated with one planet intersects the horizontal row associated with the second planet. In the example horoscope in figure 128, we found Mars conjunct Mercury in Capricorn. Follow the Mercury column down and the Mars row across until they intersect, and there you will find the symbol for conjunction.

Not shown is a biquintile from Mars to Uranus, and a "wide" biquintile from Mercury to Uranus. Can you add these aspects to the diagram in figure 129? There are also "minor" aspects between the Sun and Venus, the Sun and Saturn, the Moon and Mars and the Moon and Jupiter, which are not included here. If you can find them in figure 128, add them to the matrix in figure 129.

Exercise 13:   Find the aspects in your own horoscope. In each case, were the planets approaching partile or exact aspect when you were born (an "applying" aspect) or were they moving away (a "separating" aspect)? In each case, is it a waxing or a waning aspect? That is, was the faster-moving planet moving toward opposition (in the waxing half of the aspect cycle) or toward conjunction (in the waning half)?

What harmonics appear to be most prominent in your horoscope? Which aspects are most nearly exact?

Meditate on each pair of planets in aspect, beginning with the lowest harmonics. Review your material on the planets, signs and houses involved in each aspect, then meditate on how these factors resonate on the particular harmonic of the given aspect. What contribution does this resonance make to your character? For example, if the aspect is a square, how are effort, challenge, achievement and the other attributes of the fourth harmonic involved in the coordinated manifestation of the pair of planets through the signs and houses that are involved?

Aspect Patterns

We have used an analogy to language extensively in this book, and previously mentioned that aspects were among the "verbs" of the astrological symbol-language, since they are relationships among the "nouns," the planets. In language, sentences are grouped and linked together into paragraphs and chapters. Once more, we find in astrology an analog to language, because pairs of planets in aspect are often grouped together in various larger patterns which express the underlying themes of the horoscope.

Aspect patterns bring groups of three or more planets into mutual resonance, sometimes on one harmonic, sometimes on several. The most common patterns are as follows:

Grand Trine: Figure 130 shows the shape of a grand trine, an equilateral triangle comprised of three trines connecting three planets. It is a third-harmonic pattern. Usually three, sometimes two, signs have the same element.

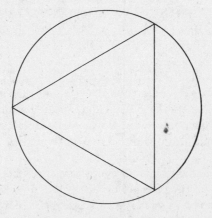

Figure 130. Grand trine

Exercise 14:   Do you have a grand trine in your horoscope? If planets are only slightly out of orb for one or more of the individual trines, their mutual resonance on the third harmonic may be sufficient for the pattern to be an active influence. If you have a conjunction, and one planet in the conjunction trines one poirít and the other trines the other point of a grand trine, but neither trines both, the conjunction serves to bridge the gap. Some astrologers figure the trines from the midpoint of the conjunction in such a case.

The horoscope in figure 128 has a grand trine between the Sun, Uranus and Neptune, with an extended orb for the Sun-Uranus relationship.

Meditate on the yin, easygoing, even lazy, Venusian qualities of a grand trine, with its emphasis on the imaginative, playful qualities of the third harmonic. Visualize and feel how the faculties involved in a grand trine work well together, how they cooperate to develop and ramify one another's activities. Can you see how it is a self-contained, largely unconscious resource, and how it needs some thorn in the side, such as a square or opposition to one of its points, to tap its juices?

In figure 128, do you see any aspects on the even-numbered harmonics that might serve to release and apply the energies of the grand trine?

If you have a grand trine in your horoscope, or in a horoscope that you are studying, meditate on the planets, signs, houses and elements involved and on how they are resonating together on the third harmonic. What is this great resource in your personality, greater than the sum of its parts and greater than you realize? What ways can you find to tap into it?

Grand square: Figure 131 shows the shape of a grand square, comprised of four squares and two oppositions. Planets in a grand square are resonating on both the fourth and the second harmonics.

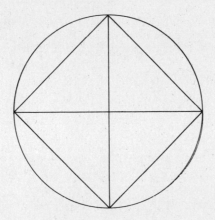

Figure 131. Grand square

Exercise 15:   Do you have a grand square in your horoscope? The mutual resonance of planets may be sufficient to bridge an orb that would otherwise be too wide for one of the squares or oppositions.

Meditate on the yang, aggressive, Martian qualities of a grand square, with its emphasis on work, adversity and achievement; meditate on its Saturnian qualities of limitation and cause-and-effect consequences. Review your material on the three modes, on squares and on oppositions. Can you see how the personal faculties represented in a grand square might get "boxed in" in an endless vicious circle of challenges and frustrations, each setting up the conditions for the next?

Which do you think would be easier to cope with, a cardinal, fixed or mutable grand square? How do you suppose each of these three types of grand square would manifest if you had it? Would you expect a mixture of modes, due to planets being near sign cusps, would it be easier or more difficult to use well?

Can you see how things would get worse if you projected your inner conflicts (squares) onto others through the oppositions? Can you see ways to use your relationships with others (oppositions) to gain insight into the inner conflicts represented by the squares in your horoscope?

Are there any "easy" aspects like the trine or sextile to provide support and assistance? Can you get help through the dispositor or benefactor structure?

T-Square: The T-square is half a grand square, a triangular pattern comprised of two squares and one opposition (figure 132). It is very closely related to the grand square, and very similar to it, but much more frequently found in horoscopes.

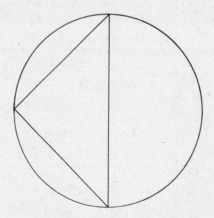

Figure 132. T-square

Exercise 16:   Do you have a T-square in your horoscope? The second-harmonic and fourth-harmonic resonances of the planets involved may be sufficient to bridge an orb that would otherwise be too wide.

Meditate on the combination of Martian and Saturnian qualities of the T-square, with its emphasis on work, adversity, achievement and limitation.

The horoscope in figure 128 has a T-square, with some stretching of the orbs of the opposition and square to Mercury. Neptune is the apex planet, at the focus of the pattern. The point opposite Neptune, at 6° Aries, is the "karmic degree" where a planet would be in a grand square. A transit over the karmic degree completes a grand square temporarily. What effect do you think this would have in a person's life? Can you see how the T-square is connected to the grand trine in the horoscope in figure 128?

Review your material on the three modes. What do you think a cardinal T-square would be like? A fixed T-square? A mutable T-square? A T-square with a mixture of two modes?

If you have a T-square in your horoscope, or in a horoscope that you are studying, meditate on the planets, signs, houses and mode involved, and on how all these factors are resonating on the second and fourth harmonics. Review your material on challenges in your life relating to those signs and houses, including the sign and house of the "karmic degree." What sorts of difficulty and what achievements have you experienced there? Is the apex planet in any way elusive or mysterious to you? How do you relate to people whose Sun is in the same or opposite sign from your T-square's apex planet? Is the opposition of your T-square much involved in your conflicts with other people? Are the apex planet and its opposite or "karmic" degree involved in those conflicts? How can your relationships with others in these four houses give you insight into your own inner conflicts, represented by the squares? In what ways do you pretend that the keys to your success lie in the hands of those other people?

Are there any "easy" aspects like the trine or sextile to provide support and assistance to one or more of the planets in your T-square? Can you get help through the dispositor or benefactor structure?

Kite: The kite pattern is a grand trine with a fourth planet opposite one of its corners, forming sextiles to the other two. It resonates on the second, third and sixth harmonics, the latter two harmonics (and the opposition and sextile aspects) being ideal channels for access to and release of the energies of the grand trine. The kite pattern is shown in figure 133.

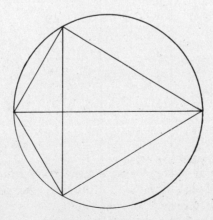

Figure 133. Kite

Exercise 17: Do you have a kite pattern in your horoscope? The horoscope shown in figure 128 has a kite pattern whose spine is the opposition between the Sun and Pluto, the major axis of the horoscope. This is a fixed Air or Aquarian kite pattern, because its spine is an opposition in fixed signs, and its grand trine is in the Air signs. The planet at the tail of the kite (in this case the Sun) is deeply connected with the purpose of the pattern and, as a consequence, of the horoscope as a whole. The planet at the head of the kite (Pluto in figure 128) shows how the energies of the grand trine are harnessed and applied.

Meditate on the kite pattern as a picture of a drawn bow and arrow, with the bowstring stretched to the tail of the kite and the arrowhead at the "working end" of the pattern, the head of the kite.

Review your material on the houses and signs at the head and tail of your kite, if you have one. What have your relationships been like in those opposite houses? What contribution have the other two points of the grand trine made to those relationships?

Kite-head: This pattern, shown in figure 128, is just the head of a kite pattern, a triangle formed of a trine and two sextiles. It occurs often in horoscopes with no oppositions. In transits, it functions much the same way as a T-square; when a transiting planet forms an opposition to the apex planet, a kite is formed.

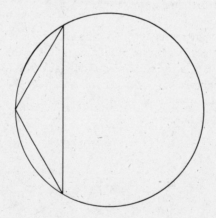

Figure 134. Kite-head

Wedge: The wedge pattern, like the kite-head, is best seen as an incomplete kite pattern. It is more versatile than the kite-head because it involves the second, third and sixth harmonics, like the kite, whereas the kite-head lacks the second harmonic. It consists of an opposition, trine and sextile (figure 135). A transiting planet can complete a kite pattern by trining both ends of the existing trine. (By forming sextiles to both ends of the existing trine, a transiting planet forms a cat's cradle pattern—see below.)

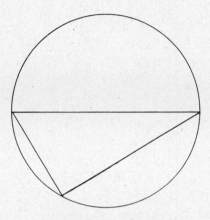

Figure 135. Wedge

Exercise 18:   Do you have a kite-head in your horoscope or in a horoscope that you are studying? What sign would a transiting planet have to be in to complete a kite pattern? Reconstruct what happened to you at the times of these transits by various planets. Did you find a particular focus on the house and sign of the apex planet at those times? Meditate on this pattern as a bow without an arrow. Do certain relationships "put an arrow in your bow"? What happens in relationships with people who have planets located opposite the apex planet of your kite-head?

Do you have a wedge pattern in your horoscope or in a horoscope that you are studying? What sign would a transiting planet have to be in to complete a kite pattern? Reconstruct what took place at the times of transits to this point by various planets. Review your experiences associated with the opposition and the signs and houses that it links. Were these relationships with other people facilitated, energized or otherwise stimulated at the times of those transits? What happens in your relationships with people who have planets located in the position that completes a kite pattern for you?

Grand Sextile: The grand sextile does not occur every day! It is quite rare for six planets to come within a few degrees of being equally spaced around the zodiac. A grand sextile consists of two interlaced grand trines, three oppositions and six sextiles; the grand trines form the six-pointed star or Shield of David. There is tremendous resonance in this pattern, on the same harmonics as the kite, the second, third and sixth; indeed, the grand sextile may be seen as three interlaced kite patterns, or, more properly, the kite, kite-head and wedge may all be seen as fragments of a latent grand sextile. Can you see how this pattern would mark the horoscope of a very diversified yet very well-integrated individual? Such a horoscope would need a square or two just to have some challenges to absorb all that tremendous creative energy!

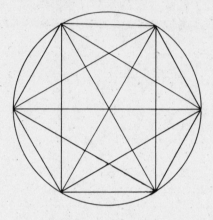

Figure 136. Grand sextile

Cat's cradle: This pattern (figure 137) can be seen as half a grand sextile or as two wedges combined in one pattern. A more complex form of cat's cradle pattern is composed of three wedges and covers two thirds of the circle instead of just half. Draw this pattern yourself. Can you see how it is made up of two kites? It also includes a mystic rectangle, to be discussed presently.

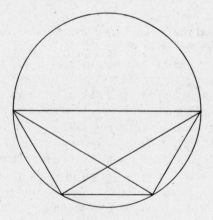

Figure 137. Cat's cradle

Mystic Rectangle: This is the last pattern we will derive from the grand sextile. It is like the mid-section of a grand sextile, omitting one of the three oppositions and the four associated sextiles. Because it has an even balance of harmonics—two each of the sextile, trine and opposition, representing resonances on the second, third and sixth harmonics—it indicates a greater degree of integration and capacity for synthesizing diverse experiences in an extremely productive way, than any of the other kindred patterns except the expanded cat's cradle mentioned above and, of course, the grand sextile itself (see figure 138). It may be for this reason that the word "mystic" has become attached to it, since people capable of synthesizing what others see as unrelated may appear to be unusually gifted or "touched by God."

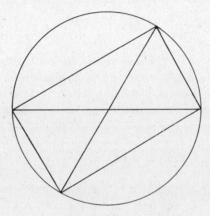

Figure 138. Mystic rectangle

Exercise 19:   Do you have a cat's cradle, mystic rectangle or grand sextile in your horoscope? Is the setting of priorities and goals an especially important issue for you? Review your experiences associated with the opposition(s) in the pattern and the signs and houses linked thereby. In those experiences, were your relationships with other people facilitated, energized or otherwise stimulated at the time of transits to points in the pattern? What happens in your relationships with people who have planets located at points in the pattern, or at points that complete a kite or other configuration that is latent in the pattern in your horoscope? Do you see how a tremendous unconscious reservoir of creative energies (the trines) is focused through specific talents and skills, ways of applying those energies in harmonious, cooperative ways (the sextiles) and comes to focus through relationships with others (the oppositions)? Meditate on the trines (the third-harmonic reservoir of creativity), the sextiles (the skills and talents) and the oppositions (the relationships) in turn, focusing on the signs, houses and planets involved at each step.

The cat's cradle has more sextiles and fewer trines than the kite: What difference do you suppose this makes? The mystic rectangle has two oppositions but has fewer trines than the kite. Does this in fact make for more ability to apply one's talents, albeit less latent creative ability? For more diversity of ability because of two oppositions involving two modes instead of just one? Can you see how the mystic rectangle and cat's cradle give a less clear and simple focus than a kite pattern, with its single-opposition "bow-and-arrow" effect? How might a T-square be added to the mystic rectangle, sharing one of its oppositions, and what effect would you expect it to have? What effect might you expect from a T-square added to a cat's cradle in the same way? Draw these combined patterns and meditate on them.

General Observations about "Major Aspect" Patterns

In patterns resonating to the second and fourth harmonics, the grand square and the T-square, the keynote is provided by the mode of the signs involved. In the grand trine, the third-harmonic pattern, it is the element of the signs that sets the theme. In the grand sextile and its derivatives, the cat's cradle, mystic rectangle and wedge, resonating to the second, third and sixth harmonics, it is the gender of the signs that characterizes the nature of the pattern. The kite (and perhaps the wedge) isolates both a mode and an element, naming an individual sign. Thus, one may have a fixed T-square, a grand trine in Air, a yin or yang mystic rectangle or an Aquarian kite.

In each case, if planets involved are near sign cusps, there may be some crossing or combining of two modes, elements or genders in the same pattern. In the case of the grand square this might make the pattern less "locked in." If the odd planet in a T-square, kite-head or wedge is the apex planet, do you think this might make the pattern easier or more difficult to deal with? If a grand trine has one planet in an odd element, how do you think this would affect the strength and consistency of the third-harmonic resonance? Do you think it might require more conscious attention, rather than functioning with so much unconscious ease?

In the diversity of a grand sextile or cat's cradle, would a planet in an odd gender provide a kind of focus, something that stands apart, or would it just add to the general confusion?

Your answers to these questions will be influenced in indvidual cases by other factors in the horoscope, such as rulerships, exaltations, dispositor structure, house position and so forth.

Patterns on Higher Harmonics

Your horoscope may have patterns. One example is the fifth-harmonic triangle between Mars, Jupiter and Uranus which you found in the horoscope in figure 128. Or you may find eighth-harmonic "wedges," "kites," "kite-heads," and other derivatives of the "grand semisquare" involving semiquares and sesquiquadrates rather than sextiles and trines. I have found seventh-harmonic triangles in the horoscopes of two talented clairvoyants.

Two twelfth-harmonic patterns deserve special mention, the yod (also called the double quincunx, finger of God, or finger of fate) and the yod kite (also called, by one writer, the tetradic yod). The yod is composed of two quincunxes and one sextile (figure 139) and resonates on the sixth and twelfth harmonics.

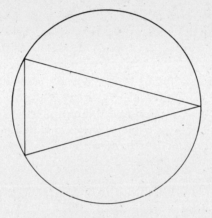

Figure 139. Yod

The yod kite, as you might guess, is comprised of a yod with an opposition from the point to the midpoint of the sextile, where it is linked by semisextiles to the other two planets (figure 140).

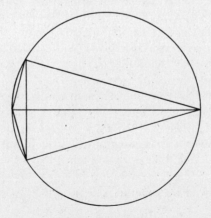

Figure 140. Yod Kite

Some astrologers give a great deal of weight to the quincunx, claiming as much influence as for a square or a trine. It is said to fluctuate in value between a trine and an opposition. From this, we may assume that the yod fluctuates in the same way. Recall that the sextile requires more attention and application of conscious choice than the trine does. When the sextile is working well, can you see how the yod might function like a grand trine? The sextile is the "driver's seat" for the yod, and the single point opposite the sextile is its point of application. Recall how, in an opposition, you tend to identify with one end and project the other end onto another person. In this case, there are two ends to identify with, and when you are not attending to the relationship between them (the sextile), there is bound to be confusion and poor judgment in relationships involving the yod.

On the other hand, if your consciousness is clearly focused in the "driver's seat" of the sextile, the grand trine character of the yod would come to the fore. Typically, there is a periodic shifting from one of these states to the other.

In the yod kite, there is a planet actually placed in the "driver's seat," at the midpoint of the sextile. This pattern fluctuates between a rather confused opposition and a kite in its effect.

Midpoints

A number of the aspect patterns we have been looking at involve midpoints. The apex of a T-square is at the midpoint of its opposition. The apex of a kite-head is at the midpoint of its trine; indeed, each point of a grand trine is at the midpoint of one of the trines, so that a kite has an opposition connecting two midpoints, one inner midpoint (linked to the trine by sextiles) and one outer midpoint (linked via the other two trines of the grand trine).

Midpoints are always significant resonance-points. Whether the aspect between two planets is a square or 133/178, at least one midpoint is a resonance point an octave higher. An opposition is a second-harmonic aspect; its midpoint, the apex of a T-square, is a resonance-point on the fourth harmonic, liked by two squares. The midpoint of a trine (third harmonic) is linked to either end by two sextiles (sixth harmonic, an octave higher).

Many astrologers who use midpoints regard them as blending the influences of pairs of planets no matter how large or small the bisected angle. (See for example, Ebertin, *The Combination of Stellar Influences*, and Hand, *Horoscope Symbols*, in the Bibliography.) The harmonics involved in the planetary relationship and in the midpoint must play a role. When we attempt to apply this principle to the interpretation of horoscopes, however, we run up against the lack of good information on the meanings of many of the higher harmonics.

Nonetheless, much good work can be done with midpoints, and I can strongly recommend the two books mentioned above for further exploration of this topic.

Transits

The meanings of aspect patterns become much clearer when they are viewed in the context of aspect cycles. We have already made reference to this dimension in the discussion of how transiting planets might "complete" a grand square or a kite where a horoscope had only a T-square or a kite-head.

The yod or double quincunx pattern displays its out-of-phase, fluctuating character very clearly in this light. Figure 141 shows a yod pattern with its focal point in Aries and the sextile planets in Virgo and Scorpio, for ease of discussion.

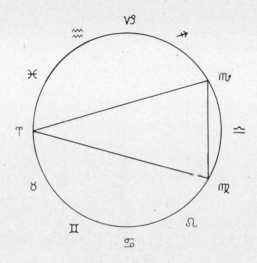

Figure 141. Transits through a yod pattern

A transiting planet in Aries is conjunct the apex planet and quincunx both the sextile planets, naturally. In Taurus, it is in opposition to the Scorpio planet while it trines the Virgo planet; one is subject to tension and stress, and the other is associated with relaxed, easygoing experiences. There is also a certain amount of stress with the semisextile to the Aries planet.

When the transiting planet is in Gemini, the trine to Virgo becomes a square, and the stressful semisextile to the Aries planet becomes a relatively easy and productive sextile. There remains some stress in relation to the Scorpio planet, through the quincunx from Gemini to Scorpio.

When the transiting planet is in Cancer, it is trine the Scorpio planet, sextile the Virgo planet and square the Aries planet. When in Leo, it is trine the Aries planet and square the Scorpio planet. And so on. In every sign (except of course Aries, Virgo and Scorpio, where it fits into the yod pattern), a transiting planet forms an "easy" third or sixth-harmonic aspect to one planet, a "hard" second or fourth-harmonic aspect to a second one and a mildly stressful twelfth-harmonic aspect to the third planet. The planets of the pattern keep swapping roles, yet always one is benefitted by the transit while another is challenged.

It is also of value to look at the orbs allowed for different aspects in terms of the aspect cycle. Figure 142 shows a grand trine in Fire signs, except for the Sun at 29° Pisces. The Moon is located at 0° Leo and Mars at 1° Sagittarius.

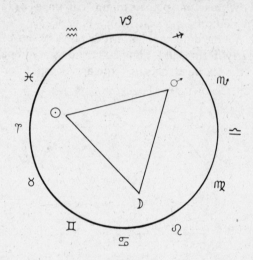

Figure 142. A grand trine with 1° and 2° orbs

The Sun, Moon and Mars are resonating together on the third harmonic, but slightly out of phase, with 1° and 2° orbs. Consequently, in each sign a transiting planet comes into exact aspect first with the Sun, second with the Moon, and last with Mars. The transiting planet resonates with all three members of the grand trine, but not simultaneously. The actual time-delay depends upon the speed of the transiting planet.

For example, the Moon takes about two hours to move 1°. When the Moon is in Aries, it forms an exact conjunction to the natal Sun about two hours before the exact trine to the natal Moon and about four hours before the exact trine with natal Mars. This would be a day with a "grand trine" mood for this person, first inspiring (Sun), then elevating the mood (Moon) and finally giving a sense of vitality and energy (Mars).

Astrologers typically allow only a degree or two orb for transits, not differentiating between transiting conjunctions, oppositions, trines, squares and other aspects; all are afforded the same orb. Now, it may be that aspects formed by transit must be more nearly exact to have an effect; practical experience of astrologers indicates this. However, one would still expect aspects on lower harmonics to be in effect over a broader orb than higher-harmonic aspects. For example, if we allow 3° for a transiting conjunction, then an opposition would get 1° 30', a trine would get an orb of 1°, a square would get an orb of 45', a sextile would get 30' and so on.

An exact or "partile" aspect tends to function automatically, without much consciousness of the relationship of the two planets involved. One reason for this is that the stimulus of transits through one planet is followed very quickly by the stimulus through the other; transits to one planet cannot be distinguished from transits to the other, so the corresponding faculties in your personality tend to operate as a unified pair, without conscious intervention or distinction between them. Then, in a manner akin to habit formation, the two faculties tend to be linked in function even at times when there is no active transit stimulus, or rather, when only higher harmonics are "tickling" them.

On the other hand, the wider the orb of an aspect, the greater the time-lag between a transit to one planet and the ensuing transit to the other. The relationship symbolized by the aspect does not function so automatically, and the pattern impressed by repeated transit experiences is not so "tight." Aspects with wider orbs may require more conscious attention on your part to have a strong impact in your life.

Continuing this reasoning, it is possible to activate aspects with wide orbs, beyond the usual limits, by paying attention to transits and consciously linking your experience of the transit to one planet with your somewhat later experiences of the transit to the second planet.

It also follows that the slowest-moving planets are strongly felt when they are transiting two or more planets in fairly close natal aspects, since the wider-orb aspects would involve too much time delay to register consciously. Yet those very aspects are the ones that most often register unconsciously, being more nearly exact. This may contribute to the outer planets being experienced as manifesting through the subconscious.

Finally, we can look at the sequence of transits to an aspect pattern as a regular sequence that is experienced with every transiting planet. The earliest planet in a pattern (e.g. the Sun in the Fire trine given as an example in figure 142) indicates how you begin your experiences associated with that pattern. Do you think it would be easier, if you have a T-square, for example, for your experiences engaging that pattern to begin with the apex planet, or to begin with an aspect to one of the opposing planets?

Exercise 20:   Draw colored lines connecting the planets that are in aspect in your horoscope. Use the colors given in the description of the aspects:

conjunction, opposition	orange
trine	blue
square	red
quintile, etc.	yellow
sextile	green
septile, etc.	violet
semisquare, sesquiquadrate	pink
semisextile, quincunx	orange-yellow

As you identify aspect patterns in your horoscope, make a separate diagram of each, like the diagram of the grand trine in Fire/Water shown in figure 142. It may not be necessary to draw separate diagrams if you can visualize each pattern clearly in your horoscope, using the colored lines that you have drawn in.

Meditate on each pattern in turn, reviewing what you know about the planets, signs and houses involved and the harmonic(s) that they are resonating on. As you review experiences which you have associated with the individual planets, houses or signs, ask how knowledge of this larger pattern could have helped you to deal with those experiences. If the orbs are very small, does the whole pattern go off at once, with little chance to discriminate one part from another; does the pattern function as a unit in an automatic or unconscious way? If the orbs are wide, does this pattern require more attention to make it work for you? Is there a mixture of narrow and wide orbs in the pattern? How does the particular sequence and timing of the parts of each pattern relate to your style of learning? To the ways that you change? To your way of conducting your life? What is the sequence of each pattern? Determine the dates of transits affecting each pattern, and review your experiences on those dates, searching for correlations. Do the sequences of events or subjective changes in yourself correspond with the planetary sequence in the pattern? Does this add further perspective and detail to your understanding of your return cycles and cycles through your houses?

Suggestions for further meditation: In each pattern, pick out the aspect(s) that seem most prominent, such as the spine of a kite or the aspect with the closest orb in the pattern. For each aspect that you single out in this way, review your material on the signs, houses and planets involved, on the aspect and harmonic, on the aspect pattern and the role of the emphasized aspect in the pattern, and so on.

Remember that a waxing aspect (before the pair of planets reaches opposition) has an inward, generative, constructive meaning (the images of a seed and sprouting plant) and a waning aspect has an outward, applied, expressive meaning (the images of a flower and fruit).

Refer to one of the many astrology manuals that offer "cookbook" interpretations of the aspects (see the Bibliography); or use the order form provided in the back of this book to purchase one of the computer horoscope delineations produced by Para Research (with texts by Robert Hand, Robert Pelletier and others). Use the suggestions in this exercise to help you prioritize the aspects in your horoscope and put them in proper relationship to each other. Otherwise, it is difficult to assimilate the wealth of diverse and sometimes contradictory interpretations that can be made of individual aspects. The task of horoscope synthesis (integrating all these meanings into a coherent delineation) is yours.

Aspect Sequence

When a transiting planet first enters a new sign, it first aspects that planet in your horoscope that has the earliest sign position. For example, a planet at 2° Leo is aspected (considering only the "major" and twelfth-harmonic aspects) before a planet at 5° Taurus, even though the sign Leo comes after the sign Taurus in the zodiac.

For many purposes, it is useful to know the twelfth-harmonic aspect sequence in your horoscope. Find the planet with the earliest sign position, that is, the smallest number of degrees in its sign, and put it at the top of the list, followed by the next-earliest planet, and so on.

For example, here is the roster of planets in the example horoscope given earlier in this chapter, in figure 128. The first list is in the "alphabetical order" of the planets, and the second is in the aspect sequence:

☉	3	♒	49		☉	3	♒	49
☽	14	♊	17		♄	5	♋	16
☿	12	♑	18		♆	6	♎	22
♀	20	♓	24		♇	9	♌	11
♂	13	♑	47		♅	9	♊	21
♃	27	♍	16		☿	12	♑	18
♄	5	♋	16		♂	13	♑	47
♅	9	♊	21		☽	14	♊	17
♆	6	♎	22		♀	20	♓	24
♇	9	♌	11		♃	27	♍	16

Transiting planets will always form aspects to this horoscope's planets in the sequence given in the second list. (Aspects on the fifth, seventh and other harmonics will follow a somewhat different sequence, but they are seldom considered in transits by most astrologers, precisely because they are more difficult to keep track of.)

This aspect sequence is a profile of the planetary positions for the entire horoscope which is, in a sense, imprinted in each of the twelve signs for this horoscope. Every time a planet reaches 3° 49' of a sign, any sign, it is forming an aspect to the Sun. The next aspect it will form will be from 5° 16' of that sign, when it forms a different aspect to Saturn. Neptune is always the third planet aspected in each sign. From the point of view of twelve signs, this aspect sequence is a perfectly regular pattern that is repeated over and over, with different aspects in each sign. The aspect sequences for other harmonics (those which are not divisors of twelve) overlay this basic pattern.

Aspect Patterns of Rulerships and Exaltations

The signs of rulership, exaltation, detriment and fall for each planet form aspect patterns that may shed light on the inner meanings of the planets themselves.

The Sun rules Leo and is exalted in Aries; these signs, together with the opposite signs of detriment and fall (Aquarius and Libra), form a mystic rectangle. Similarly, the Moon's dignities and debilities (to use the traditional term) form a different mystic rectangle. (See figure 143.)

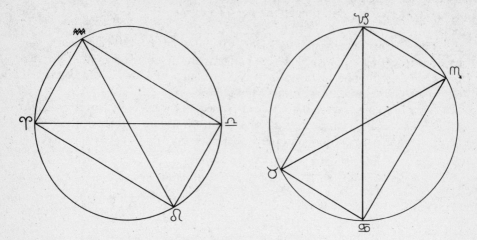

Figure 143. Mystic rectangles of the Sun and Moon

Mercury's dignities form a mystic rectangle if you exclude the Virgo-Pisces opposition; if you exclude the Aquarius-Leo opposition, they form a grand square (figure 144). This reflects the androgynous nature of Mercury. The yang, synthesizing exaltation in Aquarius gives a mystic rectangle, and the yin, analytical exaltation in Virgo gives a grand square.

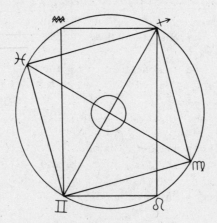

Figure 144. Mercury's mystic rectangle (yang) and grand square (yin exaltation)

The same mutable-sign grand square gives us the two rulerships of Jupiter, in Sagittarius and Pisces. Jupiter's pattern also involves a mystic rectangle, but it is due to conservative Cancer, where Jupiter is exalted; Mercury's overlaid mystic rectangle was due to forward-looking Aquarius, Mercury's yang exaltation. This tells you something about the difference between Mercury and Jupiter. (See figure 145.)

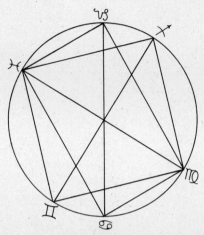

Figure 145. Jupiter's mystic rectangle and grand square

Saturn's pattern is the reverse of that of Jupiter. Saturn's exaltation in Libra plus its rulership of Capricorn together form a grand square in cardinal signs. Its Piscean-age rulership of Aquarius brings in a yang mystic rectangle (figure 146).

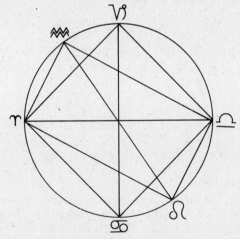

Figure 146. Saturn's grand square plus mystic rectangle

The ambivalence of the Jupiter and Saturn patterns fades with the passing of the old rulerships, as Uranus and Neptune take over rulership of Aquarius and Pisces, respectively. Androgynous Mercury will continue to have both patterns even after the new rulership of Virgo is determined. Saturn, traditionally a "malefic" planet, appropriately will retain the grand square, whereas Jupiter, a "benefic," will not.

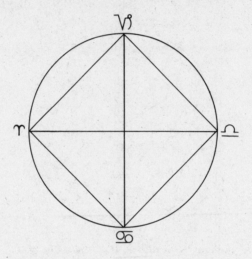

Figure 147. Cardinal grand square of Mars

Mars and Uranus both have grand square patterns. That of Mars is, appropriately, in cardinal signs (figure 147). Little ambiguity here!

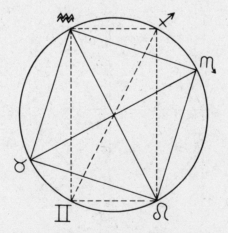

Figure 148. Grand square with mystic rectangle for Uranus

Many astrologers still consider Uranus to be a "malefic," those who still employ black-and-white, good-and-evil terms in their interpretations of astrology. Uranus' grand square is in fixed signs. A comparison with Uranus' lower octave, Mercury, is instructive. Mercury's grand square is in mutable signs, with a mystic rectangle brought in by the fixed Aquarius-Leo opposition (see figure 144, above). The proposed exaltation of Uranus in Gemini would bring a mystic rectangle into Uranus' pattern by way of the mutable Gemini-Sagittarius opposition. The parallel between Uranus and its lower octave, Mercury, is quite striking. In both cases, the yin exaltation is associated with a grand square pattern, and the yang exaltation with a mystic rectangle pattern.

Neptune's dignities and debilities form a somewhat unusual twelfth-harmonic rectangle, since its exaltation in Leo is in the adjacent sign to its detriment in Virgo (figure 149). Interestingly (since Neptune is the new ruler and Jupiter the old ruler of Pisces), there is a similar rectangle in Jupiter's pattern if you omit its rulership of Pisces (see figure 145 above).

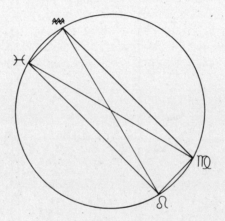

Figure 149. Twelfth-harmonic rectangle of Neptune

And if we include the proposed exaltation of Pluto in Sagittarius, Pluto has a similar twelfth-harmonic rectangle, as shown in figure 150.

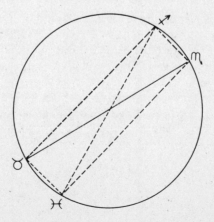

Figure 150. Twelfth-harmonic rectangle of Pluto

The exaltation of Neptune in Leo is square the rulership of Pluto in Scorpio, and the rulership of Neptune is square the proposed exaltation of Pluto in Sagittarius. On the other hand, the rulerships of Pluto and Neptune are in trine (Scorpio trine Pisces), as are their exaltations (Leo trine Sagittarius). One interpretation of this is that, as autonomous entities Pluto and Neptune are harmonious (the trines), but they are not harmonious together when either is the dispositor or the benefactor of the other.

The symbolism of the twelfth harmonic is in the nature of a challenge to recognize the higher unity of apparently disparate experiences. This stimulus for synthesis and synergy is entirely appropriate for these transpersonal planets.

The pattern for Venus is unique. Here we see a mystic rectangle pivoting about a central opposition, the Libra-Aries opposition which is the basic defining axis of the zodiac. As in the patterns of Mercury, Jupiter, Saturn and Uranus, there are three oppositions in this pattern, two of them in a mystic rectangle, but whereas the third opposition in those other patterns results in a grand square, a fourth-harmonic resonance, in Venus' pattern it introduces a twelfth-harmonic resonance.

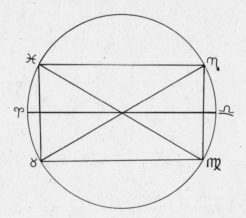

Figure 151. Venus' mystic rectangle with central opposition

If only the rulerships (Taurus and Libra) and the exaltation (Pisces) are included, and the detriment and fall are excluded, the pattern remaining is a yod, with the apex in Libra.

Martin Schulman, to whom I am indebted for pointing out this pattern, suggests that there is an implicit yod pattern wherever Venus may be in a horoscope, with Venus at the apex and two "sensitive points" at the sextile end of the yod.

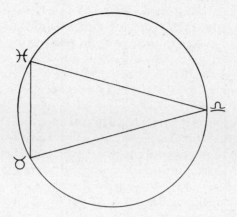

Figure 152. Yod for Venus

In his forthcoming book about Venus, *The Gifts of Love*, he suggests that a key to the symbolism of Venus is the gift of reconciling disharmony (the twelfth-harmonic quincunxes) through the power of love. Might the same principle be applied to the other patterns shown on these pages? Consider that possibility in your meditations.

Progressions

According to the theory of astrology outlined in this book, the foundation-pattern of your personality and the frame of reference within which you have perceived all your experiences is the subconsciously-remembered planetary energy-pattern of the moment of your birth. The energy-pattern attending every experience would have no meaning without that inner context in your mind. Your subconscious powers of memory and imagination compare and in a sense collate experiences, using that basic pattern as a kind of filing system. That is how your knowledge of the world is organized. (See Appendix 1 for more on this.)

In the same way, the changes in the energies that attended your experiences in the first months, following the steadily unfolding pattern of the solar system relative to your natal horoscope, provides a dynamic pattern for the unfolding of your personality through time. The transits of the first months of your life are called *progressions*, they set up inner expectations, a kind of working outline that you fill in in later years.

The most commonly used system of progressions makes an analogy between each day of those first months and each corresponding year of your life. The first day corresponds to the first year, the thirtieth day to the thirtieth year, and so on. The first three months of transits are your progressions for roughly ninety years of your life. There is an interesting symmetry in that, since nine months are spent in the womb, and three months after birth brings you to the solar return of your conception-day.

The exact timing of progressions depends upon what time of day you were born. Using the formula one day = one year, then twelve hours = six months, two hours = one month, one hour = approximately fifteen days, four minutes = one day and so on. The details of calculation are beyond the scope of this book. You can obtain a computer report of progressions for your horoscope from Neil Michelsen's Astro Computing Service or Robert Hand's Astro Graphics Services (see Appendix 3).

For the present, it is sufficient to determine one position for progressed planets per year, without necessarily knowing the exact date they correspond to within that year. To do this, write the date of your birth, and the year next to it. Below that, write the next day-year correspondence, then the next, and so on.

For example, suppose your birthday is April 15, 1948. That would be the first pair on your list. Below that, write "April 16" and "1949," then "April 17" and "1950," and so on. To bring it down to the 1980s more quickly, you might want to count by fives or by tens, but be careful to keep the correspondences straight at the end of one month and the beginning of the next. A month with thirty-one days can be especially confusing. The full example of an April 15, 1948 birthday is as follows:

April 15	1948	May 19	1982
April 16	1949	May 20	1983
April 17	1950	May 21	1984
April 27	1960	May 22	1985
April 28	1961	May 23	1986
April 29	1962	May 24	1987
April 30	1963	May 25	1988
May 1	1964	May 26	1989
May 10	1973	May 27	1990
May 15	1978	May 28	1991
May 16	1979	May 29	1992
May 17	1980	May 30	1993
May 18	1981	May 31	1994

Suppose you want progressions for 1982. In your ephemeris, look up the positions of the planets on the corresponding date, May 19, 1948. Have any of the planets changed sign or house? Are any new aspects formed, or are any old aspects left behind? Are there any relationships between progressed planets that were not there on April 15, 1948? Some astrologers would look at relationships between progressed planets for 1982 and transiting planets for the same year.

Progressions show an inner pattern of expectations, and tell you what stage of inner development you have reached at any given time. They can help you understand why you subconsciously choose to use the potential of transits in one way rather than in another, and give you the opportunity to override the subconscious expectations that you acquired as an infant, as symbolized by progressions. They can lead you to fresh insights about the unfoldment of your horoscopic patterns.

Exercise 21: Find the progressions for the current year for your horoscope. Have any progressed planets changed sign or house since your birth? If so, in what year did they change signs? The progressed Moon makes a complete circuit of the zodiac in about twenty-eight years. How closely does the return of your progressed Moon coincide with your Saturn return? If you have precise timing for the progressed Moon's positions, either by calculation or by computer report as suggested above, what does it tell you about the stages of your emotional growth? Has your progressed Sun changed sign or house? When? Can you correlate any change in the quality of your experience of life with this change? Has any other planet changed sign or house by progression? If so, what changes in your experience of the corresponding part(s) of your personality can you correlate with this change in your progressed horoscope? Are there any changes from the aspect-structure of your natal horoscope, when you look at the progressed planets? If so, review your experiences at the times of those changes.

Conclusion

Astrology is a tremendously exciting field. You may enjoy sharing what you have learned with others, either by teaching a beginning class privately or by doing horoscopes for friends and relatives. The more you do to help others with astrology, the more you will learn about it for yourself. Astrology thrives on feedback between people, and the give-and-take of sharing.

You are in a good position now to learn from other astrologers, because you can relate what they say to your own direct experience of astrology in your life. And you can ask them what the basis of *their* ideas is, how they are rooted in *their* experiences of astrology. Are they just repeating what their teachers and textbooks taught them, or have they really checked it out?

This concludes this introduction to astrology from the inside out. There are many directions that you can go from here. The exercises and images from this book will stay with you as valuable companions on your path.

Appendix 1. A Theory of Astrology

What Is Astrology?

Answers to this question that are given or implied in this book are summarized here.

Astrology is the science of cycles. Long before the advent of ecology, astrologers knew that the behavior of any system is linked to other systems in its environment, and that everything goes on in interlocking cycles. By studying the cycles of the solar system, astrologers learned to recognize, then to interpret and even to predict cycles in human affairs. Orthodox science is beginning to discover the countless interconnections of celestial and terrestrial cycles beyond such obvious relationships as tides and seasons. To an astrologer, the correspondences of macrocosm and microcosm are obvious. How could the ecology of the Earth not be influenced by the vaster ecology of the solar system?

Astrologers have long spoken of the "vibrations" of the planets and signs, and their words have been dismissed as fanciful metaphor. Now, the discovery and study of harmonic patterns in astrology indicate that what is going on can indeed best be described as vibration, as real as the vibrations of light and radio waves. All the laws of vibration apply—harmonics, octaves, resonance, dissonance, interference, reinforcement and so on. They apply to astrology as well as to the physics of electromagnetic radiation and ocean waves.

How can these vibrations influence individual human beings? We have known for many years that what appears to be solid matter really consists of concentrated points of energy arranged in various geometrical patterns. Despite what our outer senses tell us, all the atoms, molecules and masses of physical matter of the tangible world are composed solely of vibrant energy.

In terms of the four elements of astrology, the vibrant energy is Fire, the geometric patterns are Water, the processes of change and formation by which one part of the universe communicates with another are Air. Earth is the tangible outcome, the synthesis of Fire, Water and Air working together simultaneously, in synergy.

Imagine the vast, vibrating field of the universe as an ocean, and your personality as a little cove or bay in that vast sea. The changing patterns that you experience in your thoughts, feelings and actions, and in your physical body itself, cannot be separate from the patterns of waves in the ocean.

Astrology is a system of psychology. Basic concepts, such as the astrological typology of human character, have been in continuous use cross-culturally for thousands of years. No other system of psychology can claim such exhaustive clinical application.

The central hypothesis of astrology is the ancient doctrine of macrocosm and microcosm—the assumption that the energy systems of the Earth and its inhabitants resonate to the changing patterns of the solar system. How is it, then, that human beings differ from one another? If we are all resonating in unison, why aren't we all behaving in unison?

The answer is *memory*. Memory is the glue of personality. We know that the earliest memories of infancy and childhood constitute the subconscious foundation of personality. These memories establish patterns by which all subsequent experiences are interpreted.

At the very root of personality lies the subconscious memory of birth, that dramatic and, even today, often traumatic emergence from the cozy water-cushioned world of the womb. For we do remember the suffocating constriction of the birth canal, the urgent need to breathe as the head emerges, adrenalin in the blood as instinctive survival mechanisms take over from the umbilicus.

These survival mechanisms and autonomic life-support systems are ruled by the Moon, which corresponds to the faculty of memory. Other memories, memories of events before and after birth, surely must pale in comparison to this. The critical transition from fetus to infant must be deeply imprinted at the core of one's memory in every detail, including—and this is where astrology comes in—one's subconscious awareness of the exact disposition of one's energy system, resonating at that moment with the energy pattern of the Earth and of the solar system.

That fundamental, powerfully-charged memory provides a template, the frame of reference by which you recognize and evaluate all subsequent states of your personal energy system. Although your energy system is at all times in resonance with the current pattern of the solar system, your subconscious mind recognizes, analyzes and interprets it in relation to that basic pattern. Your horoscope is a map of your birth-pattern.

Are human character and experience then completely determined by the resonance between the planets and the corresponding components of personality?

The nature/nurture dispute, whether character is determined more by innate endowment or by education and experience, goes back to antiquity. Astrology has generally taken the view of its noble patrons (few, if any, commoners had horoscopes done), and they tended to view things in terms of predestination, birthright and divinely granted (or withdrawn) privilege. Feudalism lends itself to a fatalistic world-view. More deeply, God was thought to have pre-ordained every least event in His world; not to be fatalistic was felt to be impious, sinfully asserting the will of the individual against that of the Creator. In this context, the ancient maxim "the stars incline, they do not impel," meaning that astrology concerns predisposition rather than predestination, tended to be forgotten.

Fortunately, astrology survived times of superstition and the hostility of church dogmatists. Nonetheless, the popular image of astrology continues to be stained with superstitious fatalism in consequence of the expedients some astrologers have practiced in order to survive. Perhaps most people in the West today place science in one camp and astrology, along with "the occult," in another, and then feel that if they embrace one they must reject the other.

On the one hand scientists sign documents denouncing astrology without examining current evidence. On the other hand, astrologers espouse notions of astrological determinism that flatly contradict well-substantiated principles of conditioning and learning. A growing minority between these extremes senses the validity of both astrology and orthodox science, and mistrusts the unreasonable dogmas of both camps.

The conceptual framework sketched here offers a basis for working out a balanced view. Science and astrology are quite compatible. The crux of the matter is the issue of determinism versus free choice, fate versus free will, nature versus nurture.

Karma is a traditional Sanskrit term for determinism, fate, destiny and the mechanistic cause-and-effect side of things. For example, suppose your car were parked in neutral on a hill, and a child got in and released the parking brake. The car would *of necessity* roll down the hill, along a path that is predetermined by known laws of physics, until something stopped it, perhaps destroying it and injuring the child. This is *karma*, the necessary consequence of releasing the brake.

But suppose the child were alert enough to steer the car, or to pull on the parking brake again. Any such *conscious action* would change the fate of the car and of the child.

Everything we do is a mixture of conscious action with unconscious chains of cause and effect. Consider the enormous complexity involved in making a simple gesture like picking up a glass, an intricate choreography of nerve-impulses, chemical exchanges and muscular tensions that biologists say would take them years to describe with any completeness.

Your subconscious mind is the choreographer. You simply choose to make a movement, and your subconscious mind puts your intention into effect by a series of habitual, automatic patterns of action.

On a more subtle level, particular patterns in your energy system, in resonance with the planets, predispose you to follow automatic chains of cause-and-effect that have no necessary reality other than that they have become associated with those planetary patterns in your memory. However, you always have the freedom to choose whether to follow the automatic patterns, or to introduce something new. That is how you form new habits and response patterns.

For example, in resonance with the planet Mars one day, your adrenal chakra may predispose you to behave impatiently. During the course of that day, you have many options open to you when you experience frustration. You can simply lose your temper on the spot. You can deny that you are angry, pretend that the anger is not there—and later on be as surprised as everyone else when your anger explodes over some trivial issue. You can deliberately pour your aggressive energy into work, or into athletic activities, doing an end run around the frustration. You can meditatively watch your reactions in order to better learn what kind of thing "pushes your buttons," so that you can change the programming of your subconscious mind. You can just watch events and your reactions to them from a neutral point of consciousness that accompanies your "normal" consciousness, without necessarily connecting either the events or the reactions to any chains of associations in your memory.

In schools and in other social institutions we are typically made aware of our behavior only when it is being labelled as "good" or "bad," which always puts one on the spot. As a consequence, we have shied away from becoming conscious of our own behavior. However, the more conscious we are, the more choice we have. To steer the "car" of your personality, or to reach the brake pedal, you have to be familiar with how it works, what its parts are and how to locate them. To "drive" your personality you also have to see clearly where it is going and what is around you. The exercises in this book are designed to bring your unconscious awareness of these things to your conscious attention, so that you can improve your perception and your skill. Awareness is the key. This is the reason for the emphasis on meditation in this book.

Appendix 2. Meditation

What Is Meditation?

Meditation is the practice of awareness. In meditation, one becomes aware of the ever-changing activities of the mind. One becomes conscious of one's own consciousness. As a result of simple mindfulness, the mental agitation typical of "normal" day-to-day busyness lessens and the mind becomes more clear. As a consequence, life becomes less complicated as its choices become more obvious.

Meditation must be practiced to be learned. Theories accomplish nothing. Furthermore, without the direct knowledge that comes from practice, the experiences of meditators may sound fanciful, the benefits of meditation may sound like wishful thinking and all the methods and techniques of meditation may seem pointless or even pretentious.

Since we are concerned with inward experience of astrological resonances, it is appropriate to approach meditation by an account of the *inner senses.*

Imagine for a moment that we live in a country where no one pays attention to one of their senses. Let's say that everyone in this country ignores the sense of smell. If somehow you learned to cultivate and value this sense, how would you go about teaching someone else to do the same?

You might minimize distraction by having them sit in a quiet place with their eyes closed, relaxed but alert enough not to get sleepy. Then you might ask them to hold a rose under their nose and to inhale with their mouth closed and their attention focused within their nostrils. If they followed these instructions, despite their seeming complicated and pointless, they might learn to sense that rose in a new and subtle way, without opening their eyes. They might give amazing accounts of their experiences with this newly-awakened sense, which others would consider pretentious and fanciful.

This is exactly where we stand with meditation, except that we are reawakening (or waking up to) not one but a whole set of *inner senses,* including inner vision (insight) and inner hearing (intuition). Most people in our Euro-American culture discount their inner senses, or lump them under the broad and somewhat misleading category, "imagination."

Few people understand the true nature of imagination, and its importance. Imagination and the inner senses are essential to normal perception and cognition. (See for example Ulric Neisser's *Cognition and Reality.*)

When one perceives an event, sensory stimuli evoke memories of similar past experiences. The imagination—the creative, fertile phase of your subconscious mind—fabricates from these memories an image or model of what appears to be going on. It is upon this *inner counterpart*, perceived with the inner senses, that one bases expectations and responses, not directly upon the outer event itself. Most of what passes for cognition is only a rather superficial re-cognition.

I was made acutely aware of this when I read Carlos Castaneda's description of how to gain control of one's dreaming. Don Juan told Castaneda to focus his attention on a familiar object, suggesting his hands since they are most within his control. When the appearance of his hands began to shift and transform in the dream, he was to look at something else. In this way, avoiding the fascination of dream-metamorphoses, he would find himself exploring one distinct, stable locality in the world of *dreaming*.

I decided to try it. Before going to sleep, I prepared to give my subconscious mind the suggestion that I would look at my hands in a dream, and thereby gain conscious control. However, I could not visualize my hands. How could I effectively give the suggestion if I could not visualize my hands in a waking state?

Realizing that I would have to back up a step, I decided first to meditate on my hands, fixing their image clearly in mind so that I could then make the suggestion to look at them in the same way in my dream.

Look at your hands now. Study them. Are you really familiar with their unique pattern of lines and mounds? Make the experiment—put this book down now and look at your hands.

I found that I really was not familiar with my hands. In fact I had seldom really looked at them. I took them for granted. The expression came to my mind: "I know that place like the back of my hand." We think it means full, detailed knowledge. What it actually means is "I pass through that place often and never really look at it because it's familiar." In other words, if something is familiar, I can dismiss it without further attention. Another saying that came to mind is: "familiarity breeds contempt." Familiarity in this sense *is* contempt. What other familiar patterns are there in your life that you take for granted?

To improve or change any situation, you cannot take it for granted. You must first perceive it clearly and accurately. The best map in the world will not help you get where you want to go unless you know your present location on the map. The exercises in this book are designed to help you find yourself on the astrological map, then to decide where you want to go, and finally to get there. In all three stages of your process of change, the essential activity is paying attention or meditation.

There are two main branches of meditation practice: *concentration* and *insight*.

Insight meditation aims to uncouple your inner senses from memory and imagination, so that they resonate with your outer senses in a very clear, direct way, without mental or emotional intervention. By so doing, you perceive what is going on as if it had never happened before (as of course it has not). A good example is the Zen Buddhist practice of "just sitting," where no single object of meditation is isolated.

A form of *concentration meditation* is adapted in this book. The aim of concentration is to limit both inner and outer senses to one object, so that they come into clear resonance by eliminating distractions. Objects of meditation include physical objects, visual images, symbols, sounds, internal feeling-states, processes such as the process of breathing or the heart beating, and so on. Concentration sharpens the mind and makes it an effective tool. Your meditation-object provides an anchor and a point of reference, so that you are able to experience clearly both the contents of your memory and the working of your imagination, while poised in a good position to improve both.

In Buddhist practice, the aim of concentration meditation is to watch these mental processes, to witness them without attachment, thus training the mind not to cling to hopes, fears, expectations, doubts and all the rest of the paraphernalia of cognition, until insight (wisdom) arises naturally. The two techniques, insight and concentration, are thus complementary phases of one thing, the practice of mindfulness.

There are also immediate, practical results to be gained from the type of concentration meditation that is developed in the exercises in this book. You use the object of your concentration as you might use a reference number in a library, to retrieve the information relating to that symbol. You will find that you already know a great deal more than you realized you did. You already have all the information you need. Subconsciously, you knew how to use astrology and your natal birth-pattern when you were a child, and you have that knowledge now—subconsciously. The symbols of astrology will help you to recall that information accurately and systematically, so that you can use it consciously.

In most of the exercises, you explore your horoscope as a circular space around you, moving around in it, taking the perspective of each of its component parts in turn. At first it may feel a little silly (remember the person smelling the rose? See Appendix 1), but in a short time astrology begins to come alive in your mind and in your life. When it does, magical changes take place in your perception and understanding.

For this purpose, arrange to have a regular meditation space set aside at certain times, such as a particular room in your house. Your space should be quiet, and large enough to place objects in a circle around you. When you sit, your seat should be comfortable and supportive, not too soft, so that your posture is erect and alert, yet relaxed and free of strain; neither in danger of falling asleep nor of being distracted by your physical effort. A straight-backed chair that supports the thighs when the feet touch the floor is usually best. If noise is a problem, try earplugs, or headphones and quiet instrumental music (music without words).

At first, it is important to have a familiar, supportive environment to reinforce your efforts, but later, with practice, you will be able to close your eyes anywhere and visualize your meditation space around you. Then it is a living tool that you always have with you whenever you call it to mind.

Dedicate a regular time to daily meditation. If you miss your appointment with yourself, fit it in some other time during the day. Daily practice, even for only fifteen minutes, is much more valuable than hours of practice once or twice a week. First thing in the morning is often a good time, because imagination, memory and the inner senses are more open then, and closer to the dream state.

Most of the exercises in this book suggest a variety of objects for meditation, to help you realize and integrate the information given in the preceding text, including physical objects, words, ideas, images, symbols, feelings and problems that commonly arise in human experience. Your reading may suggest other relevant objects for meditation. Choose one of significance or value for you, each time you do a given exercise.

To integrate what you have learned thus far, and to practice the technique of concentration meditation used in this book, meditate on "astrology." What does the word mean to you? What images, ideas and feelings are associated with astrology in your mind? What concepts and preconceptions are you aware of in your study of astrology?

The following exercise focuses on "astrology" as a topic, but you can substitute any other topic and follow the same exercise format for any exercise in this book, if you wish.

Exercise 1: Meditate on the nature of astrology, your present understanding of what it is and how it works, your associations with the word.

Sit in your meditation space, close your eyes and take four very deep, slow breaths. Be sure to breathe all the way out before each inhalation.

If you find this preliminary slow breathing difficult, you may find it helpful to sigh a couple of times, heavily, to break up tension; or stretch and rotate your neck and shoulders gently before breathing deeply.

After the four deep breaths, relax and feel your breathing become quiet and regular, then count your slow, relaxed breaths from ten to one. When you reach "one," allow your attention to focus on the object of your meditation, astrology.

If you have trouble seeing the word in your mind's eye with your inner vision, print it carefully on a card and look at it with your outer, physical vision, until you can see it clearly when you close your eyes again. If you lose it, open your eyes and look outward again.

If you cannot hear the word "astrology" with your inner hearing, say it aloud a few times, then continue repeating the word to yourself. If you lose it, and drift from the topic, repeat it again, either aloud or to yourself.

In this way, focus your attention through your inner senses, hold astrology at the center of your attention in your mind, and watch what flows past it in the stream of consciousness.

This is like watching a boulder just at the surface of a running stream of water: Your attention tends to drift with the flow of the stream. You may suddenly become aware that you are thinking about your argument with your boss just after his secretary left, the one who reminds you of Aunt Edith who was always reading the astrology column in the papers—Ah yes! Astrology.

Your thoughts may have wandered far away from your chosen topic, astrology, and you may have little memory of how they got there or even of how much time has elapsed. Events of the day, problems, worries, plans, desires and so forth may capture your attention by the emotional energy associated with them. No matter. If you have let go of your anchor and allowed yourself to drift on the stream of consciousness, simply notice what it was that attracted your attention and why. Thank your subconscious mind for bringing it to your attention. Make a definite resolution to consider it in detail at an appropriate time, and gently but firmly re-focus your attention on the object of your meditation, astrology.

It may be that a "distracting" chain of associations began with an idea or image that was related to astrology. When the flow of your mental process does bring you something connected with your chosen object, explore the connection until their relationship becomes clear and you can see how the new material really is a part or aspect of the object of your meditation, astrology, after all. Then, with this enlarged grasp of your object, wait for the next bit of related material to present itself to your attention. Use your "distractions." Follow them back to their origins close to the object of your meditations, so that they reveal ideas and images with valid relationships to that object, astrology. Don't get lost in the process of backtracking, however. That process might be a fruitful subject for meditation on another occasion, but this time the object of your meditation is astrology.

In this way, as you persist, the object of your meditation, astrology, will unfold itself, petal by petal, disclosing its inner nature to you.

At the close of your meditation period, review the unfolded "petals" of your meditation object and their relationships, to be sure that you recall them clearly.

Then use the power of autosuggestion to set a firmer basis for future meditations. Speak directly to your subconscious mind, as if to another person within you, thanking it for its gifts (including the "distractions"). Feel warm appreciation for the rich mental processes that you have just explored.

When your period of inner focus is finished, describe your findings about astrology in the first pages of a loose-leaf notebook, the same notebook that you will use for all the exercises in this book, and that will become your astrological journal.

Develop the ideas and images that came to you, and the relationships among them. What do they tell you about your conceptions and preconceptions of astrology?

You may have difficulty at first remembering your inner experiences following meditation. If so, keep a small notepad at hand while you meditate. Energetically grasp the essence of each image or idea that you want to remember, and when you feel you are at the heart of it, some image will come to the foreground of your consciousness naturally as a label or tag. These are the keys that your subconscious mind is offering you. Do not demand that they be intellectually adequate in some sense of logic or verbal completeness. They are only reminders. The intellectual, logical and verbal processes come later, after your period of inner focus, when you record and develop your discoveries in your notebook.

The attention you give to distilling key images will ensure that you remember each one clearly. As a byproduct, your normal day-to-day memory will improve. Soon, you will not need the support of the notepad, which can interfere with meditation.

Your mind may wander, but to become impatient or angry with it is not helpful. Simply make mental note of each distraction, ask your subconscious mind why it found these images more important than your chosen focus, make a definite resolve to give your attention to it at a later time, and return to your chosen object of meditation. Later, after you have developed the fruits of your meditation in your notebook, spend some time with these distractions. You may discover some relationship after all with your topic. If one of them falls within one of the areas of astrology that you learned about prior to that particular exercise, you may want to use it as the object of a future meditation. In any case, ask yourself why this matter is so important to you now, and what you can do about it. If you ask seriously, and then listen, your subconscious mind will convey an answer.

Over time, the inner and outer processes of living and meditating become progressively easier. As your mind becomes accustomed to the new habit of attending to one thing at a time, you experience greater simplicity and clarity in all your affairs. With the new habit of attending to the things that actually concern you at the moment, instead of flitting distractedly from one thing to another, there is less and less unfinished business floating around loose in your life, clamoring for your attention.

You may experience doubts from time to time. Am I doing this right? Is this worth doing? Am I wasting my time? What would my friends or family think? Don't worry about doubts. Doubting is a natural byproduct of an agitated mind. It is a kind of mental equivalent to pain.

The analogy to pain is useful. I remember, while meditating, suddenly noticing that a pain that had been quite intense and sharp in my left shoulder was gone. When I sat to meditate and encountered this pain, I knew from prior experience that stretching or rubbing the sore area would not help. The pain would become negligible, and would simply be replaced by some other distraction. As I waited, imagery arose that was relevant to the topic of my meditation and took the foreground of my attention, so that the pain was relegated to the background. Later, I noticed that the pain had gone. Reflecting on this, I wondered if I had ever observed the actual arising or going away of such pains. Or did they come and go only when I wasn't looking?

You may want to make the actual process of doubt an object of meditation. You can gain insight into the nature of doubting, just as you can for any other phenomenon. When your attention is focused on doubt, you experience doubt;

when it is focused on some other phenomenon, that is what you experience. Simply dwell on something about which your mind generates a cloud of doubt. As the doubt arises in your mind, observe it, see how it wraps itself around the forms of your thoughts like clothing—or like a disguise. When it goes away, where does it go?

Doubt, like pain, functions as an alarm clock. Once you have waked up, you turn your alarm clock off. There is no special virtue in letting it ring on and on. To dwell on doubt or pain is like carrying your alarm clock, still ringing, to the breakfast table. Are you sleepwalking?

Stop feeding the process of doubting (or feeling pain) with your attention. Instead, turn your attention to the causes of the process. Then, having attended to that, turn your attention to things that you care about. The doubt (or pain) will fade away of its own accord.

Protection: Some people feel disorientation, confusion or vertigo on occasion during the course of meditation. These are symptoms of imbalance in your energy system which are easily corrected.

In meditation, your energy system (your chakras and the flow of energy through them—see Chapter 2) becomes more receptive. If you feel that you might be subject to intrusion or interruption, visualize a protective cocoon of white light surrounding your meditation space. It is a good idea to make this a regular preliminary to meditation, particularly in an urban environment or in an emotionally complex household.

Do not worry about whether or not your shield against psychic intrusion is "really there." Such doubts confuse the imagination, and thus become self-fulfilling. And do not try too hard to exert your will. One sees great exertions of will in comic books and melodramatic films, where the hero or heroine is resisting the Forces of Evil and so forth. Although these flamboyant manifestations are designed to convince the audience that something "real" is going on, they are really expressions of doubt. It is not a matter of will-power, for imagination is more powerful than personal will. And imagination depends upon confident expectation, or faith.

Simply feel and think that your visualization is there, confidently, and it is. Remember that these are inner experiences, perceived through your inner senses, which are not yet fully awake. Proof comes with practice, not beforehand! What matters is not the vividness of your inner perceptions, which depend upon the acuity of your inner senses, but rather your deliberate intention and definite effort to visualize. This applies to all your visualizations, as well as the white light. And the more you do it, the easier it is.

If there is anything you do not understand in this book or in your own experience, formulate it as a question for meditation. You will probably be answered directly, or at least your subconscious memory, with its perfect recall, will provide you with some clues, perhaps an indication of an appropriate exercise in this book, to gain the necessary background knowledge. As the *I Ching* states so many times, "perseverance furthers."

Grounding: Other practices are helpful in stabilizing your energy system and promoting clarity and ease in your meditation. One of these is grounding, connecting with the Earth.

As you sit with your eyes closed in meditation, visualize and feel cords or rods of energy projecting down into the Earth from the minor chakras in the balls of your feet. Talk inwardly to your body; say "Foot chakras, open up!" and feel energy from the center of the Earth warmly flowing up through your feet, through your legs, into your root chakra at the base of your spine. Feel the energy circulating through the root chakra, filling it and strengthening it; visualize and feel it returning down a large cable or pole from the base of your spine like a root penetrating deep into the depths of the Earth, forming a complete circuit.

If you are one of the many people who habitually are not properly grounded, you will experience no giddiness or instability if you commence your meditation periods with this exercise. Grounding is also an excellent way to return from meditation (or from sleep) to customary states of consciousness.

Chakra cleaning and balancing: Begin with the grounding exercise, above. While the current of Earth energy is running, visualize and feel a shaft of white light descending through the transpersonal point above your head and through each of your major chakras in turn.

Pause at the solar plexus chakra. Visualize the color violet (attributed to Jupiter, ruler of this chakra) filling a sphere in that part of your body between your navel and your heart, pouring in from the flowing stream of white light. Ask for any blockages of energy, or any unwanted connections with any other people's energy systems, to be dissolved and washed away in the descending stream of white light. Your subconscious mind will see that this is done, as you visualize and feel it happening: Such is the power of imagination.

Pause then at the adrenal chakra below the navel and visualize the color red filling it in a brilliant scarlet sphere, pouring in from the stream of white light. Red is the color associated with Mars, ruler of this chakra. Ask for this chakra to be cleaned and balanced also, and for any unwanted or unneeded energies to be washed away in the descending stream of white light.

At the root chakra, visualize and feel how the two streams of energy merge, one from the Earth and one from above, and swirl together in a sphere of dark blue-violet or indigo light, almost black, the color of Saturn, ruler of the root chakra. Ask that your root chakra be cleaned and balanced. Feel and see how the two streams of energy separate again, the Earth energy continually flowing out and down that descending cable or shaft into the Earth, and the white light returning up the sequence of chakras, each stream enriched and balanced because they came into contact through you.

At each point where you pause, the energy continues flowing; you just pause to attend to its activity in a particular chakra. When the ascending white light reaches your heart chakra, pause and feel your heart filling with golden light, color of the Sun, which rules the heart chakra. Ask that your heart energies be cleansed and balanced, and any unnecessary energies washed away in the ascending flow.

Turn your attention to your throat chakra, ruled by Venus, and visualize and feel it filling with emerald green light from the ascending flow of white light. Ask that your throat chakra be balanced and washed by that stream of energy. Do likewise with the brow chakra, ruled by the Moon (silver or blue light) and your crown chakra, ruled by Mercury (yellow light). Then return your consciousness to the transpersonal point about twenty inches above your crown chakra.

The transpersonal point is an excellent starting place for meditation, particularly if interpersonal issues of any kind are involved. At the close of your meditation, use the grounding exercise or one of the other exercises given here to return to a customary state.

To help you visualize and feel the energy flowing, coordinate it with your breathing. When you breathe out, the Earth is exhaling too, but the solar system is inhaling from the Earth through you. When you inhale, the solar system is breathing into the Earth through you, and the Earth is inhaling through you. Do nothing, just allow breathing to happen, and watch it happening. Think: "It breathes me," and visualize the colors in each chakra in turn as your natural rhythm of breathing carries the flow of energies through your system.

When you are running or working, concentrate on your exhalations, your breathing out instead of your breathing in, and notice how the Earth gives you added strength and stamina. Let the inhalations happen easily and naturally, and put whatever energy is needed into the exhalations.

Centering: As you sit with your eyes closed in meditation, visualize and feel your meditation circle around you, with your heart chakra at its center. Visualize and feel a warm golden glowing flow of unconditional love and compassion flowing into your heart chakra from the Sun and from the other stars of the universe through each of your houses. Allow your heart chakra to fill and to radiate that compassion and unconditional love outward again. Feel it first suffusing your body; register compassion for your own person. Really feel compassion for yourself, and accept it for yourself. Then visualize and feel this golden Sun light flowing out through each part of your life, as symbolized by your twelve houses. Feel compassion for others there.

Use this exercise any time and any place that you feel the need of strength, courage or centeredness. It is an excellent way to close a meditation period.

Shielding: In addition to the coccoon of white light described above, which protects your meditation space, you can shield particular areas of your person. You can place a coccoon of white light around your body as a whole (not forgetting your feet and behind your back!), or you can put a ring or band around any chakra where you feel discomfort or vunerability.

It is quite common for people unconsciously to project cords of energy, particularly from the solar plexus, into other people's energy systems. This is a natural part of rapport between people. It can be abused, however. For example, people with low self-esteem often tap into other people's energies to feed their own. Having surrounded themselves with negative imagery, they have cut off their imaginations and other subconscious faculties from the universal supplies of energy. After a period of time in the company of such people you can feel drained. You might have a headache or a stomachache. If you feel this happening, put a band around the area you feel might be tapped. Just visualize a ring of white light. Nothing can penetrate this shield unless you intend it to.

In general, you are vulnerable to such intrusion only if you open yourself to it. If you seek manipulative advantage over another person, you may open your third (Jupiter) or sixth (Moon) chakra to intrusion. If you crave emotional responses, you may open your second (Mars) or fifth (Venus) chakra. Information or communication relates to your crown (Mercury) chakra. Desire or fear is what opens your energy system and invites intrusion. Desire or fear arise when you feel inadequate or incomplete in some way. Consequently, other energies come into your life to attempt completion. But energies from outside, however well-intended, never quite do it. You can learn from them what it is that you lack, and then satisfy the lack for yourself with your own access to universal energies; but sometimes these outside influences can be disruptive, too.

Group Meditation: It is often helpful to meditate together with other people. Your energy systems resonate and reinforce one another. Sharing your experiences is fun, and hastens your progress. A good plan is to meet once a week, choosing a mutually interesting object for meditation. Meditate for a half hour or so, using a timer or having one person check the time. As you get used to working together, increase the time to forty-five minutes, then to an hour. When each of you has finished writing, after the meditation session proper, share your discoveries with each other. Follow this with a shared, potluck meal and you have a wonderful addition to your week's activities.

You may move ahead of the others in the sequences of exercises, or others may move ahead of you, in your individual work. It never hurts for those who have moved rapidly ahead to review. You are never really finished with any of the exercises in this book, in the sense of having no more to learn from them. On the contrary, a review is always richer and more rewarding than the first time through.

Some of the exercises may be read as guided meditations; for example, the first exercises in Chapter 1. Experiment with having one member guiding the group through these exercises.

You may prefer meditating once or twice a week with a partner, spouse or friend in the same way. There are excellent benefits to such practice. However, be sure to reserve some of your meditation time for your own personal work alone.

If you meditate regularly each day, you will have few difficulties. Regular meditation changes your mental, emotional and physical constitution, as does any habit. The changes brought about by meditation will enable you to experience directly what you would otherwise know about only intellectually, by hearsay. These changes take time, but they begin the moment you begin.

Appendix 3. Resources

Several computer services are available that will cast accurate horoscopes and other astrological materials for you very inexpensively and with truly marvellous accuracy. Some of these are:

Para Research, Inc., Dept. H
Whistlestop Mall
Rockport, MA 01966

Astro Computing Services
P.O. Box 16297
San Diego, CA 92116

Astro-Graphics Services
217 Rock Harbor Road
Orleans, MA 02653

Astro-Graphics (AGS) also markets some very fine software for small computers such as the Apple or the Radio Shack TRS-80. And Para Research provides a unique delineation and interpretation assembled by computer from materials written by some of the finest astrologers in the world. These are described in the last pages of this book.

For any of these services, you will first have to know the exact time, as well as the date and place of your birth. Try to find a record of this time in a baby book or on your birth certificate. Do not rely on the memory of older family members unless you have no other recourse. Even mothers have been known to make mistakes in this area!

If you have no such document, write to the government agency concerned with vital statistics in your state. These are listed in a pamphlet called "How to obtain birth and death information" that is available from the U.S. Government Printing Office in Washington, D.C. They are also listed in Robert C. Janksy's "Getting Your Correct Birth Data," available from Astro-Analytics Publications, P.O. Box 991, Venice, CA 90291. Or you may be able to get the address for the appropriate agency by calling Directory Assistance in the state capitol of your birthplace and asking for the office of vital statistics.

When you do contact the office of vital statistics, sometimes a friendly clerk will give you your information over the telephone if she or he knows you are just looking for the birth time.

If a phone call does not get you the information you want, ask for an application form for requesting a copy of your birth certificate. The full birth certificate has more information on it than the abbreviated form that people commonly have to document their citizenship for passports and so forth. There is usually a fee (generally about $2) for making the certified copy.

If you write first to one of the astrological computing services, asking for an order form and list of services offered, you will have it in hand and will be ready to order your horoscope by the time you confirm your birth time.

It is important that the time be as accurate as possible. Every four minutes, on the average, there is another degree rising on the Ascendant. Planets can change houses and even signs if they are near the cusp.

If you don't know your birth time and can't find it out for some reason—for example, if you were adopted—all is not lost. A horoscope cast for sunrise the day and place of your birth is highly significant. This is the so-called "solar" horoscope, commonly used in studies of historical figures for whom the birth time is not known. Working with your sunrise chart, exploring the positions of the planets at various times of day and their meanings in different houses, you should be able to get a pretty good idea when you were born. Astro Computing Service offers a "rectification assist," a series of horoscopes for the same day at twenty-minute intervals. After you have completed Part I of this book with a sunrise horoscope, you should be in a position to judge which of these alternative horoscopes most closely fits your experience best. The study of astrological cycles in Part II will help you pin it down even more exactly. This is the process known as "rectifying" a horoscope. The more skills you develop, such as progressions in Chapter 6, the more basis you will have for your rectification.

Ephemeris

Figure 153 reproduces a page from *The American Ephemeris* (Astro Computing Service, 1977). It shows where the planets were at midnight Greenwich time each day in October, 1929. (Greenwich time is the local standard time at the 0° meridian, which passes through Greenwich, England. It is also called Universal Time, and on occasion even "Zulu time," referring to the "Z" sound in the "zero" of 0°.)

The table at the top of the page has columns giving the daily positions of the Sun, Moon and planets. The actual daily position of the Moon's north node is listed in the "TRUE ☊ " column; the "MEAN ☊ " column gives its position according to its average speed of travel. Astrologers used the latter until recently, when lists of true node positions became available. The "SID. TIME" column lists the sidereal time that corresponds to midnight Greenwich time each day. Sidereal time is measured according to the daily revolution of the stars, whereas our clock time is solar time, measured according to the daily revolution of the Sun. Since the Sun moves relative to the stars, sidereal time agrees with solar or clock time only once a year, when the Sun is at 0° Libra (the Autumnal equinox). In October, as shown in figure 153, solar time is already one or two hours out of phase with sidereal time. The discrepancy increases by two hours each month until the Sun is at 0° Aries, when the two kinds of time are twelve hours out of phase; thereafter the discrepancy decreases by two hours each month.

The glyphs for the signs are given only at the tops of the columns, and at those points where a planet changes signs, so if there is a blank between the first number (the number of degrees) and the second (the number of minutes of arc) on a given day, look for the closest zodiacal glyph higher up in the column.

The large table in the middle of figure 153 shows the declination and latitude of each planet each day at 0 h. UT (midnight Universal Time or Greenwich time). Declination is the angular distance between a planet and the plane of the Earth's equator. Latitude is the angular distance between a planet and the plane of the Earth's orbit around the Sun, the ecliptic. The Sun is by definition always exactly on the ecliptic, so no latitude is given for it. The letter "N" indicates that a given angle is north of the plane of reference and the letter "S" indicates that the planet is so many degrees south of the plane of reference. (The plane of reference for declination is the equator, and for latitude it is the ecliptic.)

The "Daily Aspectarian" at the bottom of the page shows the exact time (at the Greenwich meridian) that aspects are formed among the planets each day. These aspects influence everyone, but they influence you strongly only if the planets involved also aspect points in your horoscope. (See Chapter 6 for details.)

The small table inset at right-center page shows various lunar phenomena. The box on the upper left of this table shows the date and time of each quarter of the Moon. The central box on the left shows the date and time (to the nearest hour) when the Moon crosses the equator (0°) and when it has its greatest declination and is furthest from the equator (27S32 and 27N34 in this case). The bottom box on the left gives the corresponding information for latitude, showing when the Moon crosses the ecliptic (0°) and when it is furthest from the ecliptic (5S14 and 5N17).

The larger box on the right side of this inset table of lunar phenomena shows in its left half the date and time (to the nearest minute) when the Moon last forms an aspect before entering a new sign. This is the "void of course Moon" which some astrologers have found significant. The right half of this "void of course Moon" box shows the date and time of the Moon's ingress (entry) into a new sign, after which it is no longer "void of course." Immediately below these two columns are shown the dates and times when the Moon is furthest from the Earth ("apogee") and closest to the Earth ("perigee").

OCTOBER 1929

LONGITUDE

DAY	SID. TIME	☉	☽	☽ 12 Hour	MEAN ☊	TRUE ☊	☿	♀	♂	♃	♄	♅	♆	♇
	h m s	° ' "	° ' "	° ' "	° '	° '	° '	° '	° '	° '	° '	° '	° '	° '
1	0 36 57	7♎ 19 32	12♍ 28 1	19♍ 29 7	13♉ 49	12♉ 37R	21♎ 43R	6♍ 27	26♎ 16	16♊ 22	24♐ 46	9♈ 29R	2♍ 26	19♋ 33
2	0 40 54	8 18 33	26 26 53	3♎ 20 48	13 46	12 31	21 1	7 40	26 57	16 23	24 49	9 26	2 28	19 33
3	0 44 50	9 17 40	10♎ 10 26	16 55 28	13 42	12 27	20 11	8 53	27 37	16 24	24 52	9 24	2 29	19 34
4	0 48 47	10 16 47	23 35 38	0♏ 10 48	13 39	12 24	19 15	10 6	28 18	16 24	24 56	9 21	2 31	19 34
5	0 52 44	11 15 56	6♏ 40 56	13 6 6	13 36	12 23D	18 14	11 19	28 58	16 24R	24 59	9 19	2 33	19 35
6	0 56 40	12 15 7	19 26 27	25 42 15	13 33	12 23	17 7	12 33	29 39	16 24	25 3	9 16	2 35	19 35
7	1 0 37	13 14 20	1♐ 53 50	8♐ 1 34	13 30	12 24	15 58	13 46	0♏ 20	16 24	25 6	9 14	2 37	19 35
8	1 4 33	14 13 35	14 5 57	20 7 28	13 27	12 26	14 47	14 59	1 0	16 24	25 10	9 12	2 39	19 36
9	1 8 30	15 12 52	26 6 40	2♑ 4 9	13 23	12 27	13 37	16 13	1 41	16 23	25 14	9 9	2 40	19 36
10	1 12 26	16 12 10	8♑ 0 29	13 56 18	13 20	12 29R	12 29	17 26	2 22	16 22	25 17	9 7	2 42	19 36
11	1 16 23	17 11 30	19 52 13	25 48 50	13 17	12 29	11 26	18 40	3 3	16 21	25 21	9 4	2 44	19 37
12	1 20 19	18 10 52	1♒ 46 45	7♒ 46 33	13 14	12 28	10 29	19 53	3 44	16 20	25 25	9 2	2 45	19 37
13	1 24 16	19 10 16	13 48 45	19 53 54	13 11	12 26	9 39	21 7	4 25	16 19	25 29	9 0	2 47	19 37
14	1 28 13	20 9 42	26 2 25	2♓ 14 44	13 7	12 23	8 59	22 21	5 6	16 17	25 33	8 57	2 49	19 37
15	1 32 9	21 9 9	8♓ 31 10	14 52 1	13 4	12 20	8 29	23 34	5 47	16 15	25 38	8 55	2 50	19 37
16	1 36 6	22 8 38	21 17 27	27 47 34	13 1	12 17	8 10	24 48	6 28	16 13	25 42	8 53	2 52	19 38
17	1 40 2	23 8 9	4♈ 22 25	11♈ 1 55	12 58	12 14	8 2D	26 2	7 9	16 11	25 46	8 50	2 54	19 38
18	1 43 59	24 7 42	17 45 56	24 34 15	12 55	12 12	8 5	27 16	7 50	16 8	25 51	8 48	2 55	19 38
19	1 47 55	25 7 17	1♉ 26 32	8♉ 22 28	12 52	12 11D	8 19	28 30	8 32	16 6	25 55	8 46	2 57	19 38
20	1 51 52	26 6 54	15 21 37	22 23 32	12 48	12 11	8 44	29 44	9 13	16 3	26 0	8 43	2 58	19 38
21	1 55 48	27 6 33	29 27 45	6♊ 33 49	12 45	12 11	9 18	0♎ 58	9 54	16 0	26 5	8 41	3 0	19 38R
22	1 59 45	28 6 14	13♊ 41 13	20 49 30	12 42	12 12	10 0	2 12	10 36	15 57	26 9	8 39	3 1	19 38
23	2 3 42	29 5 58	27 58 15	5♋ 7 1	12 39	12 13	10 51	3 26	11 17	15 53	26 14	8 37	3 2	19 38
24	2 7 38	0♏ 5 44	12♋ 15 27	19 23 12	12 36	12 14	11 49	4 41	11 59	15 50	26 19	8 34	3 4	19 38
25	2 11 35	1 5 32	26 29 55	3♌ 35 21	12 33	12 14R	12 54	5 55	12 41	15 46	26 24	8 32	3 5	19 38
26	2 15 31	2 5 23	10♌ 39 13	17 41 17	12 29	12 14	14 4	7 9	13 22	15 42	26 29	8 30	3 7	19 38
27	2 19 28	3 5 15	24 41 20	1♍ 39 8	12 26	12 13	15 20	8 23	14 4	15 38	26 34	8 28	3 8	19 37
28	2 23 24	4 5 10	8♍ 34 29	15 27 13	12 23	12 13	16 39	9 38	14 46	15 34	26 39	8 26	3 9	19 37
29	2 27 21	5 5 7	22 17 8	29 4 2	12 20	12 12	18 2	10 52	15 28	15 29	26 44	8 24	3 10	19 37
30	2 31 17	6 5 6	5♎ 47 47	12♎ 28 14	12 17	12 11	19 28	12 7	16 9	15 24	26 50	8 22	3 12	19 37
31	2 35 14	7♏ 5 7	19♎ 5 13	25♎ 38 40	12♉ 13	12♉ 11	20♎ 56	13♎ 21	16♏ 51	15♊ 19	26♐ 55	8♈ 20	3♍ 13	19♋ 37

DECLINATION and LATITUDE

DAY	☉ DECL	☽ DECL	☽ LAT	☽ 12hr DECL	☿ DECL	☿ LAT	♀ DECL	♀ LAT	♂ DECL	♂ LAT	♃ DECL	♃ LAT	♄ DECL	♄ LAT
1	2S55	11N 2	4N30	7N59	11S45	3S33	10N 6	1N 1	9S56	0N13	21N57	0S48	22S24	0N57
2	3 18	4 51	3 44	1 41	11 23	3 26	9 41	1 4	10 12	0 13	21 57	0 48	22 24	0 57
3	3 41	1S29	2 47	4S35	10 55	3 16	9 15	1 6	10 27	0 12	21 57	0 48	22 25	0 56
4	4 4	7 36	1 41	10 30	10 23	3 5	8 50	1 8	10 42	0 11	21 57	0 48	22 25	0 56
5	4 28	13 16	0 31	15 50	9 48	2 52	8 24	1 10	10 57	0 11	21 57	0 48	22 25	0 56
6	4 51	18 13	0S39	20 22	9 9	2 37	7 58	1 12	11 12	0 10	21 57	0 48	22 25	0 56
7	5 14	22 16	1 45	23 54	8 26	2 20	7 31	1 14	11 26	0 10	21 57	0 48	22 26	0 56
8	5 37	25 14	2 45	26 17	7 42	2 2	7 5	1 15	11 41	0 9	21 57	0 49	22 26	0 56
9	5 60	27 1	3 37	27 26	6 57	1 43	6 38	1 17	11 56	0 8	21 57	0 49	22 26	0 55
10	6 23	27 31	4 19	27 18	6 12	1 23	6 11	1 19	12 11	0 8	21 57	0 49	22 27	0 55
11	6 45	26 46	4 50	25 55	5 29	1 2	5 43	1 20	12 25	0 7	21 57	0 49	22 27	0 55
12	7 8	24 47	5 9	23 22	4 47	0 42	5 16	1 22	12 40	0 7	21 56	0 49	22 27	0 55
13	7 31	21 42	5 14	19 46	4 9	0 21	4 48	1 23	12 54	0 6	21 56	0 49	22 27	0 55
14	7 53	17 38	5 5	15 16	3 36	0 2	4 20	1 25	13 8	0 5	21 56	0 49	22 28	0 55
15	8 15	12 44	4 42	10 2	3 7	0N17	3 52	1 26	13 23	0 5	21 56	0 49	22 28	0 55
16	8 38	7 12	4 5	4 15	2 43	0 34	3 24	1 27	13 37	0 4	21 56	0 49	22 28	0 54
17	8 60	1 13	3 14	1N52	2 25	0 50	2 56	1 28	13 51	0 4	21 55	0 49	22 29	0 54
18	9 22	4N58	2 11	8 2	2 13	1 5	2 27	1 30	14 5	0 3	21 55	0 49	22 29	0 54
19	9 44	11 4	0 59	13 58	2 7	1 18	1 59	1 31	14 19	0 2	21 55	0 49	22 29	0 54
20	10 5	16 44	0N18	19 17	2 6	1 29	1 30	1 31	14 33	0 2	21 54	0 49	22 29	0 54
21	10 27	21 35	1 34	23 34	2 10	1 39	1 2	1 32	14 46	0 1	21 54	0 49	22 30	0 54
22	10 48	25 11	2 46	26 25	2 20	1 47	0 33	1 33	14 60	0 1	21 54	0 49	22 30	0 54
23	11 9	27 13	3 47	27 33	2 33	1 53	0 4	1 34	15 13	0S 0	21 53	0 49	22 30	0 53
24	11 31	27 26	4 34	26 52	2 51	1 59	0S25	1 34	15 27	0 1	21 53	0 49	22 31	0 53
25	11 52	25 51	5 5	24 26	3 13	2 3	0 54	1 35	15 40	0 1	21 53	0 49	22 31	0 53
26	12 12	22 38	5 16	20 32	3 38	2 5	1 23	1 35	15 53	0 2	21 52	0 49	22 31	0 53
27	12 33	18 9	5 9	15 32	4 5	2 7	1 52	1 36	16 6	0 2	21 52	0 49	22 31	0 53
28	12 53	12 44	4 44	9 48	4 35	2 7	2 21	1 36	16 19	0 3	21 51	0 49	22 32	0 53
29	13 13	6 46	4 2	3 41	5 7	2 7	2 50	1 36	16 32	0 4	21 51	0 49	22 32	0 53
30	13 33	0 35	3 8	2S31	5 41	2 6	3 19	1 36	16 45	0 4	21 50	0 49	22 32	0 52
31	13S53	5S33	2N 4	8S31	6S16	2N 4	3S47	1N37	16S57	0S 5	21N50	0S49	22S32	0N52

DAY	♅ DECL	♅ LAT	♆ DECL	♆ LAT	♇ DECL	♇ LAT
1	3N 5	0S44	11N10	0N36	21N40	0S21
5	3 1	0 44	11 8	0 36	21 40	0 21
9	2 57	0 44	11 5	0 36	21 40	0 21
13	2 54	0 44	11 3	0 36	21 40	0 21
17	2 50	0 44	11 1	0 36	21 41	0 20
21	2 46	0 44	10 59	0 37	21 41	0 20
25	2 43	0 44	10 57	0 37	21 41	0 20
29	2N40	0S44	10N55	0N37	21N41	0S20

☽ PHENOMENA			
d	h	m	
2	22	20	●
10	18	5	☽
18	12	6	○
25	8	21	☾
d	h	° '	
2	18	0	
9	22	27S32	
17	5	0	
23	15	27N34	
30	2	0	
5	11	0	
12	21	5S14	
19	19	0	
26	3	5N17	

VOID OF COURSE ☽ LAST ASPT		☽ INGRESS		
1	9pm10	2	♎	6am10
4	9am 1	4	♏	11am40
6	0am16	6	♐	8pm19
8	10pm13	9	♑	7am50
10	11pm28	11	♒	8pm26
13	11pm 3	14	♓	7am40
16	8am12	16	♈	4pm 2
18	2pm19	18	♉	9pm29
20	7am18	21	♊	0am55
23	2am 2	23	♋	3am24
24	12pm24	25	♌	5am55
27	3am15	27	♍	9am 9
29	7am55	29	♎	1pm39
31	2pm26	31	♏	8pm 2

d	h	
10	15	APOGEE
22	22	PERIGEE

DAILY ASPECTARIAN

Day	Aspect	Time
1 T	☿∠♀	3am21
	☽∥♀	4 0
	☽#♂	4 10
	♀#♂	5 38
	☽□♃	6 40
	☉#♅	10 21
	☽⚹♇	12pm 7
	☽⚺☿	3 6
	☽□♄	9 10
2 W	☽⚺♂	0am54
	☉#☽	5 32
	☽∥♅	6 45
	☽⚺♆	10 29
	☿#♆	11 54
	☽⚺♀	9pm30
	☉☌☽	10 20
	☽☍♅	10 38
3 Th	☉☍♅	2am23
	☽#♅	6 3
	☉∥☽	9 5
	♀⚺♅	9 43
	☽△♃	11 4
	☽∠♆	1pm 3
	☿∥♂	2 52
	☿□♇	4 11
	☽☌☿	4 42
	☽□♇	4 45
4 F	☽⚹♄	2am26
	☽∠♀	3 1
	☽#♀	4 39
	☽☌♂	9 1
	☽∥☿	10 27
	☽∥♂	1pm24
	☽⚻♃	2 15
	☽#♆	2 41
	☽⚹♆	4 21
	☉⚺♀	5 59
5 S	☽⚺♅	4am53
	☽∠♄	6 11
	☉⚺☽	9 16
	☽⚹♀	9 35
	♃SR	9 55
	☿∠♆	2pm24
	♂#♆	5 16
	☽⚺♃	6 14
	☽⚺☿	7 57
6 Su	☽△♇	0am16
	☽⚻♅	9 13
	☽⚺♄	10 47
	♂ ♏	12pm27
	☿△♃	3 1
	☉∠☽	4 17
	☽#♇	8 5
	☽⚺♂	8 46
	☽#♃	9 54
	☽∠☿	10 21
7 M	☽∥♄	1am 8
	☽□♆	1 24
	☽⚻♇	5 16
	☽△♅	2pm20
	☿⚺♀	10 0
8 T	☉⚹☽	0am17
	☽⚹☿	1 15
	☽□♀	1 58
	☽∠♂	4 1
	☽☍♃	4 33
	☉☌☿	6 13
	☽⚺♇	10 57
	♂⚻♃	1pm35
	☽☌♄	10 13
9 W	♀□♃	3am20
	☽⚹♂	11 54
	☽△♆	1pm15
	☉#♀	6 15
	☉∥☿	8 25
	♀∠♂	8 50
10 Th	☽□♅	2am14
	☿#♀	2 44
	☉△♃	4 0
	☽□☿	8 18
	♂⚹♆	12pm21
	☽⚺♃	4 54
	☉□☽	6 5
	☽⚻♆	7 40
	☽△♀	9 17
	☽☍♇	11 28
11 F	☽⚺♄	11am 8
	☉∠♆	1pm25
	♀⚹♇	6 37
	☽⚻♃	11 6
12 S	☽⚺♆	1am58
	☽□♂	4 9
	☽⚻♀	6 56
	☽⚹♅	2pm28
	☽△☿	4 15
	☽∠♄	5 22
	☽∥♄	6 46
	☽#♃	10 22
13 Su	☽#♇	0am 9
	☽△♃	4 55
	☉□♇	10 52
	☽⚺♇	11 27
	☉△☽	11 30
	☽⚺♀	3pm59
	☽∠♅	7 57
	☽⚻☿	8 11
	☽⚹♄	11 3
14 M	☿☍♅	1am27
	☽☍☿	1pm 7
	☽⚻♇	4 34
	☽△♂	6 28
	☉⚻☽	7 6
	☽∥♂	9 10
	☽⚺☿	11 57
15 T	☽⚺♅	0am45
	☽#♆	7 40
	☽□♃	2pm34
	☿#♅	3 1
	☉∥☽	6 24
	☽△♇	8 54
16 W	☽⚻♂	0am21
	☉⚺☽	1 43
	☽☍♀	7 11
	☽□♄	8 12
	☽#♀	4pm42
	☽#♅	5 38
	♀□♄	6 35
	☽∥☿	7 4
	☽⚺♆	9 18
17 Th	♀∥♅	5am 2
	☽⚺♂	5 18
	☿SD	5 22
	☽☍☿	6 37
	☽☌♅	8 2
	☽#☿	1pm40
	☽∥♀	2 59
	☽∥♅	3 48
	☽⚹♃	9 7
18 F	☽⚻♆	0am16
	☽□♇	3 18
	☉☍☽	12pm 6
	☿⚺♂	12 6
	☽△♄	2 19
	☿#♀	4 11
	☉#☽	6 19
	☽⚺♀	6 22
	☽∠♃	11 24
	☽∥♆	11 45
19 S	☽△♆	2am37
	♂⚺♅	7 44
	☽⚺☿	12pm14
	☽⚺♅	12 38
	☽☍♂	12 54
	☽#♂	2 1
	☽⚻♄	4 29
	☉⚹♄	8 57
	☽⚻♀	10 49
	☿☍♅	11 54
20 Su	☽⚺♃	1am11
	♀ ♎	5 12
	☽⚹♇	7 18
	☽∠♅	2pm14
	☽⚻☿	2 50
	☽⚺♄	6 14
	☉⚺☽	7 43
21 M	☽∥♇	0am34
	☽∥♃	1 51
	♇SR	1 58
	☽△♀	2 47
	☽#♄	5 19
	☽□♆	5 59
	☽∠♇	8 44
	☽⚹♅	3pm32
	☽△☿	5 27
	☽⚺♂	6 32
	☉⚻☽	10 57
22 T	☽☌♃	3am47
	☽⚺♇	10 0
	☉#♆	10 59
	♀⚺♆	4pm 9
	☽⚻♂	9 2
	☽☍♄	9 4
	♂∠♄	9 54
23 W	☉△☽	2am 2
	☽⚹♆	8 32
	☽□♀	10 3
	☿#♅	2pm59
	☽□♅	5 49
	☉ ♏	9 42
	☽□☿	11 13
	☽△♂	11 31
24 Th	☽⚺♃	5am59
	☽∠♆	9 47
	☿⚺♂	10 39
	☽☌♇	12pm24
	☉⚻♃	4 38
	☽⚺♄	11 50
25 F	☽∠♃	7am11
	☉□☽	8 21
	☽⚺♆	11 10
	☽⚹♀	5pm28
	☽△♅	8 21
26 S	☽#♄	0am44
	☽⚻♄	1 25
	☽∥♃	4 35
	☽□♂	4 52
	☽∥♇	5 39
	☽⚹☿	6 23
	☽⚹♃	8 34
	☽⚺♇	3pm19
	☽∠♀	9 33
	☽⚻♅	9 54
27 Su	☉⚹♆	1am 6
	♀☍♅	1 24
	☽△♄	3 15
	☿△♃	5 23
	☽#♂	9 5
	☽∠☿	10 43
	☽☌♆	2pm35
	☉⚹☽	3 36
	☽∠♇	5 8
	☉#☽	11 25
	☽⚺♅	11 45
28 M	☽⚺♀	2am 1
	☽#♆	7 29
	☽⚹♂	11 22
	☽□♃	12pm 7
	☽⚺☿	3 40
	♀#♅	4 2
	☽⚹♇	7 18
	☉∠☽	7 49
29 T	♂⚺♃	0am45
	☿∠♆	2 31
	☽#☿	5 55
	☽□♄	7 55
	☽#♀	2pm13
	☽∠♂	3 16
	☽∥♅	3 59
	☽⚺♆	7 21
30 W	☉⚺☽	0am33
	☿□♇	2 32
	☽☍♅	4 35
	☽#♅	12pm30
	☽☌♀	12 32
	☽∥♀	4 24
	☽△♃	5 12
	☽⚺♂	7 43
	☽∠♆	10 25
31 Th	☽□♇	0am57
	☽∥☿	3 9
	☽☌☿	3 48
	☽⚹♄	2pm26
	☽⚻♃	8 30
	☽#♆	10 1

Figure 153. Ephemeris page sample

Horoscope Forms

Figures 154 and 155 are examples of blank horoscope forms.

Figure 154 is an example of an American-style horoscope blank, with the twelve equidistant house cusps pre-printed on the form and spaces provided for recording their zodiacal positions.

Figure 155 is an example of a European-style horoscope blank, with the cusps of the signs and the individual degrees of the zodiac (in groups of five for easier counting) pre-printed around the circumference. With this type of chart form, one must first enter one of the signs in its appropriate location—usually the sign of the Midheaven, because it is at the top of the chart, whereas the horizon varies its location—then enter all the other signs in their proper sequence. (This is more attractive and in many ways more interesting if the zodiacal colors are used.) Then one must draw in the house cusps at their actual zodiacal locations, noting the positions in degrees and minutes of arc where these lines intersect the circumference (see figure 72, Chapter 4 for an example).

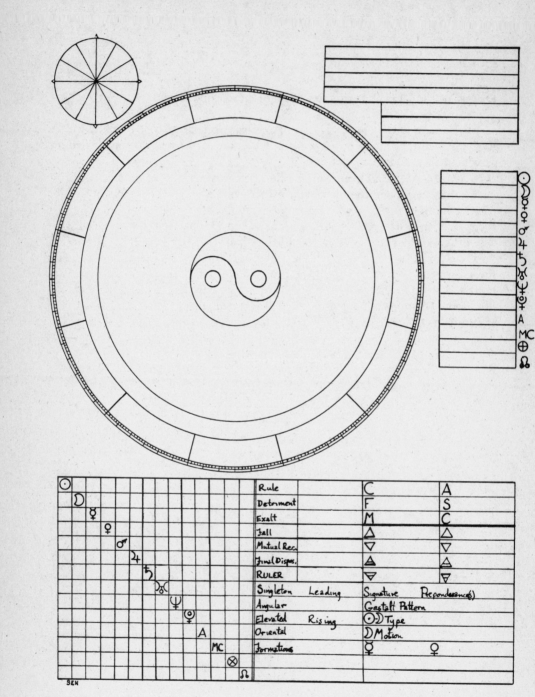

Figure 154. American-style horoscope blank

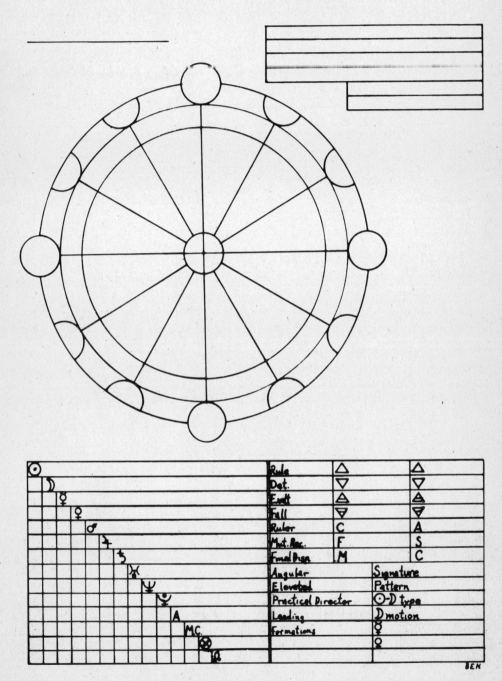

Figure 155. European-style horoscope blank

Bibliography

Bailey, Alice. *Esoteric Astrology*, Lucis Publishing Company (New York), 1951.

Bendict, Ruth. See Maslow and Honigman.

Bentov, Itzhak. *Stalking the Wild Pendulum*. E.P. Dutton (New York), 1977; Bantam paperback, 1979.

Brau, Jean-Louis, Weaver, Helen and Edmands, Allan, *Larousse Encyclopedia of Astrology*, McGraw-Hill (New York), 1980.

Capra, Fritjof. *The Tao of Physics*. Shambhala (Boulder, Colorado), 1976; Bantam paperback, 1977.

Case, Paul Foster. *Highlights of Tarot*. Builders of the Adytum (Los Angeles), 1970.
———. *The Book of Tokens, Tarot Meditations*. Builders of the Adytum (Los Angeles), 1960.
———. *The Tarot, A Key to the Wisdom of the Ages*. MaCoy Publishing Company and Masonic Supply House (Richmond, Virginia), 1947.

Castaneda, Carlos. *The Teachings of Don Juan, A Yaqui Way of Knowledge*. Simon & Schuster, (New York), 1968.
———. *A Separate Reality: Further Conversations with Don Juan*. Simon & Schuster (New York), 1970.
———. *Journey to Ixtlan: The Lessons of Don Juan*. Simon & Schuster (New York), 1972.
———. *Tales of Power*. Simon & Schuster (New York), 1974.
———. *The Second Ring of Power*. Simon & Schuster (New York), 1978

Ebertin, Reinhold. *The Combination of Stellar Influences*. Ebertin Verlag (Aalen, Federal Republic of Germany), 1972.

Erlewine, Michael. *The Sun is Shining, Heliocentric Ephemeris 1953-2050*. Heart Center/Circle Books (Ann Arbor, Michigan), 1975.

Erlewine, Michael and Erlewine, Margaret. *Astrophysical Directions*. Heart Center (Ann Arbor, Michigan), 1977.

Erlewine, Steven. *The Circle Book of Charts*. Circle Bookstore, Inc. (Ann Arbor, Michigan), 1972.

Golas, Thaddeus. *The Lazy Man's Guide to Enlightenment*. Seed Center (Palo Alto, California), 1971.

Goleman, Daniel. *The Varieties of Meditative Experience*. E.P. Dutton (New York), 1977.

Haich, Elizabeth. *Initiation*. George Allen & Unwin, Ltd. (London), 1965; Seed Center (Palo Alto, California), 1974.

Hand, Robert. *Planets in Transit*. Para Research, Inc., (Rockport, Massachusetts), 1976.
———. *Horoscope Symbols*. Para Research, Inc. (Rockport, Massachusetts), 1981.

Jones, Marc Edmund. *The Guide to Horoscope Interpretation*. Sabian Publishing Society (New York), 1941, 1969.
———. *How to Learn Astrology*. Sabian Publishing Society (New York), 1941, 1969.

Joy, W. Brugh. *Joy's Way, A Map for the Transformational Journey*. Tarcher/St. Martin's (Los Angeles), 1978.

Keyes, Ken, Jr. *Handbook to Higher Consciousness* (fifth edition). Living Love Center (Berkeley, California), 1975.

Leonard, George. *The Silent Pulse.* E.P. Dutton, (New York), 1979.

LeShan, Lawrence. *How to Meditate.* Bantam (New York), 1974.

Marks, Tracy. *The Art of Chart Synthesis.* Sagittarius Rising (Natick, Massachusetts), 1979.

Maslow, Abraham H., and Honigman, John J. "Synergy: Some notes of Ruth Benedict," foreword by Margaret Mead, in: *American Anthropologist,* 1970.

Meyer, Michael R. *A Handbook for the Humanistic Astrologer.* Anchor (New York), 1974.

Neisser, Ulric. *Cognition and Reality. Principles and Implications of Cognitive Psychology.* W.H. Freeman and Company (San Francisco), 1976.

Rodden. Lois M. *The American Book of Charts.* Astro Computing Service (San Diego), 1980. Distributed by Para Research.

——. *Profiles of Women.* AFA (Tempe, Arizona), 1979.

Index

How To Order Your Astral Portrait

Use the coupon on the previous page or, if you prefer, another piece of paper. Send the following information plus $20 for each Astral Portrait to Para Research, Dept. IO, Rockport, Massachusetts 01966. Add 1.50 for shipping and handling, for each Astral Portrait you order. The price is subject to change.

Name, Address, City, State, Zip Code

The address to which the Astral Portrait(s) should be sent.

Time of Birth

Accuracy to the minute is important. Don't rely on parent's memory. Consult hospital records or birth certificate. Midnight and noon are neither A.M. nor P.M. A.M. is between midnight and noon; P.M. is between noon and midnight. To avoid confusion, if you are submitting a noon birthtime, please write "noon." If you are submitting a midnight birthtime, please write "midnight" and two dates: the day that was ending and the day that was beginning. For example: "June 19/20, 1947, 12:00 midnight."

Please do not convert from daylight saving time to standard time. Just send us local clock time and we will convert. Or if you cannot do this, please explain. If you do not send birthtime, we will use 12:00 noon.

Date of Birth

Month, day and year.

Place of Birth

If you were born in a small town that may not be on our maps, please give us the name of the nearest city.

Please Print Clearly

Keep a copy of the birth information you send us for comparison with the computer printout. Notify us in case of error.

Guarantee

Para Research guarantees every horoscope. If for any reason, you are dissatisfied, please return the Astral Portrait for a full refund.

Please allow two weeks for processing and delivery.

Para Research, Inc. Dept. IO, Rockport, Massachusetts 01966

Please send me my personal Astral Portait. ☐ I enclose $20 plus 1.50 for shipping and handling. ☐ Charge 21.50 to my Master Charge or VISA account.

Credit Card Number_____Expires_____

N a m e_____

A d d r e s s_____

City_____ State_____ Zip_____

Birth Information:

Born (month)_____(day)_____(year)_____(time)_____A.M./P.M.

City_____State_____

. . . .

Para Research, Inc. Dept. IO, Rockport, Massachusetts 01966

Please send me my personal Astral Portrait. ☐ I enclose $20 plus 1.50 for shipping and handling. ☐ Charge 21.50 to my Master Charge or VISA account.

Credit Card Number_____Expires_____

N a m e_____

A d d r e s s_____

City_____ State_____ Zip_____

Birth Information:

Born (month)_____(day)_____(year)_____(time)_____A.M./P.M.

City_____State_____

Other Books from Para Research

PLANETS IN ASPECT: Understanding Your Inner Dynamics
by Robert Pelletier

Explores aspects, the planetary relationships that describe our individual energy patterns, and how we can integrate them into our lives. Undoubtedly the most thorough in-depth study of planetary aspects ever published. Every major aspect— conjunction, sextile, square, trine, opposition and inconjunct—is covered: 314 aspects in all. Paper, $12.95

PLANETS IN COMPOSITE: Analyzing Human Relationships
by Robert Hand

The definitive work on the astrology of human relationships. Explains the technique of the composite chart, combining two individuals' charts to create a third chart of the relationship itself, and how to interpret it. Case studies plus twelve chapters of delineations of composite Sun, Moon and planets in all houses and major aspects. Paper, $13.95

PLANETS IN HOUSES: Experiencing Your Environment
by Robert Pelletier

Brings the ancient art of natal horoscope interpretation into a new era of accuracy, concreteness and richness of detail. Pelletier delineates the meaning of each planet as derived by counting from each of the twelve houses and in relation to the other houses with which it forms trines, sextiles, squares and oppositions, inconjuncts and semisextiles. Seventeen different house relationships delineated for each planet in each house, 2184 delineations in all. Paper, $12.95

PLANETS IN LOVE: Exploring Your Emotional and Sexual Needs
by John Townley

The first astrology book to take an unabashed look at human sexuality and the different kinds of relationships that people form to meet their various emotional and sexual needs. An intimate astrological analysis of sex and love, with 550 interpretations of each planet in every possible sign, house and aspect. Discusses sexual behavior according to mental, emotional and spiritual areas of development. Paper, $13.95

PLANETS IN TRANSIT: Life Cycles for Living
by Robert Hand

A psychological approach to astrological prediction. Delineations of the Sun, Moon and each planet transiting each natal house and forming each aspect to the natal Sun, Moon, planets, Ascendant and Midheaven. The definitive book on transits. Includes introductory chapters on the theory and applications of transits. Paper, $19.95

PLANETS IN YOUTH: Patterns of Early Development
by Robert Hand

A major astrological thinker looks at children and childhood. Parents can use it to help their children cope with the complexities of growing up, and readers of all ages can use it to understand themselves and their own patterns of early development. Introductory chapters discuss parent-child relationships and planetary energies in children's charts. All important horoscope factors delineated stressing possibilities rather than certainties. Paper, $13.95

THE AMERICAN ATLAS
by Neil F. Michelsen

Provides all American time changes and time zones from 1883 to 2000 for over 100,000 birthplaces, virtually every incorporated or unincorporated city, village, neighborhood, airport and military base in the United States. "Whether or not you already have an atlas, buy Neil Michelsen's American Atlas if you're serious about computing horoscopes."—Richard F. Nolle. Cloth, $19.50

THE AMERICAN EPHEMERIS
by Neil F. Michelsen

Has everything you need to cast horoscopes. Perfect for beginners, with its chart casting instructions and Placidus house tables, it is the required tool for practicing astrologers. Daily midnight positions: Sun and Moon longitudes to the nearest second of arc, true *and* mean node of Moon, planetary longitudes, latitudes and declinations. Also includes a complete aspectarian, Moon phenomena and much more. The combined volumes of the American Ephemeris cover the 20th century.

1901 to 1930 paper, $14.95	1931 to 1940 paper, $5.00	1941 to 1950 paper, $5.00
1951 to 1960 paper, $5.00	1961 to 1970 paper, $5.00	1971 to 1980 paper, $5.00
1981 to 1990 paper, $5.00	1991 to 2000 paper, $5.00	1931 to 1980 & Book of Tables, cloth, $25.00

THE AMERICAN EPHEMERIS FOR THE TWENTIETH CENTURY
by Neil F. Michelsen

For the first time, an inexpensive paperback ephemeris which covers the entire 20th century with the accuracy and detail you expect from *The American Ephemeris*. Sun and Moon longitudes to 1 second; planet longitudes to .1 minute; calculated for GMT time; Solar and Lunar eclipses; aspectarian of Jupiter through Pluto and much more. Noon or Midnight, each volume: Paper, $15.95

ASTROLOGY BOOKS IN PRINT
by Para Research Staff

A comprehensive annotated listing of all astrological books available to the public as of early 1981 and including projected publications from major publishers. Collected by our research staff and collated through computer control, this inexpensive bibliography will not only be in high demand by astrologers, but also by all bibliophiles, librarians, bookstore clerks and researchers. Paper, $3.95

ASTROLOGICAL INSIGHTS INTO PERSONALITY
by Betty Lundsted

This book combines principle and practice. The first section introduces the author's basic concepts in a clear and readable way. The second and largest section discusses each of the major planetary aspects as a context for personality development. The third section presents the author's approach to chart analysis and synthesis and uses two case histories to illustrate how you can use the material in this book.

Betty Lundsted says that the symbols in your natal chart paint a picture of your early childhood environment which influences you for the rest of your life. She presents a unique approach to understanding how this effects your expectations, relationships, self-esteem and sexuality.

Betty Lundsted applies her training in metaphysics and eastern philosophy and her interest in psychological motivation to her astrological investigations. In this book she shares the interdisciplinary approach she has developed in years of counseling and teaching. The reader with a grasp of the fundamentals of astrology will use this book to grow as an astrologer and as a person. Paper, $9.95

THE AMERICAN BOOK OF CHARTS
by Lois Rodden

Have you ever wanted to study the chart of someone like Marilyn Monroe, Albert Einstein or Michelangelo but not known how accurate your data was? Lois Rodden, author of the astrology book *Profiles of Women*, decided to do something about uncertain birth times. In the *American Book of Charts*, Lois Rodden presents 500 accurate and verifiable birthcharts, citing sources for her data (i.e. birth certificates, family records, etc.). This means that for the first time, we have a collection of charts which has been fully researched for accuracy. Any data which the author could not verify is contained in an additional 700 biographical sketches.

The significance of *The American Book of Charts* is that Lois Rodden provides verification of previously suspect birth data and introduces a system of ranking verifiable data, which will become standard procedure among practicing astrologers. Paper, $15.95

HOROSCOPE SYMBOLS
by Robert Hand

This book, representing four years of writing and twenty years of research, presents an in-depth reexamination of astrology's basic symbols. Core meanings are analyzed in detail so that the astrologer can see for himself why traditional meaning and significance have been attributed to each astrological symbol. In many cases, these core meanings also establish new interpretations as the author develops the substance and symbolism of images which astrologers have employed for centuries. Paper, $14.95

To Order Books: Send purchase price plus fifty cents for each book to cover shipping and handling to Para Research, Dept. AIO, Rockport, MA 01966. Massachusetts residents add 5% sales tax. Prices subject to change without notice.